SONNY

The Last of the Old-Time Mafia Bosses
JOHN "SONNY" FRANZESE

S. J. Peddie

CITADEL PRESS
Kensington Publishing Corp.
www.kensingtonbooks.com

CITADEL PRESS BOOKS are published by

Kensington Publishing Corp.
900 Third Avenue
New York, NY 10022

All Kensington titles, imprints, and distributed lines are available at special quantity discounts for bulk purchases for sales promotions, premiums, fund-raising, educational, or institutional use.

Special book excerpts or customized printings can also be created to fit specific needs. For details, write or phone the office of the Kensington sales manager: Kensington Publishing Corp., 900 Third Avenue, New York, NY 10022, attn: Sales Department; phone 1-800-221-2647.

CITADEL PRESS and the Citadel logo are Reg. U.S. Pat. & TM Off.

First Citadel hardcover printing: April 2022

First paperback printing: May 2024
ISBN: 978-0-8065-4161-7

ISBN: 978-0-8065-4162-4 (e-book)

10 9 8 7 6 5 4 3 2 1

Printed in the United States of America

CONTENTS

One of the challenges of writing this book was the long life of my subject, John "Sonny" Franzese. By the time he died in February, 2020, he was 103 years old (even though on his last birthday, Sonny tried to tell me he was really 104). Many of the key players in his life had predeceased him. I'm used to getting around reporting obstacles, but death is a tough one.

The other challenge was that for many of the people I interviewed—130 in total—the events in question were so long ago. When someone would complain that I was asking about something forty, fifty, or even sixty years ago, my standard response became "You're alive, you're lucid, you're ahead of the game. It's better than the alternative."

With a little prodding, they remembered. The events in this book are based on hundreds of interviews, including six extensive conversations with Sonny Franzese—his first and only extended interviews. Most of my interview subjects, including the ones with criminal records, were remarkably candid and consistent in their stories. They wanted me to get it right.

Street guys don't put things down on paper. Fortunately, government bureaucrats and journalists do. I fleshed out the narrative, wherever possible, with sworn court testimony, archived court proceedings, other federal and state court records, transcripts of undercover recordings, depositions, police reports, indictments, FBI records, testimony before the U.S. Senate and Congress, U.S. Bureau of Prison inmate data, state investigative reports, New York State prison records, marriage licenses, U.S.

Census records, U.S. Bureau of Labor Management reports, property deeds, government press releases, the archived papers of columnist Jack Newfield, and accounts in books, magazines, and newspapers.

The quotes in this book are culled from interviews, court records, transcripts of recordings, and newspaper accounts.

This book is the story of a unique American family.

FRANZESE FAMILY

Sonny Franzese—The handsome and charismatic underboss of the Colombo family reigned over his illegal rackets with ferocity and guile.

Tina Franzese—She was Sonny's beautiful and tough-minded second wife.

Michael Franzese—The son of Tina and her first husband, he made millions running a gas tax scam on Long Island.

John Franzese Jr.—Sonny and Tina's first child and seen as the one most like his father.

Gia Franzese—Sweet and caring to her friends, she was attracted to bad boys.

Christine "Little Tina" Franzese—The youngest of their children, she had health problems throughout her life.

Maryann, Carmine, and Lorraine—They are Sonny's children from his first marriage to Anna Schiller.

THE CRIME FAMILIES

The New York Mafia is comprised of five criminal families, or *borgatas*, overseen by a commission of family bosses. Although they operate their own rackets, they work closely together. New members are assigned to a family when they are inducted.

COLOMBO FAMILY—Joseph "Olive Oil King" Profaci was the original boss of the family, then known as the Profaci family, until he died in 1962. Profaci's brother-in-law, Joseph Magliocco, briefly became boss after his death. In 1963, Joseph Colombo, Sonny's friend and business partner, took over the family, and it was renamed for him.

GENOVESE FAMILY—Founded by Charles "Lucky" Luciano, the family was taken over by Vito Genovese and then Frank Costello after Luciano's conviction for promoting prostitution. Costello retired after being shot in 1957 by Vincent "The Chin" Gigante. .

GAMBINO FAMILY—Albert Anastasia is believed to have killed the family's original boss, Vincent Mangano, in 1951 as part of a coup. By 1957, other mobsters, led by Carlo Gambino, staged their own coup against Anastasia. Sonny, who was close to Anastasia, opposed it, but to no avail. Anastasia was shot to death as he sat in a barber's chair. Gambino took over the family, and it was renamed for him.

BONANNO FAMILY—Joseph "Joe Bananas" Bonanno, the family's original boss, was forced out after he plotted to kill rival bosses. Sonny despised Bonanno.

LUCCHESE FAMILY—Gaetano "Tommy Three-Finger Brown" Lucchese took over the family in 1951 and ran it until he died in 1967.

SOME OF THE GANGSTERS

Carmine "the Snake" Persico—He took over the Colombo family in 1972 after Colombo was shot at an Italian-American celebration in New York City. He acquired his nickname, which he loathed, after betraying the Gallo brothers in an internal Colombo war.

Gregory "the Grim Reaper" Scarpa—Nicknamed "the Grim Reaper" because of his love for killing, he became a top-echelon informant for the FBI in 1961. As a capo in the Colombo family, he was well-positioned to give the FBI valuable information. Sonny never trusted him.

Sebastiano "Buster" Aloi—He sponsored Sonny's induction into the Cosa Nostra when Sonny was just fourteen years old. Aloi became the family's underboss and was the father of Vincenzo "Vinny" and Benedetto "Benny" Aloi, who sided with Victor "Little Vic" Orena in the 1990s Colombo war.

Anthony Carfano—Also known as "Little Augie Pisano," he was a capo in the Luciano family and was unhappy when Genovese took over. In 1959, he and a former beauty queen, Janice Drake, were shot to death in his black Cadillac.

Felice "Philly" Vizzari—He was an active loan shark and book-maker who worked under Sonny. Vizzari's name surfaced in a State Investigations Commission hearing in 1964.

Frank "Franky Camp" Campione—Fiercely loyal to Sonny, he was his sometime driver and later helped nurse Sonny back to health when he became ill in prison.

Ernest "the Hawk" Rupolo—Called "Ernie the Hawk" or "the Hawk" because he never missed a shot, even after losing his right eye, he was killed in grisly mob hit in 1964.

William Rupolo—He was the Hawk's brother and testified at Sonny's trial for the murder of the Hawk. Eight years later, William, his wife, and daughter-in-law were found bound, gagged, and stabbed to death in their burning Brooklyn apartment. Police believed the killings were mob-related. He and his brother are buried in the same plot at Green-Wood Cemetery in Brooklyn.

Joseph "Little Joey" Brancato—Brancato served as acting boss of the Colombos and was close to the Franzese family.

Andrew "Mush" Russo—Persico appointed Russo, his cousin, as acting boss in 2009. More polished than the average street guy, Russo had ties to the entertainment industry and was close to Sonny.

John "Johnny Irish" Matera—Sonny's longtime bodyguard and driver, he also was one of his codefendants in the bank robbery and homicide cases. A solid earner, he became a capo and moved to Florida. In 1981, he was summoned to a meeting with Persico and never seen again.

Lawrence "Champagne Larry" Carrozza—Extremely close to Michael Franzese, he fell in love with Gia Franzese.

Victor "Little Vic" Orena—After Persico was imprisoned on a racketeering conviction in 1986, he named Orena acting boss. In 1991, Orena tried to wrest control of the family from Persico, sparking another internal Colombo war. Sonny was key to negotiating peace after that war.

THE BANK ROBBERS

Four street hoods testified against Sonny in three criminal cases against him. Sonny denied ever meeting any of the men. Some people believed that they only testified because a rival gangster, who was deeply jealous of Sonny, provided them with protection.

James "Smitty" Smith—Known as "the vault man," because he was the guy designated to jump over the bank counter to scoop up the money, his eyesight was so bad he seemed to be perpetually squinting. During one heist, he hurdled the counter, but only grabbed one-dollar bills. After that, he always wore his glasses.

Richard Parks—He was the oldest of the bank robbers and seen by investigators as the most cunning.

Charles "Blackie" Zaher—Bushy-haired and lanky, he was an unstable drug addict. He tried to commit suicide in jail after a prison chef passed on a threat to his life. He managed to escape from jail and stayed on the lam until a couple of sharp-eyed patrolmen spotted him hanging around a bank in a ski mask. He insisted he wasn't there to rob the bank, but police arrested him anyway.z

John "Blue Boy" Cordero—He was able to tie Sonny directly to the bank robberies. Although he was a drug addict, he came across well on the stand.

Eleanor Cordero—The Hawk's widow, she married John Cordero about a year after Ernie's death. She was the driver in two of the bank robberies. Brash and loud, she would show up at the prosecutors' offices with pillows and sheets for her conjugal visits with John. After John Cordero tried to kill her with an ax, she said Sonny was framed.

THE SONGBIRDS

Joseph Valachi—A Genovese soldier, he made international headlines when he broke the mob's code of omertà and testified before Senator John McClellan's committee in October 1963 about the inner workings of the Mafia.

Michael Franzese—After being convicted of racketeering and facing ten years in prison, Michael signed a cooperation agreement with federal investigators and provided information on mob bosses across the country.

John Franzese Jr.—He became an informant for the FBI in the mid-1990s and then wore a wire against his father, beginning in 2005. He later testified against his father, who was ninety-three, helping to send him back to prison. John went into the Witness Protection Program but later left it.

Gaetano "Guy" Fatato—A hulking former standout football player, he and Sonny got to know each other while serving time in prison. Fatato agreed to wear a wire and recorded Sonny making numerous incriminating statements.

THE INVESTIGATORS

Bob Greene—A hard-charging investigative reporter for *Newsday*, he pursued Sonny and other mobsters relentlessly, and had to have police protection for his wife and children as a result. He went on to win two Pulitzer Prizes.

Michael Gillen—He was the shaggy-haired Assistant U.S. Attorney who prosecuted Sonny in the bank robbery conspiracy. Gillen was capable of courtroom theatrics, once pulling out an M1 semiautomatic rifle to make a point.

James C. Mosley—Cerebral and committed to seeking justice, on behalf of the Queens district attorney's office, he prosecuted Sonny for the homicide of Ernest "the Hawk" Rupolo.

Robert Lewicki—He was the FBI agent who became John Franzese Jr.'s handler.

THE JUDGE

Jacob Mishler—The U.S. District Court judge who presided over Sonny's bank robbery trial, Mishler refused to be cowed by threats to kidnap his daughter. Sonny hated him with a passion he reserved for few other people. Sonny vowed that if ever given the chance, he would find Mishler's grave and "pee" on it.

"SONNY" FRANZESE SAT in his wheelchair in the lounge of a Queens nursing home, where he had lived since his release from prison in 2017 at age 100, the oldest inmate in the federal prison system. He hated the place, though he didn't complain to visitors. Accustomed to far worse after his many years in prison—"I wouldn't put a dog in a jail pod"—the nursing home was at least an improvement.

Jammed onto a busy block dotted with stores hawking cheap clothes and delis selling canned beans and frozen pizza, the facility's location made it easier for people to get there to see him. The nurse's aides, too, tried to be cheerful, even though there seemed to be little they could do to get rid of the odor of urine that hung in the air. It was a place that lacked the sparkling amenities of its counterparts in the wealthier suburbs of New York. It was time-worn and frayed around the edges, or, as an old friend of his indignantly put it, appeared to be "a home for indigents."

The friend was indignant because of who Sonny was. John "Sonny" Franzese was the last of the great Mafia bosses, a protégé of Albert Anastasia, friend of Vito Genovese, ally of Carmine Persico. At the peak of his power in the 1960s, he generated millions in income for the mob, and himself, through illegal rackets, like bookmaking and loan-sharking, and legitimate businesses, like independent record labels and nightclubs. Men on the street both revered and feared him for his ruthless ferocity. Organized-crime investigators believe he killed or had killed as many as fifty people. Because he steadfastly refused to rat on his confederates, despite repeated entreaties from FBI agents, he earned a grudging respect from law enforcement and near-mythic status on the street.

And yet here Sonny was, hobbled by a litany of physical ailments, stuck in a nursing home because no one in his large family was able or willing to take him home. He had outlived most of the people who wanted to see him behind bars or dead, something he considered a victory in itself. Musing a bit about "all the guys I left behind," he chuckled and said, "But I'm still alive. Ain't that something?"

Even at his advanced age, Sonny had a full head of hair— something he was very pleased with—and a thick neck and strong jaw. The years hadn't really worn down his appearance. His health was another matter. He had a pacemaker, one kidney, hearing loss, false teeth, spinal stenosis, and a host of other conditions, but he didn't complain. Sonny exuded a zest for life, laughed easily, and was a great storyteller, with a comic's sense of timing. In every one of his stories, he won the fight, got the girl, secured the better part of the business deal.

But his charm masked the darker reality of his life in the Mafia: a life full of betrayal, treachery, and petty grievances resulting in often-lethal consequences. He could trust no one, not even his beloved sons. As he sat at a table, he cast glances behind him to see who was there. In the end, many of his old friends who were still alive didn't bother to come and see him. His children were scattered and busy with their own lives, and his once-elegant wife had died destitute and estranged from him.

His life had reached both the pinnacles of high society and the depths of years of being locked away in prison. As he reflected on his past, Sonny expressed no regrets about his career in crime— "I never hurt nobody that was innocent"—but he never once acknowledged even the existence of the Mafia. "Omertà? What's that?"

He was true to his oath until the end.

Shown a picture of himself from his heyday, when he cut a ruggedly handsome figure in his perfectly tailored suits, with a jaunty smile for photographers, Sonny grinned and said, "Hey, let me ask you: A face like that, could he be a murderer?"

Yes, he could.

What was I doing, sitting down with a killer?

I grew up in Minnesota, a pretty sheltered existence, far away from the Mafia. What I knew about the Mafia was the little I had seen in movies, and I wasn't impressed. I saw nothing glamorous in preying on other people. When I moved to Long Island for a reporting job at *Newsday*, I was appalled at the respect, and deference, shown to the mobsters who operated freely on the margins of local governments. They sucked up lucrative paving and garbage contracts, and blocked legitimate contractors, as the mob padded the bills and provided substandard service or worse. That any politician would even talk to these thugs shocked me, but they did more than that. Often they were friends.

Over the years, I interviewed some bona fide mobsters, and they were, for the most part, not very interesting. They were greedy and violent, and there was no code of honor among them. They were out only for themselves. I knew enough to stay away.

And yet here I was, interviewing a man who had murdered and hurt countless people in pursuit of power and money, and I was enthralled.

It started when I interviewed Michael Franzese, Sonny's adopted son, for a story that would touch on the Mafia's influence on Long Island in the 1980s and '90s. Michael had once been a huge earner for the Colombo crime family. However, when law enforcement caught up with him and he faced years in prison, he cooperated, feeding federal authorities information about Mafia leaders all over the country. That put a target on his back, and he left the life. After serving time in prison, he moved to California far away from the mob and became an evangelical pastor. Handsome, articulate, and comfortable with the press, he has turned his time in the Mafia into a profitable personal brand.

After our interview, Michael mentioned that he was going to visit his father, who was due to get out of prison in a few months. Because of Sonny's deep Long Island roots, it was an obvious story for *Newsday*, and I jumped at it.

In doing the story of his release, I was struck by the respect Sonny had both from street criminals and people in law enforcement. That's unusual. Cops and prosecutors typically are dismissive of mobsters because so many of them are like the ones I've met—greedy, violent, and dangerous. Sonny was different. He was tough and self-disciplined and inspired loyalty among his men. He had been a massive celebrity in his day and had spent years in prison because, unlike Michael, he had refused to rat out his confederates. I had to get an interview with him.

I tried the usual channels—his lawyer, family members, and friends—but few were willing to talk. Finally, "Frankie Blue Eyes," Sonny's longtime friend, emerged. In the traitorous world of the Mafia, Frankie Blue Eyes was pure in his devotion to Sonny.

Frankie—to this day, I don't know his last name, and he likes it that way—asked Sonny if he wanted to talk to us. He said he would. I'm not sure why. Frankie said he remembered the old *Newsday* stories about him, when he was frequently front-page news. I think it may have been that Sonny was simply ready. He knew he had a great story to tell.

When we arrived at the nursing home, Sonny was out for an appointment. As we waited for him at the deli across the street, Frankie Blue Eyes talked about his regrets in his own life, but remained proud of his friendship with Sonny. It pained him deeply that his old friend was stuck in a nursing home.

After three hours of waiting, we gave up and started to leave. I went to the front desk to leave a platter of freshly baked Italian cookies for Sonny. My thinking was that, at the very least, the prospect of meeting a gangster of Sonny's stature was an occasion and that I should bring an offering. The only thing I could think of was a platter of cookies. I'm sure other people thought bringing cookies to a mobster was laughable, but the gesture paid off.

The nursing-home employees had been strict about adhering to patient privacy guidelines. But upon seeing the cookies, one aide pulled me aside and whispered, "If you wait a little longer, he just might be coming back in twenty minutes in the next ambulette."

So we continued to wait, until it finally seemed inevitable that we had missed him. We got up to leave again. Then Sonny rolled in. Though in a wheelchair, he looked far younger than his years because he exuded vigor. He quickly took command of the situation. He eyed each of us, appraisingly, smiling, but reserved. Frankie Blue Eyes stepped forward. "These are the people from *Newsday* I told you about," he told him.

Sonny relaxed, smiling broadly. He wanted to talk.

I had come armed with court records, old newspaper and magazine articles, and photos of Sonny. I had thought they might help break the ice, and they did. He dove into the records with gusto, occasionally asking me to read sections, because his eyesight was failing. When I read him the notes FBI agents had written while listening in on private conversations at his home through illegal bugs, his jaw clenched. For a moment, I thought he would erupt, but ever disciplined, he remained calm. His mood lifted when I showed him his rap sheet, with crimes dating back to 1938. It was as if I had shown him his high-school yearbook. He went through each crime, filling in details, laughing at the memories.

Sonny was unabashed about being a bad guy.

"Every night I sleep good," he said.

The stories came tumbling out—his time in the army, his affairs with famous women, his tense friendship with Frank Sinatra. He spoke about prison, his family, even his regrets. I found him to be surprisingly open, but still cagey. He was far less willing to talk about money—"I don't want the IRS coming after me"—and he only admitted crimes for which the statute of limitations had expired.

He spoke fondly of Bobby Darin, whom Morris "Mo" Levy, of Roulette Records, had "given" him. He was really impressed with his talent, which he thought far outstripped Sinatra's. And he genuinely liked Darin's first wife, Sandra Dee—"She was a nice girl, couldn't sing, though, couldn't sing." Unlike all the other famous women he told me about, he never claimed to have had an affair with her.

We were together for several hours that day, and he never tired. Both avuncular and crude, he recalled long-ago events with startling clarity. He was keenly aware of his place in the annals of American crime and expressed pride that he had never ratted on anyone. "No one in history" had done what he had done, and a comparison to Jesus Christ was apt, in his view. "Jesus suffered. He didn't squeal on nobody."

An aide brought him dinner, and he slapped the tray in disgust. "Rice again! I'm so sick of that crap."

I don't know if he was performing for me, but it worked. I immediately offered to bring him food the next time we saw each other. After going through several options, we settled on *pasta e fagioli*, his favorite.

"My mother used to make it good," he said. "A lot of people don't realize it. They don't put garlic in it, it don't taste good."

When I left, Frankie Blue Eyes turned to me and said, "You made his day."

"No, Frankie," I replied. "He made mine."

We would meet five more times, always with *pasta e fagioli*, pizza, meatball hero sandwiches, and more from the one pizza place left in the neighborhood actually run by an Italian. Sonny had an enormous appetite, and he often looked over to my plate to poach a bite. One time, a bunch of his old friends showed up. Sonny performed for them, telling vulgar and ugly stories, as they hooted their approval. For some reason, I wasn't repelled. It was fascinating to see this completely different facet of his personality.

In between visits, Sonny would hear from others I had contacted for interviews. They weren't calling to let him know; they were calling to ask his permission. He never denied it, and his friends kept talking to me.

I couldn't help but like Sonny. It might have been because I never spoke to any of his victims, because they were either dead or too terrified to talk to me. Or perhaps it was because he was so good at reading me. His ability to read people, after all, was part of what kept him alive for so long. Years ago, I rejected the chance to talk to guys like him, but Sonny had the ability to draw you in. He was the kind of guy you'd want to invite over for a backyard barbecue, until you remembered that you'd be crazy to let anyone you loved anywhere near him.

Maybe the simplest explanation for my liking Sonny is that I fell in love with his story. His life was an epic adventure, and he knew it. Just before his last birthday, he sent word through a mutual acquaintance that he wanted me to come to the celebration at the nursing home. A coworker was convinced that Sonny didn't mean it and said I shouldn't go. But the invitation was so specific and intentional, I was pretty sure he did mean it. When I arrived, Sonny looked delighted to see me, which immediately put his wary relatives at ease. He was recovering from pneumonia and looked pale and tired. We chatted for a while, and though his relatives invited me to stay, I didn't want to intrude on a family gathering. I left.

Besides, the message had been sent: Sonny wanted me to tell his story.

A little more than two weeks later, he died.

CHAPTER 1

The House on Shrub Hollow Road

"They wanted me to roll all the time. I couldn't do that."

THE WHITE HOUSE on Shrub Hollow Road was not unlike the other houses on the winding street on suburban Long Island. A newly built Colonial, with a two-car garage, it was set back on a half acre of manicured lawn about forty minutes east of New York City in Roslyn. The family, a husband and wife and five children, went about the normal business of life in the well-heeled sub-urbs—Little League games, parent-teacher conferences, and Sunday dinners. But inside the house, life was far from normal.

In fact, someone was listening.

It was the early 1960s, and the FBI had placed bugs in the kitchen wall while the house was under construction. After the family moved in and went about their daily routine, FBI agents listened in on a special line that went to their Manhattan office, taking notes. The bugs were entirely illegal, but that didn't stop agents from eavesdropping on the family's conversations. The family didn't know.

Agents had bugged the home because it was owned by John "Sonny" Franzese, the notorious Mafia up-and-comer who had murdered his way up through the hierarchy of what was then known as the Profaci family. Sonny committed his first murder at the age of fourteen. Aspiring wiseguys did not get to choose their Mafia family; the mob hierarchy assigned them to families. Sonny became affiliated with the Profaci family. The New York City Police Department heard rumors that the young Italian from Greenpoint, Brooklyn, was involved, but his father, Carmine "the Lion" Franzese, moved quickly to shut down any investigation. In those days, a well-placed bribe in the NYPD worked wonders.

It became a singular point of pride for Sonny, because as a result of that act, he was "made," or inducted into the Mafia, which at the time was still a secret society unknown to the general public. Because Sonny was so young and because of law enforcement's interest in the murder, the family decided to keep his new status under wraps for two years. Secrecy was one of the Mafia's most important currencies, and Sonny was more disciplined than most in adhering to his oath. Over the coming years, as mob boss after mob boss rolled and violated omertà, the Cosa Nostra's vow of silence, Sonny was steadfast. He never ratted, even though his refusal would come at a great personal cost.

"They wanted me to roll all the time," he said years later. "I couldn't do that. Because it's my principle."

As Sonny rose through the ranks, he enforced his discipline with a bloodlust that terrified even the toughest of gangsters. Once, he sold his car to a Long Island dealership, which, in turn, put it up for sale. A car salesman told the buyer to have it swept for bugs because it had belonged to "a hoodlum named Sonny Franzese." Whether the salesman had merely been making an offhand remark or having a little fun by passing on underworld gossip, he had made a profoundly stupid mistake. Word got back to Sonny. Days later, three thugs showed up at the dealership with baseball bats. They beat the salesman savagely, nearly killing him, and left him bleeding and broken on the floor. The man survived, but was crippled for life.

Authorities believed Sonny personally killed or ordered the murders of scores of people. He admitted as much in a boast to a young hustler he was mentoring, but who was secretly taping him. "I killed a lot of guys . . . You're not talking about four, five, six, ten."

It wasn't just the body count that excited him. He took pride in his methods of disposing of bodies. When he stopped into a body shop he owned, he always pointed out the vats of acid to his youngest son, John. "Oh, that's good, that's good," he told him. "Acid, that's good. Remember that." John understood that his father was referring to dissolving bodies with it.

Keeping tabs on Sonny was so important to the FBI that agents' Airtel memos went directly to FBI Director J. Edgar Hoover. "Hoover would give his left nut to get Sonny Franzese," proclaimed one FBI agent.

Sonny was keenly aware of law enforcement's interest in him. Years later, he said he had suspected that the government was eavesdropping on him: "I didn't know. Had an idea, but they denied it, so I couldn't use it because they said it wasn't true."

He didn't worry about it anyway because he prided himself on his discipline. He had two separate phone lines installed at his house and still kept his phone conversations short and vague. When he was on the streets of Manhattan, he never used the same phone booth twice. If he wanted to have a business conversation with an associate at home, he'd pull the man into the bathroom and run the water. Even with that, he would still whisper. And he never discussed business with a woman.

For Sonny, eluding the government and beating the system was part of the endgame. One day, a friend stopped by with his nine-year-old son. Sonny noticed that the boy looked glum and asked him, "What's wrong with you?"

"My dad hit me because I was charging people to be my friend, and if they didn't pay me, I'd fight them," the boy replied.

Sonny slapped the boy on the side of his head. Stunned, the boy said, "What was that for?"

"For getting caught," Sonny replied.

By the 1960s, Sonny was at the peak of his power. In his mid- to late forties, he cut a handsome figure in finely tailored suits.

Thick-necked and built like a boxer, he walked with an athlete's natural grace. When he walked into a room, he would survey it, always calculating his edge. Without a word, he could dominate a room. Conversations would quiet down and people would steal glances his way. He knew the effect he had on people, and he relished it.

If he had any weakness at all, it was for his second wife, Tina, a lovely and lissome brunette he had fallen for when she was just a teenager, seventeen years his junior, and he was married to someone else. They met in 1950 at the Stork Club, a swanky Manhattan hot spot frequented by celebrities. Friends thought he'd like to meet a pretty young cigarette girl there, sixteen-year-old Tina Capobianco.

"So they told me, the guy said, 'Sonny, why don't you come along? She's a nice girl, and you'll like her. She's a pretty son of a gun.'

"I says, 'All right, if I got nothing to do, I'll meet you.'

"So then I came, and I went to the club, and I saw her. If I hadda married her that minute, I woulda been married from that day on. I fell in love with her the second I saw her. Isn't that something? That's how it went. Love at first sight. She was very pretty, a very pretty girl. She knew how to dress, she knew how to walk, every goddamn thing."

Tina was the perfect partner for his ambitions. Smart and status-conscious, she kept up appearances, dressing her children in expensive clothes and schooling them in social graces. They were the only children in the neighborhood who said "yes, ma'am" and "no, ma'am" to adults. When guests visited their home, which was always immaculate, Tina had coffee cake and fresh coffee on hand. And like Sonny, she immediately sized up anyone who came into their home.

Tina had no illusions about who her husband was. When Sonny was courting her, he took her to Manhattan's hottest clubs, flaunting his ties in the entertainment business, as well as his other connections. On one date, Albert Anastasia, then the boss of not only "Murder Inc.," but also of New York's waterfront, came over to their table to say hello to Sonny. Tina was impressed.

The two of them made a dazzling pair—with movie-star looks, smarts, and charm that inevitably drew people into their orbit. In fact, when he and Tina first met, movie producers offered her a contract. Sonny hated the idea.

"She knew I was against it," he recalled. "I told her, 'You do that, we'll break up. You're not gonna be my girl.'

"Every girl that went into the movies hadda be a whore . . . That's what I was worried about. I'm a die-hard guy. You're my woman, you're my woman, nobody else's. She didn't take it."

By the time the family moved into the house on Shrub Hollow Road, Sonny controlled gambling, extortion, and loan shark rackets throughout Brooklyn, Queens, and much of Long Island. An informant told FBI agents that Sonny and his pal, Joseph Colombo, were paying New York City police $1,500 a month for the protection of a single craps game in Brooklyn.

One day, a profitable trucking company came to his attention. Mobsters always look to see who's making money, and Sonny wanted in. He sent two of his men over to explain that the trucker was going to have a new business partner.

Bemused, the trucker told them, "Hey, I don't need a business partner."

Sonny's men laughed and looked at each other. "Oh, yeah, you do."

He kicked them out. The next day, one of his new trucks didn't start. Someone had poured sand into the carburetor. He cleared it out and went about his business. A few days later, four men burst into his office with baseball bats. Before he could run, they launched their attack, beating him mercilessly with the bats. The last thing he remembered before losing consciousness was one of the men shouting, "Sonny wants to talk to you!"

As they had at the car dealership, they left him on the floor, bloody, broken, and barely alive.

The next thing he remembered was waking up at the hospital.

But it wasn't over. Several very large men stopped by his hospital room with some paperwork. That's when he signed over half his business to Sonny.

In the 1960s, truckers knew the risks they faced from organized crime, but the injustice of it rankled the victim. He complained to an Internal Revenue Service agent, who contacted Gerald Shur, then an attorney in the U.S. Justice Department's organized-crime and racketeering section. "We got a promising lead," the agent told Shur. "How fast can you get here?"

Around that time, in October 1961, the U.S. government, prodded by U.S. Attorney General Robert F. Kennedy, was ramping up its efforts against organized crime. Shur saw the trucking company owner's story as the perfect opportunity to make a case against a major organized-crime figure. He asked him to testify against Sonny.

"Testify?" he responded. "I thought just telling you would be enough. The mob will kill me and my entire family if I testify. No way am I speaking out against Sonny Franzese!"

Shur was dumbfounded. He pushed hard, but a government bureaucrat was no match for the Mafia. The trucking company owner, understandably, refused.

Shur, a serious man who believed deeply in the power of government to do justice, fumed on the way back to his office from the meeting. "There's got to be a way to get witnesses to testify against the mob," he said.

"Would you?" asked one of the agents in the car.

Shur turned to what he knew best: government bureaucracy. He began writing memos urging the Justice Department to create a program to protect government witnesses. It was the only way, he argued, that they could make headway against gangsters like Sonny Franzese.

His argument resonated with like-minded attorneys in the department. Within a decade, the Witness Security Program (WITSEC), or the Federal Witness Protection Program, would become a reality. The program, which became a critical tool to keep witnesses who testified against organized crime and other violent criminals out of harm's way, would come back to haunt Sonny years later in a way he never could have imagined.

Sonny had no idea that his little trucking-company takeover had caught the attention of the U.S. Justice Department. He wouldn't have worried about it anyway, as he was preoccupied with something far more important in his life at that time.

A war had broken out within the Profaci family after one of its soldiers, Joe "Crazy Joe" Gallo, made a move to take over the family. And Sonny was at the center of it.

Gallo had been angry for years. He felt that family boss Joseph "Olive Oil King" Profaci treated him like a peasant and favored his relatives and sycophants over the men who did the real work. Making money under him was tough, too. Every time Gallo tried to move in on a racket, he discovered it was under some other wiseguy's control. He and his brothers had had enough.

Sonny warned Profaci that the Gallos were going to make a move; but Profaci, by then rumored to be ailing with cancer, didn't act.

The Gallos struck in February 1961. They kidnapped Profaci underboss Joseph Magliocco and bodyguard John Scimone, but failed to grab Joe Profaci, who had gone to a Florida hospital for cancer treatment.

As they demanded a bigger piece of the numbers racket, and amnesty for the kidnapping, they held their hostages at a Manhattan hotel. Tense negotiations followed, with Sonny acting as emissary. Profaci passed word that he would negotiate, only after his men were released, but Crazy Joe insisted that they kill one of the hostages as a sign of their resolve.

Joe's older brother, Larry, nixed that plan. After two weeks, they released three of the hostages, but hung on to Scimone, whose toughness they had come to admire, for another week.

The Mafia commission, or bosses of all five families, weighed in. The Gallos' revolt clearly had violated Mafia rules, but the bosses believed they had a legitimate complaint about not getting their fair share. The commission decided not to intervene, ruling that it was an internal matter of the Profaci family.

Negotiations between the boss and the rebels dragged on. Profaci promised concessions, but never came through. The Gallos felt squeezed financially; but unlike the ailing and older Profaci, they were young and strong and had struck up new alliances, most notably with Carmine "Junior" Persico, who was known for a particular bloodlust. "He likes to kill," one friend said of Junior. The Gallos waited, stocking up on guns.

Profaci, however, had his own plans.

One Sunday afternoon, in October, Scimone called Larry Gallo and asked him to meet him at the Sahara Lounge in Flatbush, Brooklyn. Larry trusted Scimone, believing they had bonded during the kidnapping. He went to meet him. While he was chatting with the bartender, two men emerged from the shadows and looped a rope around his neck—they had opted for a rope, rather than a gun, for the killing to be more discreet. They didn't try to kill him right away. They pulled the rope tight until he was gasping for breath and then loosened it ever so slightly, enough to let him gulp some air. Their torture had a point: They ordered Larry to summon his brothers to the bar.

He refused, evidently ready to accept his fate. Just as they pulled the rope tighter to kill him, a patrolman, who had noticed that the side door to the bar was ajar, walked in to check on the place. Larry was saved.

One of the two men who had pulled the rope around Larry Gallo's neck was none other than Junior Persico, their supposed ally. From then on, the Gallos called him "the Snake," a moniker that stuck, and one that Persico loathed throughout his life. Though Sonny and Junior Persico were closely allied, Sonny would come to understand the "Snake" epithet years later.

Persico was arrested and charged in the garrote attack, but refused to testify.

The attack sparked a vicious internecine battle within the Profaci family, resulting in at least a dozen murders. New York tabloid newspapers covered the war with gusto, sparing no grisly detail. Readers lapped it up.

In the Franzese household, though, the stories were far more than simply lurid headlines. They were disturbingly real.

FBI agents could hear the tensions simmering in their house. Sonny and Tina, who had gotten married in 1959, fought constantly. They fought over money, taking care of the children, even whose mother was better. It became clear to the agents, however, that the ever-present threat of violence often ignited their arguments.

One day, FBI agents heard Tina scream, "Your mother hates you, and I have to put up with you."

With that, Sonny slapped her. Tina, unafraid, threatened to leave him. "Where's your gun, big man?" she yelled.

Sonny left, and Tina called her mother, Antoinette Capobianco. She was furious about the argument and still seething over something that had happened earlier.

"I'm definitely leaving him," she told her, explaining that they had had a violent fight after John, their first child and then just a toddler, walked into the bedroom and saw Sonny sitting on the bed with a gun next to him. John, a bright and curious child, asked what it was. Tina was horrified.

"That's a fine thing for a father to show his baby," Tina spat.

"Hide the gun, Tina," Antoinette replied.

"I will not hide it. I will have nothing to do with it. Besides, it's never loaded," Tina said. "You know what he did? While I was holding the baby in my arms, Sonny held the gun up to my eyes! If he ever does that again, I'll cut his hand off."

Tina meant it. For all her husband's ferocity on the street, she wasn't cowed by him. She continued to fume to her mother. "Nobody ever bothers him. He's a big man!" she said, her tone oozing with sarcasm.

"He's always playing with that gun."

After getting off the phone with her mother, Tina called another woman and related the same story about their fight, but then confessed to a deeper worry.

"He's out tonight," she said. "Tomorrow I'll be reading about all the murders, and I won't sleep nights."

At times, the tensions would ease. One night, Sonny kissed Tina good-bye, put two guns in his pockets, and left. Tina silently watched him go. For all her rages, her terror of his being killed trumped everything. Neither one of them knew whether he'd come back alive.

When Sonny stayed away for days at a time, two bodyguards kept watch over Tina and the children; but Sonny knew that might not be enough.

When he finally came home days later, tense and unshaven, he confessed to his own worry: "I was on pins and needles. I didn't know if something had happened to you."

Tina, too, was racked with worry. She turned to her mother; they spoke every day.

"Every time he goes out, I'm afraid," she told her. "I expect to read in the paper that he's been murdered."

CHAPTER 2

Making His Bones

"I was a pretty good fistfighter."

SONNY WAS BORN in Naples during one of his family's sojourns to their native Italy, but he grew up in Greenpoint, Brooklyn, a tough neighborhood teeming with Italian immigrants who had fled World War I in the 1920s. His father, Carmine "the Lion" Franzese, who had been a Cosa Nostra don in Naples, was well-respected in America. He owned eighteen buildings, including the spartan three-apartment building on Leonard Street where Sonny grew up and opened his own social club at Leonard and Jackson Streets. The club, though unassuming on the outside, was an important place to be seen for local gangsters. Al Capone, a fellow Neapolitan, carved his initials, A.C., into a wooden counter there.

To the world outside the Mafia, the Lion was a simple baker, which could account for Sonny's lifelong fascination with ovens. But to those who knew him well, he was tough and treacherous. A man once came to his store to beg forgiveness for witnessing something he shouldn't have. The Lion smiled, reassured him everything was all right, and invited him to relax with him in the back of the shop. The relieved man followed him back there, and the Lion promptly killed him.

The man had witnessed Sonny committing his first murder at age fourteen.

*   *   *

Sonny was the youngest son of eighteen children, only ten of whom survived to adulthood. His sisters fussed over the beautiful baby, and his older brothers carted him to baseball games at Ebbets Field, the Major League baseball stadium in Crown Heights, Brooklyn. But the bloody undercurrents of his family's life were never far away. When he was two years old, Sonny was eating *pasta e fagioli* and playing cards with a girl—family members say it was a sister, but he said it was a neighbor—and they fought over a card. "She lets go of the fork, and boom! It went right in my eye."

His mother, Maria, rushed him to the hospital. "They wanted to take the eye out. And my mother's crying, 'Please, Doctor, please don't take his eye out! Please save it. Do something! Do something!' The doctor got so impressed, he said, 'All right, Mom, I'll try very hard to save it,' and he saved it. I still got the eye. Can't see as good with it, I can't see good, but I still got it."

There was no coddling in the Franzese family, his eye notwithstanding, and he quickly picked up the code of the street. He became a fighter.

"In our neighborhood, you had to be a fighter because the whole neighborhood was fighters. And if you didn't fight, you got your lumps, so you hadda be a fighter. That's how I wound up fightin'."

Sonny's older brother Onofrio, known as "Nufrio," was someone nobody in the neighborhood messed with. He was small, but people knew what he was capable of. He managed to win over at least some of his neighbors by hosting block parties, staging fireworks on the Fourth of July, and opening the hydrants—called "Johnny pumps" in those days—for the kids on hot summer days.

He also staged fights "to prove that their neighborhood didn't have a better fighter than us," and because a little wagering made it more interesting. Sonny was the star. Although he complained to his brother—"them punches hurt"—boxing held him in its thrall. He loved the two-man contest, the primal nature of it.

Unsanctioned fights were popular in the neighborhood, and word spread about the young Italian. One day, Sonny, still a teenager, had a fight set with a much larger guy at the Broadway Arena in the Bushwick section of Brooklyn. He was apprehensive—"How am I into this one?"—but could not refuse, because his friends would think he was a coward.

"Now there's all guys around. I look around, I see all my friends. I said, 'I can't say no, they'll think I'm afraid.'"

The fighters weighed in. Sonny was 147 pounds, his opponent 169—too much of a weight difference for a fight.

"So the guy said, 'We can't make the match.' 'Oh,' I said, 'thank God.'"

The promoter had other ideas, however. "So he said, 'No, no, no.' He said, 'Something's wrong. The guy had his foot on the scale. He must have been touching it. Let's do it again.' So he makes me one seventy-one . . . and the guy one sixty-nine. And I fight the guy."

The other fighter came on strong, trying to overwhelm the smaller teenager.

"And when I fight him, as soon as I walk in the ring, he hits me, a shot on the nose. I thought I was knocked out on my feet, standing up. As soon as I come to, I went at the guy like a maniac. I hit him; he goes down. When he goes down, I jump on him on the floor and I start hitting him. That's where Rocky Graziano got that stuff from hitting a guy on the floor, he got it from me.

"And I start hitting him on the floor, I was banging him out till the referee comes over. 'You guinea bastard!'

"I said, 'Screw you, you rat son of a bitch, I'll fight you next, you bum.'

"'You gonna fight me next?'

"'Yeah, I'm gonna fight you next. Get out of the way!' And I knocked the guy out."

The referee backed out of a fight with Sonny. He said he was a police sergeant and, thus, couldn't fight.

"You know something, I'll be honest—not that I'm bragging. I hate to brag, because you brag, then you go out on the street, you fight with a guy, you get knocked dead—I was a pretty good fist-fighter."

Even as a young man, Sonny carried himself with an easy authority. He was nearly five-ten and solidly built. An avid sports fan, he loved listening to boxing matches on the radio. He had a broad grin and always greeted his neighbors with respect. Schoolwork came easily to him, as did the girls. "I was in demand, believe me. I never knew why. I never thought I was good-looking. I never really did. As time went on, I became overcome with the attention I got, you know."

For a while, Sonny dated a "cute Irish girl," and he really liked her. But her father barred him from their house: "I'm not pure-blood. What kind of blood do I got? I thought there was only one kind of blood, red."

Furious, he confronted her. "Did you tell him I went to bed widja? I aint pure-blood! I'm more red-blooded than anybody. I'm a die-hard American!"

Normal boundaries didn't apply to Sonny. He went wherever his appetites led him, even trying to seduce a teacher in high school. "It made me a little nervous. I'm a kid, but I know enough about life to know what to do. When she heard me talking like that, she buckled away. She was afraid . . . She used to always come near me, and I'd say, 'Let's do something.' God bless her, she held her place."

By then, life at Eastern District High School in Brooklyn seemed small and dull compared to life on the street. Another boy's cigarette lighter caught Sonny's eye, when he was fifteen. "It was stolen," he said, never explaining just how he happened to wind up with it. When the lighter's owner saw Sonny playing with it, he challenged him to a fight. This was no idle threat; the boy was the school's entry in the Golden Gloves tournament. Naturally, Sonny couldn't refuse a challenge. By his telling, he easily dispatched his opponent.

Although he won the fight, he lost any future in high school. He was expelled.

"When my father heard I was fighting, he went crazy . . . 'Look,' he said—in Italian, he couldn't speak English—'if you wanna fight, I'll make you fight. You fight with me. I'll beat you up. Nobody's gonna beat you up, but me. Either you stop, or I'll break both your legs.' So I stopped. He was a firm believer in that. He didn't want to see any of his children hurt."

After leaving high school, Sonny ostensibly had gone to work in his father's bakery, but his real job was running a craps game in Brooklyn—the biggest game in New York. Sonny had an intuitive feel for business and powerful backing. Although the craps game was under the aegis of an older wiseguy, "I was the one running it."

Sonny was a soldier in the Profaci family. To move up in the family ranks, he needed to make money, and he was very good at that. He was making an impression on the adults around him, even the principal who expelled him from Eastern District High School. "He comes back into the neighborhood and starts asking questions about me. When they told him that I ran the neighborhood, that I become a wiseguy, he said, 'I expected him to become something big, but not that.'"

The principal wasn't the only person who noticed Sonny's success. Powerful mobsters did, too.

Albert Anastasia, who ran a hit-man-for-hire organization, nicknamed "Murder Inc." in the press, and Vito Genovese, a longtime associate of Charles "Lucky" Luciano, clashed in a dispute over turf. Both were powerful men, and they eyed each other's activities warily. Sonny idolized both men, and soon found himself in the middle of a precarious standoff that would test his ability to navigate the treacherous byways of the mob.

Anastasia had asked two brothers from Genovese's neighborhood to tell him whenever Genovese was on his turf. Instead, they reported it back to Genovese, who was furious at the affront. Genovese called Sonny and said, "You busy?"

Sonny told Genovese, a fellow Neapolitan, "No, no, no, for you, I'm never busy."

He went to see Genovese, who asked him if he knew anybody around Anastasia. Sonny said he did. Genovese asked him to set up a meeting with Anastasia's people.

Sonny brought two of Anastasia's hoods to the meeting and then expected to leave. His family, the Profacis, was not part of the dispute; and he didn't want to know what was discussed. He knew that that could only create problems for him.

But the men insisted that he stay. The meeting lasted two hours and culminated with a succinct order from one of Genovese's men: "Tell him (Anastasia) to fucking stay away from this neighborhood."

Sonny left, but it wasn't over. Someone from his crew heard about the meeting, and he was summoned to another meeting to explain what had happened. Sonny was in a tough spot: He knew he couldn't reveal what had happened at the meeting, nor could he show a lack of respect to his own crew. He danced around it, insisting that he hadn't really heard anything.

He handled himself with enough aplomb that both Genovese and Anastasia were impressed, and Genovese became his lifelong champion. Men on the street viewed Genovese as a homicidal maniac, but Sonny admiringly called him "the toughest cocksucker I ever met."

The guys in Sonny's own crew weren't sure he was leveling with them, but they let it go, because he was earning too much money.

Gambling was big business, and floating craps games—a dice game that never remained in the same place, but changed locations frequently—were especially popular. Players would arrive at a predetermined location and were taken to wherever the game was being held. Food and entertainment, usually in the form of prostitutes, were often provided. Such setups invariably attracted the attention of authorities, but liberal payoffs to police ensured that the wiseguys would be tipped off to any planned raids. More than once, detectives assigned to the NYPD's elite gambling squad would break down the door of a game, only to find that the players and hosts had vacated the premises moments before their arrival.

Sonny, too, was becoming adept at evading the legal consequences of his illicit activities. He loved besting the cops. His first arrest was for felonious assault in Brooklyn on January 7, 1938. A day later, the charge was dismissed. Two more arrests followed in the same year. Each one was for disorderly conduct and resulted in a $10 fine and a day in jail. He was twenty-one years old.

So began a pattern of arrests over the next twenty-eight years in which he displayed a remarkable ability to dodge jail time. Each time he was arrested, he was acquitted, the charges were dismissed, or he was let off with a nominal fine. For Sonny, the arrests were a brief interruption of business. Anytime he got into a jam with the police, he could turn to the mob's vast network of snitches and cops receptive to bribes and friendly judges, when necessary.

Secure in his chosen career, Sonny took up with a pretty and voluptuous blond teenager, Anna Schiller, who gave birth to their first daughter, Maryann, in February 1941. Anna was fifteen. Sonny was twenty-four. Throughout his life, Sonny would favor younger, but not necessarily docile, women. Although he considered himself a traditionalist, he didn't legalize their union until November 1942.

Their marriage was volatile. Anna and Sonny fought often, and he threatened to disfigure her face with a knife.

Sonny's newfound domesticity, as tenuous as it was, was soon eclipsed by world events. The Japanese surprise attack on the U.S. naval base at Pearl Harbor in Honolulu pushed the previously neutral United States into World War II. Sonny wanted to join the fight. He went to a recruiter's office to sign up, only to be rebuffed after the recruiter decided he had to talk to a psychiatrist, who didn't think he'd be a good candidate for the Army.

Furious, Sonny lunged at the psychiatrist, grabbed his arm, and demanded that he let him enlist. They fought for about fifteen minutes, until the doctor got up, left the office, and told him to wait. Sonny expected him to return with military police to arrest him. Instead, "He comes back with two more doctors. They sit down and says, 'What's on your mind, soldier?'

"I says, 'What's on my mind? Nothin' is on my mind.'

"'Then what are you arguing with the doctor for?'

"'He says he wants to reject me. I don't want to be rejected. I want to go overseas and fight.'

"So he looks at the guy and he says, 'What the hell are you getting mad about? What do you want to reject him for? He wants to go and fight, let him go.'"

Things were no less contentious once he successfully enlisted in May 1943. He had frequent scrapes with other soldiers. By Sonny's account, he won every fight, and they were always against bigger and better-trained fighters. Once, while stationed in South Carolina, he got into a fight and ended up with two guys holding his arms while a third punched him. Another soldier persuaded the group to settle their beef with a fair fight, so they went to the gym. They squared off, and Sonny, of course, knocked out his rival.

Not surprisingly, Sonny's combativeness came to the attention of the military brass; in his view, they were impressed. "They liked me because I had guts. Now I could fight with everybody. I didn't care for nobody. I figure I'm going to die, I'm going overseas and dying. I wasn't worried about nobody. You know what I mean?"

The top brass weren't his only admirers. "My major's wife fell in love with me. I was having sex with her all the time. I didn't know they'd shoot you if you have sex in the wartime."

Army officers tried to get Sonny to make a career of the army, he said, but he told them, "'I ain't a career man. I'm not. I just joined the army to fight for my country. Help them to win or lose,' I said. 'I can't be the guy. Once the war is over, I'm out.'"

Years later, he wasn't sure he had made the right decision. "I should have took it. I'd have been a general today."

When his unit boarded a train to go overseas, a lieutenant pulled him off the train. "He said, 'We have to hold you.' Somebody told them that if I went overseas, that I was going to shoot all the officials. I never said that. I never would shoot them . . . How could I shoot them? They made up stories about me that were never true. They took me off and they put me in the hospital."

He was dishonorably discharged for "pronounced homicidal tendencies" in 1944. He had been in the army a little over a year.

Once he was out, Sonny was back on the street. One night in the late 1940s, he was sitting in a back corner of the Orchid Room, a bar he owned in Jackson Heights, laughing and talking with a younger man. Everything seemed friendly.

All of a sudden, a shot rang out, and the man slumped to the floor. Sonny signaled to an associate, and the body was quickly removed and dumped on the street.

What struck observers who later recounted the scene was that afterward, Sonny resumed talking and laughing, as if nothing had happened.

That steely resolve—Sonny would later call it "determination"—caused others to recall a certain look he had, the kind that when he flashed it at you could make your blood run cold. He could toggle from telling a funny and folksy anecdote to an ice-cold stare. Anyone who saw that stare remembered it.

Meanwhile, his marriage to Anna was crumbling. Once he met Tina, it was all but over, though it would be years before they got married.

Like Sonny, Tina had grown up in Brooklyn, but under very different circumstances. Her father, Rocco, was a school bus driver, and her mother, Antoinette, worked in a textile factory. They were hardworking people and ran a strict household. They had high expectations for their children and disciplined them when they fell short—Tina's mother would pinch her cheeks if she earned anything less than an A in school.

Tina yearned for a more glamorous life beyond Brooklyn.

Though still a teenager, she moved easily among the celebrity patrons at the linen-topped tables of the Stork Club. Actor Montgomery Clift was said to be smitten with her. However, once Sonny saw her, he became determined to clear away any competition.

With Tina, however, that wasn't so easy. Her parents disapproved of Sonny, who was seventeen years older than their daughter, and besides that, he was married. In any case, Tina had other suitors. In January 1951, she married a soldier named Louis Grillo. Four months later, she gave birth to a son, Michael.

But Sonny would not be put off; if anything, her slipping out of his grasp only increased his ardor. He pursued her relentlessly, sending friendly neighbors as emissaries to the Capobiancos to vouch for his good intentions.

By 1959, Tina and Sonny shed their respective spouses and got married.

The two of them would become a formidable couple.

CHAPTER 3

Down to Business

"What we done in New York is unbelievable."

IN THEIR WEDDING PHOTO, Tina and Sonny look triumphant. Tina, chic with a hat perched jauntily on her head and a simple gold cross around her neck, is smiling broadly. Sonny, wearing a tuxedo and white carnation on his lapel, is positively beaming with pride. She was twenty-five. He was forty-two.

They were finally married. It was what she had wanted for years. While Sonny was still married to Anna, Tina would drive by their apartment, screaming at her to leave him. And finally, they were married. She had prevailed. She savored that victory, ready to start her new life with an important man who adored her.

All of that ruptured the moment they returned home from their honeymoon in Mexico. That's when Sonny sat Tina down to talk. "She ran off and left the kids," he told her. "We gotta take 'em."

It blindsided Tina. She had thought she was marrying a wealthy and powerful man who merely needed to divorce his first wife. She never knew Sonny had any children, let alone three. Her son, Michael, was just eight years old, and now she was expected to raise three more children from another mother—Maryann, Carmine, and Lorraine—as well. Everything she thought she knew was wrong, and the man she loved had kept this enormous secret from her. The new life she had dreamed of for so long vanished in an instant. She seethed with resentment.

But before long, her anger over her new circumstances was

temporarily alleviated by the birth of their first child together, John Franzese Jr., on April 22, 1960. Both Sonny and Tina were over the moon at John's birth. It was as if the stars had aligned perfectly to create this child. He was the spitting image of his father. A happy and energetic boy, he could do no wrong in his parents' eyes. Tina would go on to have two daughters, Gia and Christine ("Little Tina"), but John was always his parents' favorite, forgiven for any transgression.

Tina made it clear to her stepchildren that they were just that. At Christmas, they got cheap toys, while her own children were spoiled with expensive gifts. John, a sensitive boy, noticed it and didn't like it.

One wintry day, Tina pushed twelve-year-old Carmine, who had walked barefoot into the kitchen to check what was in the refrigerator, onto their snow-covered porch. She locked the door as she screamed at Sonny, "They belong with their mother!"

He responded, as he always did, that Anna wasn't cooperating. "What am I supposed to do? Throw them out on the streets? My hands are tied."

Whether that was true was never clear, and it didn't matter, since the result was the same. The argument was a routine between them and frequently ended with Sonny simply leaving the house.

Tina threw herself into decorating their home. If she couldn't have the life she dreamed of, she would at least create the façade of that life. She had exquisite, and expensive, taste. She bought the latest appliances and had washable plaid carpeting in the kitchen. Elsewhere in the house, she had their wooden parquet floors stained blue, revealing all the grains of the wood. The effect was breathtaking. With her fastidious housekeeping, their home looked like a designer showcase.

Outside, she had inground sprinklers installed, a novelty at the time. Because Tina never felt she had to pay her contractors—because she was, after all, married to Sonny Franzese—the system was poorly installed and didn't work. A couple of repairmen were summoned to fix it. As they were working, Sonny arrived home with two bodyguards. He watched them on his lawn for a while and said, "Whaddya doing?"

They chatted a bit, and Sonny learned that one of the repairmen had a fuel oil company on the side. That piqued his interest. "Oh, you got a fuel oil company? How big?"

The man, named Louie, puffed up and bragged about his fledgling business, which had all of one broken-down truck, but seemed bigger in Louie's telling. He wanted to impress the homeowner that he was more than just a sprinkler repairman. Sonny listened attentively, smiling, drawing him out. Finally, when Louie finished, he said, "Whaddya think? You wanna expand? I'm an entrepreneur. I finance young guys like you."

Fortunately, Louie was working with a friend who was savvier about street guys and knew enough to get out of there as soon as possible. The friend offered an excuse, and they finished the job and left without any complications for Louie's little business.

Sonny, for the most part, tolerated Tina's home improvements. But one day, she went too far. Disturbed by their barren front yard, she spent thousands to have trees and bushes planted all around their home. As always with Tina, she made sure it was done beautifully.

When Sonny came home and saw the new landscaping, he erupted and demanded that it all be ripped out. And so, their lovely suburban lawn was stripped of any potential hiding spots for assassins.

Sonny had reason to be cautious. He had been successful in brokering the truce in the Profaci internecine war in March 1962. Peace—always more profitable than war—was possible. Joe Gallo was in prison, having been convicted of conspiracy and extortion; Joe Profaci died shortly after the truce. Profaci's brother-in-law, Joseph Magliocco, was set to take over, but he had his own health problems. Far worse, however, was the way he had reacted when the Gallos had taken him hostage. He had shown fear. Word spread—gangsters are notoriously gossipy about such things—and Gambino, always looking for ways to knock out his rivals, pushed the commission bosses to show Magliocco that his standing had fallen.

Sonny, once again, emerged as the mediator. He began to talk to Magliocco about retiring. Sonny was one of the few people in the family with the stature to approach him; and besides, they had a long-standing personal relationship. Sonny's daughter had been a flower girl in a Magliocco family wedding.

Sonny's efforts appeased the commission. Family soldier Gregory Scarpa, who was working secretly as an informant for the FBI, told agents that "the family would be completely reorganized and that young men would be put in all of the executive positions, and the old men would act only as advisers."

Scarpa, known as "the Grim Reaper" because he loved killing, had become a top-echelon informant for the FBI in 1961. The agency considered it a coup because at the time, little was known about the key players in the Mafia or how it operated. Scarpa was intelligent, informative, and cagey enough to dangle tantalizing tidbits, while also settling scores with rivals. FBI agents filed copious reports about his information over the years, and they never balked when he whined about money, which he did constantly. They felt he was just too important an informant, and they were right.

Sonny never liked Scarpa. He didn't trust him and kept his distance. He later would tell his son John, "There's something wrong about that guy."

Sonny's instincts were right. Scarpa provided agents with valuable intelligence about him. Early on, Scarpa flagged Sonny to the FBI as an up-and-comer in the organization: "His opinions carry a great amount of weight because of his activity for the organization."

Scarpa's information was good. After helping to broker the truce, Sonny was made a capo, alongside his old pal Joe Colombo, in July 1962. It was an important promotion because it meant that he would have his own crew of men kicking up money to him. He already had a core group of men working for him, but now he was one of nine *caporegimes* in the four-hundred-man family, just below boss and underboss in rank. Below him were soldiers—all made members of the family—and a legion of associates, all involved in highly lucrative and tax-free illegal money-making operations. In addition, the bosses gave Sonny several of the illegal operations that Gallo's crew had run.

Money was rolling in.

"I started buying businesses, you know," Sonny said years later. "I started a used-car business. I started making money, and then I opened up a club, another club, another club, and I started making big money. Never under my name, though. I couldn't get a license . . . I was a bad guy."

By the early 1960s, the Mafia was riding high in New York. The syndicate had crime families throughout the country—from Chicago to New Orleans to Denver—but New York was the apex. In addition to making millions from traditional rackets, members of the city's five crime families had steadily insinuated themselves into government, labor unions, and the entertainment industry. Buoyed by money and power, mobsters enjoyed a star status all their own. From the sidelines, honest cops and prosecutors watched the mob's rise, seemingly helpless to stop it.

Even Sonny marveled at the Mafia's reach and influence— "What we done in New York is unbelievable."

And word was spreading about Sonny. Mobsters from all over the country began to hear about this rising star in New York. He was becoming known as a guy you could turn to, to take care of a problem, big or small.

That became evident one night when Frank Sinatra Jr. came to perform with the Tommy Dorsey Band at one of the nightclubs Sonny owned as a silent partner, the San Su San, a sleek dance club in Mineola topped with a huge neon sign. Built to accommodate large crowds, the club hosted big-name entertainers, like Red Buttons and actor Mickey Rooney, which was unusual for a club on suburban Long Island. That night, however, crowds were thin, and Frank Jr. was bombing. A call came in to Sonny from the Chicago outfit. The next night, the club was jammed, with a well-primed standing-room-only crowd and Sonny seated at the head table. After every song, they hooted and hollered, giving Frank Jr. standing ovations. Frank Jr., energized by the applause, rose to the occasion and gave a rousing performance. Someone alerted the entertainment press, and, miraculously, a series of rave reviews were published. Frank Jr. was a smash.

It was vintage Sonny. He was adept at fixing things behind the scenes.

It was one way Sonny separated himself. Rising to the top levels of a Mafia family and running a profitable crew required more sophisticated skills than leg breaking. It required managerial acumen, networking, and the ability to craft agreements with other families. Law enforcement recognized that and watched uneasily as Sonny moved in on what were supposed to be legitimate businesses.

Sonny opened the floodgates for organized crime in the suburbs. Not content with traditional rackets, he seized every opportunity he could to make money. While other mob bosses thought small, he thought big.

Sonny found the perfect place to expand his loan-sharking operations—banks. Banks were an obvious target; that was, after all, where the money was. But Sonny saw a better way to get in. It seemed that some banking executives found themselves getting into debt because of their own vices—whether it was an affinity for prostitutes or gambling—and had to turn to the street to get out from under. Sonny was only too happy to oblige. In return, his guys were able to take out bank loans at very reasonable interest rates and then put that money on the street for a much higher rate of return.

Sonny was a master of using OPM—other people's money.

Banks were an excellent place to do business, but labor unions were even better. Unions had a steady stream of revenue through members' dues and pension funds—irresistible to guys like Sonny. Just as significant, anyone who controlled the union controlled the associated industry. That meant the mob controlled the ability to call strikes and raise prices, giving it extraordinary power over civilian life—anyone outside the Mafia was considered a civilian. Its reach in labor ultimately extended from sanitation workers picking up garbage to the construction workers putting windows in new buildings, with the costs always passed on to the public.

To exercise that kind of control successfully, you needed someone who could think strategically, who understood what levers to pull. That's where Sonny came in.

Established unions were one thing, but Sonny wanted more. He was behind a novel plan to organize the roughly seven thousand barbers working on Long Island. The scheme had nothing to do with workers' rights or working conditions. It was about money.

Sonny's associate Salvatore "Sam the Pizza King" Calascione ran a sham union called the Long Island Barbers Guild. The guild set out to charge barbers a $50 initiation fee and $10-a-month dues, and enforce a price of $1.75 for a haircut. At the time, the going rate for a haircut was never more than $1.50. The beauty of the price increase was that the cost would be picked up by the public.

Those barbers who were disinclined to join were, of course, subject to forceful persuasion. One barber in Oceanside who didn't see the wisdom of joining the guild was physically ejected from his barbershop. On his way out of his shop, his attackers warned him that there were orders to chop off his hands. Before that order could be carried out, the barber signed up.

The sham union steadily picked up members, until one of Calascione's strong-arm men tipped off police about a plan to dynamite a barbershop. Authorities moved in quickly and shut it down, resulting in a high-profile trial. Sal Giglio, an associate of Sonny's, was expected to be a key witness in the case. Giglio never made it to the witness stand, however.

He died just two days before he was scheduled to testify, after his car crashed through a fence and hurtled into twelve feet of water in Newtown Creek in Greenpoint, Sonny's hometown. Police determined that it was an accident, and no one was ever charged.

As good as Sonny was at strategy, he was just as capable when it came to the nuts and bolts of extortion. That became obvious when some profitable hair salons in Queens caught his eye. For nearly a month in January 1961, he and an associate set loose mice in the shops to scare the hairdressers and customers, wreaking havoc.

That wasn't enough to make the owners capitulate, however, so Sonny had to come up with something else. He hit upon one that both satisfied and amused him. When shop proprietors sent out for coffee or soft drinks, Sonny sent back a surprise. He intercepted the order and substituted cups filled with bees. When the unsuspecting hairdressers opened up the cups, bees flew out. Once again, chaos ensued.

The shop owners caved. The price they paid to be left alone was hefty—$5,000 a month. Sonny netted $500,000 for himself.

Police caught wind of the scheme and arrested Sonny and a partner and charged them with extortion. Sonny insisted he was merely a salesman and labor organizer. The charge, like so many other earlier charges against Sonny, was dismissed. The judge simply voided it.

While some people resisted Sonny's brand of unionizing, others wholeheartedly embraced it. One night, Sonny attended a testimonial dinner in Brooklyn for Chuck Browne, president of Local 164 of the Hotel Employees and Bartenders Union of Nassau County. Roughly 2,500 people showed up, with Sonny and his nephew Carmine "Tutti" Franzese as honored guests. Browne did very well for himself that night: He got a thirty-foot cabin cruiser, a wristwatch, a ring, and many other small gifts.

That largesse didn't come directly from Sonny, but he allowed it to be given out. He always believed in sharing profits. "I always treated people fair," he said.

The men under him agreed. Unlike Profaci and other greedy bosses, Sonny always let them make money when they were working for him. It not only gave them an incentive to earn—and kick up more money to him—it ensured their loyalty.

But they could never get him to spring for a meal. Members of his crew made a game of trying to get him to pick up the tab when they went out to eat. It never worked. One night, Sonny invited his guys to a restaurant, promising he'd pay. Eager to see this unique event, they all showed up. After dinner, he asked the waitress for the bill. He started scrutinizing it, questioning each charge. His guys squirmed uncomfortably. They hated looking cheap. Finally, one of them couldn't stand it any longer. He jumped up and offered to pay the bill.

"Oh, no, you don't have to do that," Sonny told him.

"It's okay, it's okay," the embarrassed man replied, grabbing the bill.

Sonny's gambit had worked.

Unlike his mob contemporaries, Sonny never flaunted his wealth. Luciano crime boss Frank Costello, who craved acceptance in the legitimate world, lived in a sprawling estate in tony Sands Point on Long Island's Gold Coast. Carlo Gambino summered in a stately mansion on the water on the South Shore in Massapequa. Not Sonny. He preferred maintaining the veneer of middle-class respectability and dressed like an IBM executive. Besides, picking up a check wasn't the only way in which he was cheap. He hated spending his money, period.

It drove Tina crazy. She pressured him to take the family on vacation—like other suburban families—and he would oblige, as long as it was a free resort or complimentary plane ride. When they went to a restaurant, they would order, eat, and walk out without even being presented with a bill. It was just assumed that they wouldn't pay.

Tina didn't mind stiffing restaurant owners, but it infuriated her that he didn't want to spend money on his family. She'd spend more money just to get under his skin.

It worked. One day, Sonny demanded to know why their checking account was overdrawn. He complained about a returned check. "Does it cost a lot to support me?" Tina shot back.

More than anything, Tina hated being shut out. He never confided anything truly important to her. As he told John when his son was older, "You never tell a woman anything. You never trust them with nothing. And if something isn't right, lie to them and never admit it."

Sonny shook off her complaints. He was too busy with more important things, running his businesses and dealing with the bosses' machinations.

One night, he had to attend a sit-down with Gambino. The conversation got heated. Sonny, who carried tissues all the time, reached into his pocket for one. The moment Gambino saw Sonny reaching into his pocket, he dove to the floor.

Startled, Sonny said nothing. But everyone else in the room saw what Sonny saw.

As Sonny later told John, "That fucking guy ain't got shit."

Gambino was the very same man who had shamed Joseph Magliocco out of a permanent leadership position because Magliocco hadn't demonstrated sufficient toughness during the Gallo kidnapping. Now, here was Gambino, humiliated by a man whose fearlessness on the street was legendary.

Gambino never forgot it.

CHAPTER 4

Dazzling Nights

"People just liked me, you know what I mean?"

IN THE GALAXY of New York City nightclubs, the Copacabana burned brightest.

Getting in wasn't easy. Celebrities, socialites, and sports stars all jockeyed for a coveted table amid the faux palm trees. But one particular patron never had a problem. When he made his entrance—striding briskly, confidently, and with a slight smile—a frisson of excitement rippled through the crowd. Patrons of the club knew exactly who he was.

Asked where he sat when he went to the Copa, Sonny smiled and said, "Wherever I wanted."

Sonny frequented all the city's top clubs, but he felt most at home at the Copacabana, with its roster of glittering acts and Copa Girls dance line. If the club was filled, he would go to the back door and tell workers to set a table on the stage; and they did.

"People just liked me, you know what I mean? I was just like a big hit with them," he said.

Located on East 60th Street, the Copacabana had the feel of a private club. Patrons and performers were solicitously attended to by a fleet of uniformed employees, all overseen by the vigilant eye of manager Jules Podell. Although the name on the lease belonged to an English press agent named Monte Proser, Podell ran the show—with the strong backing of his silent partner, Frank Costello. Because their criminal pasts made it illegal for them to get a liquor license and run a nightclub, they allowed Proser to be the front man—for a while.

Podell, a former butcher, had a hard-knocks background, with bootlegging arrests, jail time, and a gunshot wound in the leg. For all his murky past, he was a stickler for outward appearances. He held his staff to high standards and involved himself in all the minutiae of running a club, from supervising the kitchen staff to picking the talent.

When he saw something not quite to his liking, Podell tapped the large onyx pinkie ring he always wore on a glass, and an employee would come running, Sonny recalled, impressed. "He would see everything. He was smart."

Podell became a staple in gossip columns, which, naturally, boosted his business. It didn't hurt that he set aside a nightly table for gossip king Walter Winchell, who liked to mix up his column with items about New York City's underworld. When Costello went to prison, Winchell wrote: *[The] New York situation is fluid. Younger men are springing up on all sides, including Joey Gallo, Sonny Franzese, etc.*

Podell also kept close to Sonny. "Julie Podell thought I was the best thing that ever happened to him."

It undoubtedly had a lot to do with business. Gangsters added to the noirish glamour of the club, and Sonny exuded the kind of power that people immediately recognized. Customers came to see the glittering roster of performers onstage, but were just as thrilled when they spotted celebrities, and mobsters, in the audience.

"People would come there to see me, too," Sonny said. "They didn't come there just to see the show . . . You thought I was the star sometimes."

The people who knew who he was and his position in the family, like Gianni Russo, who as a teenager worked as a messenger for Costello well before he portrayed Carlo in *The Godfather*, didn't dare approach him. It would have been impertinent for a mere messenger to even talk to a man of Sonny's stature. But entertainers, oblivious to the rules of Mafia hierarchy, gravitated toward him. Celebrities like hanging out with other celebrities.

The Copacabana was a launching pad for careers, from Sammy Davis Jr. to Wayne Newton to June Allyson, who got her start on the Copa dance line. Dean Martin and Jerry Lewis, with their vaudeville-style act of songs and jokes, were regulars onstage. Sonny knew them well—"He was a good guy, Dean Martin." Once you appeared at the Copa, you could go anywhere in the world.

"All the top entertainers in the country, in the world, they all wanted to work there," Sonny said. "That was the Madison Square Garden of show business."

Part of the Copacabana's appeal was its exclusivity. Podell insisted that employees and customers alike adhere to a strict dress code. Sonny was always nattily dressed and knew full well that reporters would describe his wardrobe in detail, his cashmere coats included: "In those days, cashmere was expensive."

Tina, too, dressed beautifully, always in the latest designer clothing. She was never overdressed or flashy. "She had class, she had class," Sonny said. And she mingled easily with the celebrities who would come up to meet Sonny, often charming people with her intelligence and humor. She held her own.

Everyone knew, however, that they weren't like other couples. Tina and Sonny rarely arrived at the club together. He would walk in through the back entrance, and she would go to the front door. Podell didn't allow unescorted women in the club, but made an exception for Tina's entrance. A doorman would greet her and usher her to Sonny's table.

Sometimes they sat at Podell's table—"He used to invite me to eat a lot there with him. He was a good guy, Julie"—a savvy move on his part because Copa customers took note.

By his account, Sonny drew more customers to the Copa than Frank Sinatra did to Jilly's Saloon, another celebrity hangout in Manhattan, run by Ermenigildo Rizzo, known as "Jilly." Sinatra was close to Jilly, but Sonny had little use for him. "Jilly, I never liked. Jilly was a rat." Sonny was suspicious of him because "he hung out with the cops." Years later, Jilly would be convicted in an $8 million-dollar fraud scheme and sentenced to one thousand hours of community service, a comparatively light sentence given the scope of the crime—and an indicator to Sonny, who watched such things very carefully, that he was right.

Sinatra, even more than other entertainers, was comfortable around mobsters. He had grown up with street guys and had had his own youthful run-in with the law. He and Sonny, though, had an uneasy relationship, as each jousted to assert dominance.

"He wanted to be catered to all the time. See, I used to play it right. When I used to see him, I made out (like) I don't see him. I did it on spite. He used to come back to me and talk loud, so I could hear him. I wouldn't turn around."

Sinatra was used to being in charge, but not when Sonny was around. Some of their shared friends were put off by Sinatra's arrogance. To them, it was clear who the top man was, but Sonny, ever magnanimous, quieted them.

"What do you expect a guy to turn out to be?" Sonny told them. "Youse made him a superstar. Now what do you want him to do? Act like a dumb son of a gun and cater to you people?"

Sinatra might have been high-handed, but Sonny felt a certain affinity for the singer. They had met years earlier when he was performing at the Rustic Cabin, a roadhouse in Englewood Cliffs, New Jersey, and a fight broke out.

"It was a free-for-all," Sonny recalled. "So I jumped in and started helping him. I figured he's a skinny guy, they'd kill him. So I got very close to him. He was a good guy. I liked him."

That didn't mean that he wouldn't try to move in on Sinatra's girlfriend. He was, after all, Sonny Franzese. When Sinatra was dating actress Ava Gardner, she would come to the Copa to watch him perform. Gardner was beautiful and tempestuous, and everyone knew Sinatra was hopelessly in love with her. One night while the singer was performing onstage, Sonny struck up a conversation with her.

"Ava Gardner, I started to talk to her. The more I'm talking to her, I realize she's getting friendlier and friendlier. So I got her in the back room behind the bar . . . And I get her close and I'm kissing her and I got my hands on her backside and I put them under her dress. She had a miniskirt on. And I got in her, her drawers. I got my hands in there. I'm feeling her ass. She was hard as a rock."

Her boyfriend was not far away on stage, but Sonny was not at all concerned. "The hell with him. He was arrogant. He thought every girl was, was in love with him. Nutty son of a gun."

Sonny and Gardner never did anything more than the few moments of groping each other in a back room, but it was still a conquest to Sonny.

Sonny had no compunction about asserting his dominance over Sinatra, but when it came to business, he helped him out. Intensely ambitious and cutthroat, Sinatra eyed other Italian-American singers warily. Worried about competition from popular singer Jimmy Roselli, he insisted that his records be removed from New York jukeboxes, which were a significant revenue stream for the Mafia in the 1950s and 1960s. Sonny made one phone call, and Roselli's records were out.

And when Podell needed help with an uncooperative entertainer—like singer Bobby Darin—he knew where to turn. One night, Podell wanted Darin to take a picture with him, but Darin refused. Podell complained to Sonny.

"I go, 'You're kidding me. He told you that?'

"He says, 'Yeah.'

"'So what do you want me to do?'

"'You're the only guy he listens to.'"

Sonny went upstairs to see Darin in his dressing room and told him, "Jules is the boss here. You can't turn him down."

Darin immediately had a change of heart. "Wait awhile, Sonny. You want me to take a picture with him? Anything you want."

Darin was, according to Sonny, "with" him and couldn't refuse.

Sonny genuinely liked Darin, whose real name was Walden Robert Cassotto. Darin's maternal grandfather, Saverio "Big Sam Curly" Cassotto, died in prison a year before he was born. He never knew his biological father. His mother had gotten pregnant as a teenager, and he was raised thinking she was his older sister.

A talented musician, he had started out writing jingles. Darin's career took off in 1958, when he recorded "Splish Splash," a novelty rock song. Performing at the Copacabana, he broke attendance records. The rivalry between him and Sinatra was palpable.

"Sinatra had a voice that was unbelievable, but this kid had a voice that Sinatra couldn't reach the notes he reached. Sinatra could never sing 'Splish Splash,' 'Mack the Knife.' Bobby Darin's voice, he coulda sang anything. He was a very good . . . a nice kid. As a matter of fact, he hated Sinatra, and Sinatra hated him, because he knew he was a threat to him."

Their rivalry would never be fully tested. In 1973, Darin died at the age of thirty-seven after complications from open-heart surgery.

Entertainers loved Sonny, and he loved them. He opened his own booking agency and started pitching little-known acts to big clubs. He had a sharp eye for talent and a soft spot for underdogs, especially ones he thought might hit it big someday. He used to tell his sons, "Life is like a wheel. Whoever is on the bottom could be on the top the next day."

He got interested in Black performers, like soulful singer Sam Cooke, who had none of the connections of a Sinatra to get a foot in the door, and Johnny Nash, who hit the charts with "I Can See Clearly Now." And he became a fierce advocate for a little-known trio of Black women singers—the Supremes. In Sonny's telling, he was the one who persuaded Podell to book the Supremes at the Copa.

"He says, 'Sonny, I've got a white club. I ain't got a Black club.'

"I says, 'Yeah, but this ain't a Black act. This is a white act.'

"He says, 'I don't know, Sonny. If I put in a Black act, I'll have to close up my place.'

"I said, 'Look, check it out.'

"So he checked it out, and he put them into the club."

What followed was a thunderously successful appearance, igniting the Supremes' rise to stardom. The group's success also paved the way for other Black groups, like the Temptations, to appear at the Copa.

Sonny's account of his conversation with Podell doesn't ring entirely true, because other Black performers—like Sammy Davis Jr., Nat "King" Cole, and Ella Fitzgerald—had appeared at the Copacabana before the Supremes. But it is true that Podell originally had a policy of banning Blacks. And there's no doubt Sonny helped the careers of Blacks in the music business at a time when others wouldn't. He loaned seed money to music producer Danny Sims, who would later go discover reggae singer Bob Marley; Sims felt a lifelong debt of gratitude to Sonny. Moreover, Sonny and Sammy Davis Jr. became good friends, particularly after Sonny helped Davis's protégée Lola Falana get out of a one-sided music contract.

Through such friends, Sonny met and struck up relationships with beauties like actress Diahann Carroll. Gorgeous and glamorous women were inevitably drawn to Sonny, something he said he never fully understood. Years later, he would talk about it with genuine disbelief.

"They [would] come up to me, actually pick me up. They hit on me like I was Rudolph Valentino. I couldn't believe it myself sometimes."

One of his paramours was Jayne Mansfield, the buxom blonde star of the 1950s and '60s who was one of *Playboy*'s early centerfolds. She was "madly in love with" him.

He met her at the Latin Quarter, a Manhattan nightclub opened in 1942 by Lou Walters, Barbara Walters's father. "When the show starts, over there, you know, in the Latin Quarter, the stage goes up, as the show starts, all the lights go out. So I look up and who's looking at me—Jayne Mansfield. So I says, 'What the F are you doing up there?'

"She said, 'I don't know. I don't know. I don't know.'

"I said, 'After the show, come down here.' She says, 'All right, I'll be down.'"

He thought it was a joke. Then his friend said she really was coming to their table. He laughed along with his companions; they were always kidding around. "So all of a sudden, boom, boom, boom, Jayne Mansfield comes walking out."

Sonny needed to make room for her at his table, so he told his friend Johnny to leave. Johnny got up, but couldn't help but protest: "Sonny, you're too much. What the hell are you doing? You're chasing me off the table."

Sonny replied, "I can't have sex with you. I'm going to have it with her. Get the hell off the table."

The table erupted in laughter, but Johnny made his exit. Jayne sat down, and they began flirting. Before long, he asked her, "Who's taking you home?"

She replied that her husband, Mickey Hargitay (who was 1955's Mr. Universe), would take her home. To Sonny, that was tantamount to throwing down the gauntlet.

"If your husband comes here, I'm going to beat him up," he told her.

"Do you know who my husband is?" she replied.

More posturing followed, and Jayne tried to gentle Sonny, telling him not to get too excited. The night started to wind down at 4 a.m., and they left the club for a hotel.

"You know what she told me? Now you may not believe this, but, so help me God, she told it to me—she says to me, 'I made a lot of pictures. I went out with a lot of handsome leading men . . . Here I am in a place, there's three hundred fifty people here, and you're the best-looking guy here, too.'

"I says, 'What are you talking about?'

"She says, 'Sonny, you're the best-looking guy I ever went out with.'"

For Sonny, a woman like Mansfield was simply fun. "Not that I wanna brag, but I was in demand. The women went crazy."

He didn't deny himself. Nobody's girlfriend or wife was off-limits to him, not even the wife of his idol, baseball great Joe DiMaggio.

Sonny met actress Marilyn Monroe, not at the Copa, but at the Stork Club, thanks to an introduction by Frank Costello. "Marilyn was gorgeous, forget about it."

The mutual attraction proved irresistible, and their relationship led to an encounter that that left Sonny deeply ashamed. His account of what happened that evening was telling because he actually expressed remorse about it. Sonny was not a man inclined to express regret or embarrassment about anything he did.

It was May 19, 1962, when Monroe sashayed onto the stage of Madison Square Garden in a skintight, rhinestone-studded dress and sang a breathy "Happy Birthday" to President John F. Kennedy during a Democratic fundraiser. Her very personal tribute to the president shocked many of the fifteen thousand people in the audience.

Down in the darkened arena, a very different personal drama was playing out. DiMaggio—by then Monroe's ex-husband, but still carrying a torch for her—tried to approach Sonny to confront him about their affair.

"He was chasing me all over the place. He wanted to talk to me. I didn't want to talk to him. I was ashamed. What can I tell him? Your wife's a whore? You know what I mean? So I ran away. I wouldn't talk to him. I liked Joe DiMaggio. He was my hero."

Sonny was not at all ashamed of his many infidelities—"I was a run-around guy"—but it bothered him that he had hurt a man he idolized.

Later, he would become convinced that his affair with Monroe—who was rumored to have been involved with Kennedy's brother, U.S. Attorney General Robert F. Kennedy, too—was what brought the wrath of the U.S. government down on him.

But it wasn't just law enforcement that he had to worry about. When people came to a nightclub, they'd walk right past a guy like Joe Colombo and go straight for Sonny.

Colombo noticed, as did other men. It made Sonny uneasy, but he wasn't sure he could tamp down the attention he got.

"All of a sudden," he said, "I started to become more famous every day, and I never knew why."

CHAPTER 5

Cops Turn Up the Heat

*"I'm not a guy that scares easily. I don't
care."*

IN AUGUST 1963, Suffolk County police converged en masse on a
small house fronted by a white picket fence in bucolic Huntington, about an hour east of New York City. They smashed down
the front door and moved swiftly inside as the startled occupants
tried to scramble out the back. Betting slips were piled up in neat
stacks, and gambling ledgers tallied up staggering amounts of
money running through the operation—more than $12,000 a week
in bets.

The raid didn't rate a big news story, but it did bring the Suffolk Police Department's attention into sharp focus. Seven men
were arrested, not just for bookmaking, but for trying to bribe the
police. That might have been a common occurrence in New York
City, but not on Long Island. Moreover, the gambling operation
was so sophisticated and well-organized that authorities realized
they were dealing with a completely different kind of criminal organization. And when an informant told cops that Profaci family
boss Joseph Magliocco had turned over all his Long Island gambling operations to a mobster named Sonny Franzese, he became
a high-priority target.

Long Island in the 1960s was fertile territory for a guy like
Sonny, who had been given it as his reward for his role in negotiating peace in the Gallo-Profaci war. Thousands of families had
moved out to the suburbs to get their own little piece of the Amer-

ican dream, and the place was ripe for the plucking by gangsters on the make like Sonny.

Law enforcement knew that, too, and they weren't having it. Sonny wasn't the only wiseguy to move to the suburbs. By 1963, authorities counted more than forty-seven of the nation's top mobsters living on Long Island. It worried them. They called it an "invasion."

That little-noticed raid was only the beginning of an unprecedented law enforcement blitz against Sonny in the 1960s. Over the next few years, virtually every law enforcement agency in the state of New York and federal government tried to bring him down. Just as capable of trickery and cunning as the bad guys, they would use every means at their disposal to drive Sonny out.

Sonny, in their view, was a bloodthirsty killer and a rapist—he had been charged with rape in 1947, but never convicted. He didn't mind the killer label, but the rape charge always rankled. Years later, he described what he said happened that night:

"I was out with two friends of mine. So I hadda go to New York. So they were with a girl. They left the girl in the club with these two guys. So . . . we come back, and the girl says she's been raped. So the guy, I tell them, 'Drive her home.'

"Instead of driving her home, they dropped her off. So she went. Now, now, they come knocking on my door, and the guy said to me—uh, Detective, I think his name was Dempsey, if I'm not mistaken—he said to me, 'Sonny Franzese?'

"I said, 'Yeah.'

"He says, 'Were you in New York tonight?'

"I says, 'Why? What's that have to do with you?'

"He said, 'Well, we gotta lock you up.'

"'For what?'

"He said, 'Rape.'

"I said, 'Rape who? I never raped nobody. I don't have time to rape a girl. What are you, kidding?'

"He said, 'No, we got you.'

"So I say, 'Jesus Christ. Something's wrong someplace. I said, I never raped no girl.'

"So sure enough, I find out, my two friends raped the girl. Now they tell me, if you don't tell us who the guys are, we're gonna hit you with the charge. So I said to him, 'No, I don't know who the guys are, and I don't know who the girl is. I ain't gonna admit to nuthin'.'

"And they booked me under the goddamn charge. Now we go to court, and the girl won't show up. We go to court again, and the girl won't show up. The judge got aggravated and he threw the case out. So, how the hell, now I got a record for a rape charge that I never committed?

"What am I gonna rape a girl for? I didn't have to.

"In those days, you couldn't be a rat. I couldn't be a rat, so I got stuck with it."

Sonny professed not to understand why law enforcement was so interested in him. "They all hated me for some reason. I never done nothin'. I never hurt none of them or nothin,' but they all come after me like I was the last gangster in the world," he said.

He refused to let them drive him away. He was at the peak of his game, making a lot of money. He knew that he had gotten to where he was by being who he was, a guy who wouldn't back down.

"I'm not a guy that scares easily," he said. "I don't care."

Just two days after the Suffolk raid, William Cahn, the district attorney of neighboring Nassau County, made a splash by launching a highly publicized hood roundup, sending out detectives before dawn with "invitations" to more than twenty men, among them hoodlums with monikers like "Tony Fats," "Joe Adonis," "Joe Pitts," "Tony Guns," and "Johnny Dio."

Sonny was the fourteenth one hauled in, and, as always, he cut a dapper image before the cameras. In fact, the caption under his photo described him as "Suave Sonny." DA Cahn wanted to know about Sonny's gambling operations, but Sonny didn't have a lot to say. He conceded that he had visited his friend Magliocco at his home—nothing criminal in that—but said he couldn't discuss his own business activities because he was under investigation by the IRS. Meanwhile, the day before, Magliocco had told Suffolk authorities that he didn't even know Sonny.

Cahn's interest in Sonny wasn't just because of the gambling raid. He had recently returned from Washington, D.C., where he met with Joseph Valachi, a low-level Genovese soldier. A deeply paranoid and bitter man, Valachi had decided to talk to authorities because he was terrified that he'd be killed in prison. It was the first time any made guy actually broke ranks and revealed the secrets of the Mafia. It was a huge coup for law enforcement.

When Cahn met with Valachi, he hadn't gone public yet. That would come a few weeks later, in October 1963, when he would testify before a U.S. Senate hearing on organized crime initiated by Senator John McClellan in a spectacle that riveted the nation. For the time being, Valachi was meeting quietly with fascinated prosecutors, like Cahn, filling them in on Mafia secrets, as well as unsolved murders.

Cahn wanted to know who was moving up in the New York organization.

Valachi fingered Sonny.

"He's one of the fastest up-and-coming men in Cosa Nostra," Valachi told Cahn. "He has a hand in everything."

Suffolk County police started hauling in Sonny's friends. One was Albert Maione, a bookmaker who ran a gas station in Jamaica, Queens, that Sonny used as a drop for bookmaking and policy slips. When rackets chief John Fay asked him about working for Sonny, Maione said he had been out of work since suffering a heart attack. Asked why he took the train every day into Brooklyn, Maione said, "I'm just visiting friends and looking for a job."

"Every day for a year?" Fay asked, incredulous.

"Yes," Maione replied, whining that the questioning was putting a strain on his heart.

Around the same time, Queens DA Frank O'Connor also met with Valachi. After their meeting, O'Connor let it slip that he had new information related to the sensational 1959 rubout of Anthony "Little Augie Pisano" Carfano and beauty queen Janice Drake, who had been shot to death outside a motel in Jackson Heights, Queens.

Carfano was a Luciano capo who had been unwisely vocal about his hatred of his new boss, Vito Genovese. In September 1959, he was enjoying a night out and ran into friends, including Drake, a striking blonde married to comedian Allan Drake. As they were eating dinner at Marino's, Carfano got a call and was told to leave immediately for "urgent business." He offered Drake a ride home.

That night, police found both shot to death in Carfano's black Cadillac. Carfano had a bullet in his neck and left temple, and his body was slumped over to the right side, his head on Drake's body. Drake, dressed in a cocktail dress and mink stole, had a bullet in her neck. Her head rested against the passenger side, with her eyes wide open. Even in death, her skin seemed to glow. She was achingly lovely.

It wasn't a robbery. Little Augie was found with $1,933 in his pocket.

Police said they were shot by people sitting in the back seat, which they scoured for evidence.

The murders went unsolved for years. Then O'Connor revealed the new information: Three people had been at the scene when Carfano and Drake were killed. One of them was Sonny, Genovese's old friend. O'Connor didn't identify the other two. Authorities didn't have enough to charge Sonny, however.

Week after week, the news stories about Sonny kept coming in the New York newspapers. His name was always mentioned in connection to something or someone else, rarely in connection with actual criminal charges. It had the feel of a campaign, almost an obsession.

Many of the stories were written by *Newsday* reporter Bob Greene, a big man—more than three hundred pounds—with an equally big personality. He reveled in chasing bad guys. "It's always been sort of understood: foxes and the hounds," he told one writer.

The relentless publicity infuriated Sonny, and he needed to shut it down. Shortly after the hood roundup, Nassau police received a warning for Greene. "Tell Bob to be careful. They're out to get him," the caller said.

The caller was a close associate of Sonny's.

Another tip came in with a little more specific information—a man with a history of blowing up things was on his way to bomb Greene's home in Smithtown, another bucolic community farther east from New York City on Long Island. Mobilizing quickly, cops pulled over three men in a white Cadillac. As police approached, one of the men tried to ditch his .22-caliber pistol. But it was the driver of the car who got the police's attention. It was none other than Salvatore "Sam the Pizza King" Calascione, the same guy who threatened to dynamite the shops of barbers who wouldn't join the sham barbers' union.

They questioned the men at the precinct, but didn't get enough to charge them. The close call, however, was enough for them to put Greene's home under constant surveillance.

Greene had always taken precautions to protect his family. When his son, Bob Jr., was in kindergarten, police drove him to school. The five-year-old chafed at the police supervision and begged his father to make it stop. Thereafter, he was allowed to walk to school with his friends, with a police car following behind.

But this latest threat had come really close. Greene sat down his then-twelve-year-old son and said, "Listen, if they kidnap you, we're not going to pay a ransom."

Bob Jr. listened quietly and said, "Okay."

Greene explained: "It's not going to make a difference. The object is to do everything you can to get away. Because once they get you, they're not going to let you go."

It pained Greene to know what he was putting his family through, but Greene, like Sonny, could not back down. Close to law enforcement after working as an organized-crime investigator, he viewed his job as a mission. As he told another journalist years later, "Organized crime was living here. If you wanted to keep [government] with the people, you had to fight these sons of bitches."

Police and prosecutors felt exactly the same way. After the nationally televised hearings with Valachi captivated the public, organized crime became a top priority. As such, Sonny became a prime target. They decided to do what they could to rattle him, hoping he'd make a mistake.

Agents sat in cars watching his house for hours, often with binoculars to make it obvious. Two men with walkie-talkies would sit there, watching, until two more men came along in another black sedan to relieve the first two. Sometimes they left a machine gun visible in the back seat, just in case any curious children walked by. Other times, they stopped schoolchildren as they got off the bus and quizzed them about the Franzese family.

It was humiliating for Tina and the children. She sometimes invited the neighbors' children over to swim in their backyard pool. That was a rarity at the time, and neighborhood kids considered it a treat. But as they got a little older and the surveillance became more obvious, their parents stopping letting them go.

Just in case that wasn't enough, police leaked details about Sonny's day-to-day routine to Greene, who gleefully included them in news stories, much to Sonny's consternation. Sonny liked to act as if the surveillance didn't bother him, but he couldn't stand the pressure on his family. Once, he was taking Tina and the children out to eat at a local diner, and, as usual, the agents followed him. He erupted.

"They threatened my kids, pulled a gun out on my kids on Jericho Turnpike. They were following me. I was with my whole family. I got, I got . . . got so mad. I stopped the car, I got out, and I started cursing them. They said, 'Don't come another step, or I'll shoot you.'

"'Shoot me, you rat bastard!' I went right back at 'em.

"He backed up. The other guy [said], 'Stop, Sonny. We could shoot you for this.'"

Worried about the safety of his family, he stopped.

Tina told the story a little differently. "He decided to take us to a diner, and they were behind us, following us. They're always following us. I can't see why they're following seven children and a mother and a father. What would anybody do with seven children in the car?

"So we got to the restaurant and got out. I'm sure, till this day, my husband hasn't said it to me, I'm sure that they made some remark about me to him. And, of course, he got a little excited. And, of course, I interrupted.

"And they said, 'Go ahead, Sonny, do something to me.'

"And the other one pulled a gun out of his pocket and said, 'Go ahead, because I'm dying to do it.'"

Sonny stopped.

Police and FBI agents kept up the surveillance, which only prompted Sonny to make a game of eluding them. He'd call up an associate and tell him to meet him at a particular diner or café in a shopping center. The associate would, of course, comply. They'd sit down and Sonny would take off his jacket and order his food. Then he would excuse himself to go to the men's room. Oddly, though, he'd take an inordinate amount of time there. The associate would have no choice but to wait. Inevitably, Sonny would return to the table as if nothing were amiss.

Years later, the associate would learn that Sonny had actually slipped out the window of the men's room, walked to the end of the shopping center, and met with the men he really wanted to talk to. After finishing, he would return to the first café through the window of the men's room—all without the watchful FBI agents being any the wiser.

In early September 1963, Scarpa gave agents an important bit of news: Magliocco had formally stepped down. He was seriously ill, so much so that his own brother told Scarpa it was like not having a boss at all. Word was that Sonny might take over the

Profaci family. Authorities started bringing him in for questioning about various unsolved murders, but never made anything
stick.

Carlo Gambino, who couldn't countenance the idea of Sonny
becoming boss, threw his support behind Joe Colombo, effectively blocking Sonny's ascent.

On December 28, 1963, Magliocco died of a heart attack at
Good Samaritan Hospital in West Islip. The commission wanted
to keep his death quiet, and only about fifty members of his immediate family attended his funeral at St. Charles Cemetery in
Farmingdale. As instructed, hoods stayed away.

When a new boss takes over, all the capos revert to soldiers because it is left to the boss to choose who he wants as his capos. By
April 1964, it was clear Sonny would remain a capo. Colombo
met with his new capos at Renato's Luncheonette in Brooklyn
and laid out new rules: They were to be at the disposal of their
men. They were to hear their problems and not move in on their
action. And soldiers were supposed to be available at all times to
carry out their captains' orders.

By June, the new capos were formally introduced at a meeting
arranged by Colombo. Persico was one of them. Although the
Persico and Franzese families socialized with one another, Sonny
viewed the Snake with suspicion.

Colombo's takeover of the family seemed to herald a new era
for the crime family. No longer would they be taxed by an inef-
fective leader derided in the press as "Fat Man." Scarpa told FBI
agents that ambitious younger men were taking over. He wel-
comed that, but he was worried. He had overheard a close associate of Sonny's, Dominick "Mimi" Scialo, saying that he thought
someone was talking to the FBI.

For all the Colombo family's new plans, law enforcement was
just as determined to beat them back. In December 1964, the
State Investigations Commission grabbed a piece of the crime-
fighting spotlight by holding a hearing on loan-sharking. The SIC
subpoenaed Sonny, who refused to testify, invoking the Fifth
Amendment against self-incrimination eighteen times. Other mob-

sters appeared as well, but it was the testimony of one of Sonny's victims that captured the public's attention.

Margaret Rudgalvis, the forty-six-year-old owner of a luncheonette in North Babylon called Peggy's, trembled as she told her story. She and her husband had bought the business with a partner and were doing well for a while. Then a road project diverted traffic, causing business to fall off. Desperate, her husband, Henry, turned to a loan shark for cash to stay afloat. Soon Sonny's friend and associate Felice "Philly" Vizzari and other mobsters took over the place. They turned it into a betting parlor.

Margaret was horrified. She sent a letter to the Suffolk District Attorney, begging for help: *I'd rather be on home relief than live like this.*

Instead of help, two men showed up at her house one night and slammed a door on her hand. They told her that was "only a little bit" of what was to come.

She and her husband fled New York and changed their names.

The spectacle of a frightened middle-aged woman telling her story of being victimized by the mob was far worse publicity than any stories of a brazen mob rubout. There was nothing glamorous about beating up a middle-aged woman.

Sonny, by all outward appearances, shook off the testimony, like all his previous scrapes with the law. But after returning home one night, he found himself in an unsettling conversation.

"As I'm coming to my house, the garbage guys tell me, 'Sonny, Mr. Franzese, make like you're talking to us, that you find that there's something wrong, an argument, because we're going to tell you something.'

"And he's telling me, 'The FBI grabs us every morning, after we leave your house. They take all your garbage. We've got to separate your garbage and give it to them.'"

"Dumpster diving," or looking through garbage, is a standard investigative technique.

This jolted Sonny. He was used to the surveillance, but agents looking through his garbage? He called his lawyer, Maurice Edelbaum, and said, "Look, I've got to see you right away."

They met at a prearranged spot, and he told Edelbaum, "Look, something is happening that ain't right. The FBI took . . . is taking all of my garbage."

Edelbaum was puzzled. "Why are they taking your garbage?"

"I don't know," Sonny said.

Sonny asked around and got his answer: "They want to find out where I spent my money, what I was eating, where I was shopping, what I was buying."

But then Sonny came to a more ominous realization: Someone had turned on him.

"One of them motherless guys, friends of mine, that wanted to be like me, but he couldn't. He was giving me up to get me in trouble, so they'd take me off the street."

CHAPTER 6

The Hawk Surfaces

"Why would I want to deal with garbage like that?"

ON A SUNNY DAY in August 1964, a sixteen-year-old boy came upon a gruesome sight on the shore of Jamaica Bay near Far Rockaway: the bloated body of Ernest "the Hawk" Rupolo, forty-eight, a one-eyed hit man from Baldwin, Long Island. A heavy rope was looped around "Ernie the Hawk's" neck and wrists and two concrete blocks were tied to his left leg. He had been shot five times, stabbed eighteen.

Despite the blocks, the body had washed up to shore because the killers had failed to slit open his stomach, a usually foolproof method of sinking a body. His corpse had been in the water about two weeks, and his wallet, with $51 and his Social Security card, was untouched.

New York tabloids pounced on the story, declaring that the Hawk had been murdered because he was a stool pigeon—A TALKY HAWK IS RUBBED OUT BY GANGDOM, proclaimed one newspaper. Many years earlier, the Hawk, anxious to get out from under a hefty prison sentence he was facing for a shooting, had testified against Vito Genovese, Sonny's lifelong ally. The Hawk told the court that in 1934 Genovese had ordered a hit on Ferdinand "the Shadow" Boccia, who had unwisely demanded his $35,000 cut from $116,000 lost in a crooked card game to Genovese's crew. Boccia felt he deserved a cut because he had steered the loser to the game. Genovese disagreed, and Boccia was found shot to death in Brooklyn. A judge rewarded the Hawk for his testimony by dismissing the charge against him.

But others, in particular, the Hawk's widow, Eleanor, said The Hawk was killed for a different reason: He had tried to muscle in on Sonny's rackets.

"They hated each other. They really, really did," she said at the time.

The Hawk had always dreamed of being a crime boss. Though he didn't have Sonny's business savvy or self-discipline, he had guts. He had been useful to the Luciano crime family from an early age. When he was twelve, he changed the year on his birth certificate so he could leave school and start what he had always aspired to—a career in crime. He began by robbing and burglarizing, specializing in what he called the "bucket racket." He and a friend would ring a doorbell. If someone answered, they'd say, "Can I have a bucket of water? The car's steaming." If no one answered, they'd bust in and burglarize the place.

The racket worked fairly smoothly until it came time to divvy up the loot. One night, the Hawk objected to cutting in the girlfriend of one of the burglars for a share. That turned out to be a nearly fatal mistake. The offended boyfriend shot him in the head and threw him out the window of the motel where they had been hiding out. Ernie survived, but lost his right eye. Miserable over being disfigured, he decided that life wasn't worth much after that. As a result, he became willing to commit just about any act of violence. Even with just one eye, he never missed a shot. Mob associates took notice of his prowess and nicknamed him "the Hawk," and the moniker stuck. He became a hit man for "the Organization," as he referred to it, at sixteen.

It wasn't long before the Hawk got locked up, and despite promises to the contrary, the Organization did nothing to help him. Nine years in Sing Sing prison deepened his bitterness. While the Hawk was in prison, Sonny, someone he knew from the neighborhood, was out on the street making money. And unlike him, Sonny never did a day. Somehow, the Organization always came through for Sonny, getting charges dismissed with a well-placed bribe.

But not for the Hawk. He had been locked away and forgotten. He could barely contain his rage and jealousy. Living on the outside, he decided to at least sate some of that rage by moving in on Sonny's rackets in Queens.

Sonny, for his part, said he never even knew the Hawk. "Why would I want to deal with garbage like that?"

But there's no question he never would have tolerated a move on his territory.

That the Hawk managed to stay alive after testifying against Genovese was at least in part a testament to his usefulness as a killer. His brother, William, known as "Willi," later claimed that another Genovese gangster, Michele "Big Mike" Miranda, had extended his protection to the Hawk.

Eleanor had a different explanation for how her husband had managed to stay alive. She said the Hawk had told her that they'd never do anything to him because of some papers he had that a woman was holding for him. She never knew what the papers were. One day, he went to get those papers, and they were gone. "And two weeks later, so was Ernie," she said.

By the time the Hawk had met Eleanor, a street-smart barmaid, he hardly seemed like marriage material. He drank heavily, disappeared for days at a time, and had been through two earlier common-law wives. Eleanor, too, was hard-drinking and loud-mouthed. Attractive and a bit heavyset, she favored garish, attention-getting clothing. She didn't take guff from anybody, not even a contract killer for the Organization. Something in the two of them clicked. They fell in love and moved in together in 1957.

Not that their union was peaceful. They fought often and hard, but the Hawk always came back to her, lavishing expensive gifts on her when he returned.

One night, she was out drinking, and the Hawk came to get her by sticking a gun in her back and saying, "Are you coming home?"

Eleanor, by then drunk, refused and screamed she'd take out his good eye. They argued until she threatened to call the cops. The Hawk gave up and went home. It was the kind of scene that repeated itself, over and over, in their relationship.

Yet Eleanor was the one who would soothe him with cold compresses on his head at night as he told her stories of murders he committed. He talked about killing his friends, explaining that, "It was him or me." She always listened, part of her captivated, part of her feeling revulsion.

About six months before he was killed, the Hawk told Eleanor that they were going to kill him. She didn't believe it. But he started to change his behavior. Afraid they'd kill her if she was in a car with him, he wouldn't drive her anywhere. The Hawk's last drive was with his best friend, Roy Roy.

"He drove for him," William explained. "He was the only one he'd've gone with. That's what they do. They take your best friend and he has to do what they say, even if he is your best friend. And they make him walk into something, take you out, wine you and dine you, and then walk you into it."

It was Eleanor who had to identify the Hawk's body at New York's Bellevue Morgue, where bodies were stacked in a cooler. For all her husband's faults, she knew that he had adored her in a way nobody else had. It gnawed at her that the Hawk's own friends had killed him, but she knew well the dangers of seeking justice for him. Besides, she and the Hawk had a young daughter. She had to make a secure home for her.

She found security, she thought, in a hood named John "Blue Boy" Cordero from Lynbrook, a village on the South Shore of Long Island. They met in June 1965, while she was working as a waitress at the Luau Club in Queens. Eight years younger than Eleanor, he was wiry and handsome in his way and completely smitten with her. He told her he made his money from owning a car wash. He loved gifting her with jewelry and cash, and their relationship was no less volatile than her union with the Hawk. Cordero was possessive, jealous, and addicted to heroin.

To feed that habit and Eleanor's expensive tastes, Cordero followed a well-trodden path of crooks in need of fast cash: He robbed banks. Eleanor first became aware of his real vocation about a month after they met. He came into the motel room where they were staying and dumped piles of cash on the bed. It didn't alarm her. If anything, it excited her.

Later that month, they went to Baltimore—staying in a Holiday Inn under the name "Capone"—because Cordero wanted to case banks there. He deemed the banks there unsuitable, and they returned to New York.

Cordero was hardly a criminal mastermind, and his henchmen were no more sophisticated than he was. There was James "Smitty" Smith, dubbed "the vault man" because he jumped over counters and scooped up money; Charles "Blackie" Zaher, who like Cordero was a drug addict; and Richard Parks, the oldest of the crew, at thirty-two, and the only experienced gunman. They were an unlikely crew of misfits whose lives would later collide with Sonny's.

Eleanor, not one to shy away from trouble, stepped in as the getaway driver because Blackie had blown it in an earlier robbery. Cordero told Eleanor what happened:

"Blackie was waiting for them to come out of a bank robbery in Queens. He's so scared that he throws up in the car. They come running out of the bank, and as Smitty and John jump into the car, Blackie drives away, leaving Richie standing on the street, and Richie is running after him screaming like a maniac to stop the car. They almost have to shoot Blackie to get him to stop the car. He never drove for them again."

The men robbed the Kew Gardens bank, and jumped into the car with Eleanor. It would have been an easy escape, except that she made the wrong turn and ended up at the very bank they had just robbed.

"I hadn't been in the neighborhood before," she said. "I pulled up to the bank and they went in, and I'm sitting there, petrified. They're back in no time. They all jump in, and John yells, 'Go!'

We make it to a switch car nearby, and John and I pull away. I make a wrong turn and end up right back at the bank.

"There are radio cars all over the place, and there I am. Stopped for a light, with money on the seat next to me. John says to keep driving like nothing happened."

And so she did. Later, they met to divvy up the spoils, a total of $8,000. But they got into a heated argument because the men didn't think Eleanor should get a split. Cordero prevailed, and Eleanor got her share.

They picked banks at random and on a moment's notice. They robbed one bank in Oceanside on Cordero and Eleanor's wedding day because it was near her beauty parlor. They had scheduled their vows for 2 p.m. that day at a Queens courthouse, so they planned to rob the bank first thing in the morning. Eleanor drove the getaway car.

"I sat outside that bank for two hours, waiting in a stolen car for them to come out," she said. "The bank was so crowded. Finally they come running out of the bank and jumped into the car. I took off, but they told me to take it easy and obey all the traffic laws. So I stopped for a light about fifty feet away, and they started screaming, 'What are you stoppin' for?!'

"So I went through this light, and this woman starts yelling that I went through the light, and I start yelling back. Now everybody in the car is yelling at me. What a scene."

They got away with $4,000 and made it to the wedding in time. Smitty was best man, and Parks was a witness. Cordero bought Eleanor orchids. "It was a nice wedding," she said.

Afterward, the men argued again about Eleanor getting a share. She got her share, but resolved not to drive the getaway car again.

Aware that they were attracting the attention of law enforcement, Cordero decided to branch out beyond New York. They hit a bank in Holyoke, Massachusetts, and then came up with what they thought was a brilliant plan: They would rob a bank in Denver because the U.S. Mint was there.

They had planned to leave early on a Friday so they could hit the bank that same day, but John and Eleanor overslept. They took a later flight, and the men spent a couple of hours casing the area. They selected the perfect bank to rob, but it was too late to do it that day. They would do it the next day. Eleanor explained what happened next:

"The next morning, they got up early and left to rob the bank. I waited at the motel. When they came back, John is steaming mad. He's white-faced and was going bananas. He said, 'They had nothing in that bank!'

"I'm not believing him, and I tell him, 'You go out to stick up a bank, and you come back with nothing?'"

They had robbed the bank on a Saturday, when it had no money on premises. It had cost them more than $600 to get there, and they netted $80.

The men were desperate. A mistake like that wouldn't look good to their New York backers, who were expecting their share. The next business day, they hit a Salt Lake City bank, netting $33,000. After their bank-financed vacation in Las Vegas, Cordero and Eleanor returned to their home in Bethel, Connecticut, thinking that they had pulled everything off without a hitch.

They were wrong. On October 1, 1965, FBI agents arrested them. They took John Cordero to the jail on West Street in Manhattan and Eleanor to the hospital, because she was pregnant and suffering complications.

For Cordero, who fancied himself a tough guy, it was a turning point. It didn't take long for him to give up the others, and they were arrested and charged with five bank robberies over forty-four days. But he was worried about Eleanor. He insisted that she wasn't involved, and she was released.

For law enforcement, it didn't seem like much of a coup to nab these bank robbers. Their ineptitude was comic, even pathetic. It seemed almost beneath the FBI to expend its resources on these guys.

It turned out that the FBI had set its sights on something far bigger.

*   *   *

Months after his arrest, Cordero gave up the information that changed everything: Sonny Franzese had been the mastermind behind the robberies. His codefendants quickly backed him up in separate FBI interviews. In one fell swoop, the hapless hoods were vaulted to star status in the federal system.

As spun out in FBI reports and news accounts, they told this tale:

Nearly a year after the Hawk's body was discovered, Cordero took Eleanor to the John Doe Room, a bar in Jamaica, Queens. They were having drinks when in walked Joseph "Whitey" Florio, a member of Sonny's crew. Whitey and Cordero knew each other casually, but when Eleanor saw Whitey, she erupted.

She shouted across the bar that Whitey was one of the men who had killed her Hawk. Words flew, and she burst into tears, as bar patrons looked on in amazement.

Whitey asked the bartender who Eleanor was. "He tells me this broad is the Hawk's wife. I say I didn't, but I don't say anything else, even though she is foul-mouth, 'cause I am a gentleman," he said later.

Cordero—embarrassed by "her dirty language and all," according to Whitey—hustled Eleanor out. In the parking lot, he heard a door open and close behind them. He turned and saw Whitey with his hand in his pocket. Afraid Whitey was going to shoot him, Cordero pulled out his gun and fired five shots at Whitey, who hit the pavement and rolled under a car. Cordero pushed Eleanor into his car and they took off.

Authorities later described it as a gun battle, but Whitey scoffed at that. "What gun battle?" he said. "This guy pegs one shot at me; I run like hell. You call that a gun battle?"

Cordero hadn't hit Whitey with a single shot, but he had committed a grave error: He had shot at a member of Sonny's crew. The incident was so serious that Sonny had to convene a mob sitdown, according to a January 1966 FBI memorandum.

They met at the Aqueduct Motor Inn, an ugly and uninviting brick building owned by an associate of Sonny's named Anthony Polisi. A sit-down is a serious affair, and not showing up is not an option. Cordero appeared, as did Whitey, still smarting from the insult of being shot at.

Whitey presented his case, and Sonny listened. Sonny turned to Cordero and said, "When you shoot at him, you shoot at me. What have you got to say for yourself?"

Cordero complained that the bank robberies, which had been committed under Polisi's supervision—something he never told Eleanor—had been poorly managed, exposing them to risk. "Two days ago, we hit the Jamaica Savings Bank. It was after we hit it that we learn it had only been hit two weeks before. We could have walked into a trap."

Sonny considered this and then passed down his judgment: "There will be no foul-ups from now on. Starting now, I am going to take personal charge of this operation. I will deal direct."

It was an extraordinary exchange, if true, because Sonny had never been directly connected to the crimes of lower-level associates. For prosecutors, it was a huge break. This was the first time they had witnesses willing to testify against Sonny, the man they had been chasing unsuccessfully for years.

But for others familiar with how Sonny operated, it was flat-out incredible. This was a man who did not deal with low-level street guys. They might have been kicking up money to him, but it was always through middlemen. When he planned something, he would give orders to an associate, who transmitted them down the line through as many as seven other people until reaching the person designated to commit the crime. If that person was caught, it would require too many other people to link Sonny to it. More important, no one who knew Sonny dared testify against him.

Years later, Sonny insisted that sit-down never happened. "Please believe me," he said. "I know it's hard to believe, but I never met them. I didn't know them."

And he understood only too well the importance of insulating himself: "I was a firm believer that if a guy knew something about you, you had to worry about it."

He came to suspect that there was something or someone bigger behind the bank robbers.

CHAPTER 7

Sonny Makes Music

*"Hey, listen, you had to make money. It was
tough."*

PAUL VANCE FUMED as he paced in the office of Roulette Records.
Morris "Mo" Levy, owner of the independent music label, was
cheating him out of his royalties. He knew it and Levy knew he
knew, but Levy didn't care, because he didn't have to.

Vance, who had penned the megahit "Catch a Falling Star,"
was a prolific songwriter in the 1960s. He had written a novelty
song, "Leader of the Laundromat," a catchy and funny parody of
the 1964 hit song "Leader of the Pack," by the Shangri-Las.
Vance's song, performed by the Detergents, had literally cleaned
up, rising to number 19 on the Billboard charts and selling nine
hundred thousand records. Vance wanted his money.

Levy, who had produced a string of bubblegum hits, like
"Hanky Panky," thanks in no small part to his mob connections,
would have none of it. He lived large and liked to gamble. He
was nearly broke, down to his last $10,000, and was about to lose
Roulette. Without the royalties from that song, he'd go under.

"They all came back," he told the Detergents, meaning that all
the records had been returned, unsold. "You kids go out on the
road and make some money with Dick Clark."

That answer was enough to satisfy most of the young and inex-
perienced artists working for him, who were thrilled at the
prospect of appearing on the hugely popular TV show *American
Bandstand*. But not Vance; he demanded his money. In a moment

of magnanimity, Levy offered to let the Detergents look at his books if they doubted him, but then quickly added, "I have two sets anyway."

The Detergents, young but not stupid, quietly made their exits. Vance stayed behind and paced, his rage building.

Sonny and some of his associates watched this scene unfold at Roulette's offices in the Brill Building in New York City. Sonny owned a couple of independent record labels, and the money was fast and easy. He didn't meddle in the creative end of things, but he was effective when they needed him to be. Usually, his mere presence in their offices was enough to settle a dispute. And given the way Levy and others ran their businesses, disputes over money were frequent.

Vance couldn't contain himself any longer. He slugged the much larger Levy, knocking him down.

The room erupted.

"The window, the window!" Sonny shouted. "You dumb bastard!"

Sonny and the other men grabbed Vance and hung him by his legs out the window of the eleven-story Art Deco building. "Give him what he wants, or I'll drop you right here!" Sonny yelled.

Vance, his head spinning, blinked at the sidewalk below. "You got it!" he yelled.

Hands started to pull him back onto firm ground. As Vance righted himself inside the building, Levy smiled at him and said, "You're the only guy who ever knocked me off my feet. From now on, you're my buddy forever."

Vance choked out a laugh.

Few people had ever dared to challenge Levy, a bear of a man with hands like catcher's mitts and a propensity for violence. More than once, Levy settled business disputes with a baseball bat. Singer Jimmie Rodgers, who sang such hits as "Kisses Sweeter than Wine," once suffered a fractured skull after he had the temerity to demand his royalties.

Levy was a brute, but he had a good ear for talent, the more malleable the better. Instead of paying his artists, he liked to make a show of bestowing them with extravagant gifts and sending them out on tour. He knew they'd be thrilled to perform on TV, and he counted on their ignorance of the business.

He was also an associate of the Genovese crime family, or, as Sonny put it, "a friend of mine," in other words, a mob associate. As a young man, Levy had gotten friendly with Tommy Eboli, acting boss of the Genovese family while Vito Genovese was in prison, and his close friend, Vincent "The Chin" Gigante, a future boss. Like Sonny, they saw the profit potential in the record business and made sure Levy cut them in. Levy had no problem spreading the money around to the right people.

Sonny didn't like Levy: "He was a thief. He robbed everybody."

But he felt bound by his oath. Regardless of his contempt for Levy, his connections to the Genovese family made it that "I couldn't do what I wanted to do to him."

Sonny was a genuine music fan, and he admired Vance's ability to churn out moneymaking hits. After their momentary disagreement, Vance found himself developing an unlikely friendship with Sonny. Although Vance wasn't the first songwriter to be threatened in a dispute over money, something about that episode bonded them. Levy thought songwriters were expendable, but Sonny knew better. When other mobsters questioned his friendship with the songwriter, Sonny made clear to them that Vance was worth more alive than dead. "You wanna know who he is? He's the guy who wrote twenty-nine gold records!"

Vance came to respect Sonny's ability to analyze a situation and how he was always straight with him. They would go out to eat, always with their backs to the wall, and discuss business. Vance knew he could turn to Sonny for help when he needed it. In the bumptious world of rock music in the 1960s, Sonny's help came in handy. More often than not, Sonny's reputation was enough. Sometimes he'd simply make an appearance, and nothing more needed to be said or done. Things were, as Detergent singer Ron Dante said, "indicated. Things were not really said. They were indicated."

Sonny, for his part, was philosophical about his role in the music industry. "Hey, listen, you had to make money," he said. "It was tough."

Speaking of his "friends" in the music business, he said, "They were all crooks."

The record business had long been a playground for gangsters, with hard-to-trace money and myriad ways to make it. The mobsters fed off exploitive contracts signed by naïve teenage performers, stolen song credits, mobbed-up jukebox companies and record-pressing plants, plus pay-for-play payoffs to disc jockeys.

Although Sonny didn't like Levy, he had his uses—"He gave me Bobby Darin."

Sonny was on a roll with the money from the music industry, and he was constantly looking for ways to make more money off it. "I'll be honest with you. If I don't get pinched, if I don't get locked up, I don't know how much money I'd be worth, you know?"

The violence was just a part of doing business, and Vance's experience of being hung out the window was not unique. A manager would sign an artist to a label, which would help him make a hit. All of a sudden, the artist would believe he was worth a lot more money and that he didn't need his manager anymore. That's when the music industry executives would turn to their friends. The artist would be given a choice—his signature on the paper or his face on the sidewalk below.

Once, certain people were aggrieved by an uncooperative singer at Universal Artists. They grabbed him and hung him out the window. Unfortunately, the man was a twin. They had grabbed the wrong guy, his brother.

Another favorite gambit was a bit more subtle. An acquaintance would approach an offending artist on the street and exclaim, "Oh, my God! Oh, wow, I'm so happy you're okay! I was really worried about you!"

Confused, the artist would ask what he was talking about.

"My God, so-and-so said he was gonna break your legs. I

mean, he showed me the baseball bat. He was, like, you know, taking the baseball bat and saying, 'I'm gonna hit a home run. I'm gonna take this guy's knees out from under his ass. He's a no-good guy.'"

Inevitably, the shaken artist would ask what he could do to prevent this. Only too happy to oblige, the acquaintance would offer to talk to the baseball bat guy and work out the disagreement. And the artist would wind up paying.

Sonny was a master of that con. But when necessary, he tapped into violence for the desired effect. When his son Michael was twelve years old, he rode into the city with Sonny and his driver because Sonny had an appointment at his record label, Kama Sutra Records. As they were driving, Sonny spotted a man on the street and ordered his driver to stop. He jumped out of the car to talk to him. He was furious. He grabbed the man by his throat and pulled him up off the ground.

The raw brutality of the moment terrified Michael. He had never seen anything like it, much less coming from the man he regarded as his father. Despite his father's tempestuous relationship with his mother, when he was home, Sonny was a doting and gentle father. Sonny's driver tried to brush off the incident, telling wide-eyed Michael not to worry. That's when it dawned on Michael for the first time that his father, the man he idolized, was a criminal.

For some music producers, that was just fine.

"Sonny at least was upfront about where he was at, what his business interests were, what his responsibilities were to the organization that he was part of," said Artie Ripp, Sonny's business partner in Kama Sutra Records.

Sonny opened the necessary doors. He wasn't the kind of mobster who tried to get a record deal for a girlfriend with a lousy voice. He was naturally drawn to talent, but he also knew that talented performers would make him money.

Ripp was just twenty-three when he partnered with two pals, Phil Steinberg and Hy Mizrahi, in the record business. Steinberg and Mizrahi had borrowed money from Sonny and were unable to pay it back. Sonny resolved the matter the way he often did:

He became their silent partner in Kama Sutra. At one point, he had an interest in Buddah Records and also was often seen in the offices of Capitol Records. It was critical that Sonny stay in the background, because the big music companies, like MGM and Columbia, wanted nothing to do with gangsters. But for some independent music labels, the Mafia's brand of mediation was essential.

In 1964, one of Kama Sutra's groups, the Shangri-Las, had a big hit with "Remember (Walking in the Sand)." The record rose to number 5 on the charts, and Mo Levy took notice. He went to Steinberg and said simply, "They're mine. I want my cut."

Steinberg demurred and said he'd get back to him, but Levy was not put off. "I'm confident you'll do the right thing," he told him.

Steinberg was worried. He knew exactly what Levy was capable of. Then Sonny came by the office.

Sonny liked dropping in on the young record producers. They were street kids, like him. Often he'd bring Tina and the children with him because they loved being around the recording studios. The Brill Building, just north of Times Square in Manhattan, was the hub of the music industry at the time, with music offices and recording studios all under the same roof. Music could be heard wafting throughout the building as songwriters worked in cubbies next to one another.

Sonny noticed the bleak mood of Steinberg and his partners. They should have been celebrating the record's success. He asked them what was wrong.

Steinberg shrugged, unsure whether he should tell Sonny.

Sonny would not be put off. "Hey, Phil, what? Am I your friend? You can't tell me your problems?"

Steinberg told him. Sonny appeared surprised, but then told Steinberg and his partners not to worry about it. When Steinberg bumped into Levy at another recording studio a few weeks later, Levy made no mention of the cut he had demanded. In fact, he made no mention of anything. He was all smiles, as if nothing had happened.

"Sonny kept the wolves away," Steinberg later told a writer.

Ripp witnessed that personally one night at the Copacabana. He was there with his wife, a buxom brunette who favored décolletage and always attracted male attention. Some men tried to start a conversation with her, and out of nowhere, "two guys appeared who took those potential pains in the ass immediately away. They disappeared," Ripp recalled.

Sonny always kept an eye on his surroundings. He had noticed the problem and taken care of it.

Sonny also liked mentoring younger men, schooling them in the business of the street. And he knew that their gratitude toward him could pay dividends later.

Tony Bruno was a songwriter who worked at Kama Sutra in his early twenties. He and Sonny clicked, and Sonny started using him for errands, like picking up checks for him. There were two brothers—Bruno called them "the Lesser Brothers," because they were both very large—who gave Sonny a check every week. Sometimes, however, they missed a week.

Sonny could have resolved the payment problem the traditional way, but one time, he decided to be a little more creative. He sent over a piano to be put in their office. Then he sent over Bruno with very specific instructions: He was to play a song he wrote, "Don't Let It Bounce," every time he picked up a check.

To Bruno and Sonny, that was hilarious. What the Lesser Brothers thought is unknown.

Bruno liked Sonny's sense of humor, but dreaded it when Sonny told him to meet him for dinner. He knew Sonny would never pick up the bill, even though Sonny was far wealthier than a songwriter who was just starting out. It didn't matter. Bruno always paid. "It's not like I had a choice," he recalled.

When it came to business, Sonny never hesitated. One day, Sonny was meeting with a man in the back of a boxing gym owned by his longtime friend Tommy Gallagher. He liked to meet people there. It was a place where he could relax, and it was also away from the prying eyes of the FBI agents and cops fol-

lowing him. As Gallagher was cleaning out spit buckets, he overheard the man tell Sonny that some restaurant owner said he was
"with" Sonny.

"What's this guy's name?" Sonny asked him.

The man told him, and asked, "Is he with you?"

Sonny replied coolly, "He is now."

Protection rackets were huge at the time. Businesses of every
stripe, from truckers to bakers, had to pay tribute to the Mafia just
to operate. Sonny had a particular fondness for that way of making money. His name was gold. He'd dispatch an associate to a
business he was interested in, and often just the mention of his
name was enough to get a business owner to cough up. If a
clearer message was needed, that could be arranged easily, too.

As his business interests were expanding, Sonny hewed to a disciplined daily routine. Every day, he left his house on Shrub Hollow Road around 10:30 a.m., after kissing Tina good-bye. His
driver typically would take him into New York City, and he'd
stop for various meetings, sometimes at the theatrical agency he
owned, other times on street corners. Sonny had the walk-and-
talk perfected. Correctly figuring that it was impossible to bug his
conversations outdoors, he'd walk down the block with an associate, finish his business, and then another underling would appear and another walk would begin.

At lunchtime, Sonny was too busy to indulge in the wine-
fueled pasta lunches his contemporaries favored. He'd usually
grab a date-nut sandwich with cream cheese at Chock full o'Nuts.
Other times, he'd send an errand boy to fetch the sandwiches for
his crew. And he, of course, didn't pay.

The details of his daily routine were known because of the constant surveillance. As self-disciplined as Sonny was, it grated on
him. One day, Nassau County detectives were following Sonny
in suburban New Hyde Park, where there were numerous pay
phones. Sonny got out of his car, walked back to their car, and
said, "Pick any phone you want. Just show me where. Because
you know that I'll use it once and never again."

Detectives had been making their presence obvious to Sonny and his cohorts for a while, but they determined the pressure wasn't good enough. They leaked what they knew about Sonny to a trusted reporter.

That reporter was *Newsday*'s Greene, who, in December 1965, wrote a three-page spread devoted entirely to Sonny. Headlined THE HOOD IN OUR NEIGHBORHOOD, the story stripped away any veneer of respectability the Franzese family had hoped to achieve in suburban Roslyn. It pegged him as the fastest-rising executive in the empire of Cosa Nostra crime.

"Sonny Franzese is the big comer in the Cosa Nostra," Sergeant Ralph Salerno, who at the time was a Cosa Nostra expert for the New York City Police Department, told Greene. "He has an extraordinary talent for organized crime. He knows when to compromise and when to get tough; he knows how to run a business, and crime is big business; and, most important, he is an expert at not getting caught."

The story, complete with undercover photos taken of him walking on his lawn and next to his garage, spilled specifics of Sonny's illegal rackets and his personal life, the kind of details Greene and the detectives knew would get under his skin. It made for compelling reading. It also upended the Franzeses' family life. Michael, always a good student, started getting into fights at school.

Far worse for Sonny, the publicity hurt his standing on the street. Members of the Cosa Nostra were supposed to keep a low profile. This kind of publicity was bad for everyone. Sonny was respected and feared enough that few people would dare say it to him directly, but he knew it was bad.

CHAPTER 8

Public Enemy Number One

"They played me real dirty."

THE INDICTMENTS came in an avalanche in a single year, 1966.

In March, the Manhattan District Attorney charged Franzese with being the "muscle man" in a $10 million Garment District bookmaking ring. Photographers snapped a photo, which made the front pages, of Sonny smiling as he buttoned his overcoat after his arrest. The captions noted that his overcoat was cashmere.

In April, the U.S. Attorney charged him with conspiring to rob banks, the first time the feds linked the Cosa Nostra to a nationwide bank-robbery ring. *Newsday*'s front-page headline trumpeted: FEDS NAB FRANZESE AS SUPER DILLINGER. Sonny, always conscious of the cameras, made sure to shake his attorney's hands in a way that hid his handcuffs from photographers.

In October, the Queens District Attorney indicted him in the Rupolo homicide, along with the four men who purportedly carried it out on his orders, including Whitey Florio. Again, *Newsday* couldn't help but take note of his looks, saying he was more "like an executive posing for an *Esquire* clothing ad than a man charged with first-degree murder."

And in December, the Nassau District Attorney accused him of engineering the home invasion of an Oceanside jukebox company owner whose two teenage sons were handcuffed and gagged.

Looking back at the indictment blitz, Sonny said, "I was in the limelight too much, and they resented it."

There could be no other reason, he said. "They were no good. They treated me bad . . . They played me real dirty."

That four different law enforcement agencies all charged him with crimes in a single year was extraordinary. It is not unheard of for local prosecutors to cede jurisdiction to federal prosecutors, who have broad legal powers and can seek tougher penalties. But not this time. Sonny was too big and too successful at eluding prosecution. Nobody wanted to take any chances of him getting away again.

"Sonny Franzese back in 1966 was one of the preeminent organized-crime figures in New York, if not the United States," said Edward McDonald, former chief of the federal Organized Crime Strike Force in Brooklyn. "And everybody wanted to get glory."

In the bookmaking case, prosecutors said Sonny provided protection for four betting parlors. Sonny, "when necessary, would direct certain persons under his influence and control to compel bettors to pay their losses," the dryly worded indictment said. Sonny's cut was a sizeable percentage of the $80,000 to $100,000 a week the parlors took in, a staggering amount of money.

"If you look at the headlines of the papers . . . they had me down as the biggest shylock of New York," Sonny marveled years later.

When NYPD gambling squad detectives caught wind of the operation, they scoped out the betting parlors. One was in the back room of a button factory on West 34th Street. Two others were in private apartments. The fourth one, a fur shop on Broadway in Midtown, proved to be the weak link. A detective posing as a fur buyer, accompanied by two policewomen posing as models, entered the fifth floor of Allied Fur Products and saw, not racks of furs, but a wire room for a full-blown gambling operation.

Prosecutors hit Sonny with forty-two counts of bookmaking and one count of conspiracy. When he was arrested, Sonny wasn't worried about the case. Two key potential witnesses in the case, Abraham Eisenberg and Dominick Cappolla, suddenly went missing.

The next month, on April 12, 1966, Sonny walked into the federal courthouse in Brooklyn to be arraigned on the bank robbery charges. As usual, he had dressed for the occasion in an expensive suit—and the judge took note.

Asked his occupation, Sonny said, "Dry cleaner."

"That suit looks like it cost five hundred dollars," the judge said. "That's a lot for a dry cleaner."

Sonny said nothing.

The judge set bail at $150,000, the equivalent today of more than $1 million. Sonny's lawyer objected loudly, but the bail stood.

Although Sonny was a wealthy man, his family and friends could only produce $96,000 in assets immediately—one of the hazards of having to hide so much income. He spent the night in the Federal House of Detention on West Street in Manhattan, but was out the next day when his family produced deeds to fifteen parcels of land in Brooklyn and on Long Island as collateral. Photographers followed him as he walked out of the courthouse with his family.

When they reached his house in Roslyn, Sonny bristled at the thought of photos being taken of him at his home. He told Tina to get out of the car and open the garage door while he waited in the car. Then he drove in, himself, slamming the garage doors behind him, denying the photographers their shot.

Out on bail, Sonny got back to business, conducting his routine walk-and-talks in Brooklyn and Manhattan. He had been fending off criminal charges since he was fourteen years old. He wasn't going to let a couple of court cases interfere with business.

But the police had other ideas.

In September 1966, New York City cops arrested him again, this time for consorting with other known criminals, Joseph "Little Joey" Brancato and Gennaro "Jerry" Galtieri, in front of Bickford's, a luncheonette at West 34th Street and Ninth Avenue in Manhattan. It was a low-level crime at best, but because of who was involved, it became a news story. *Newsday*'s Greene couldn't resist taking a dig at Sonny for the "kindergarten-type crime," and lamenting: *There used to be a certain class about Cosa Nostra Luminary John (Sonny) Franzese of Roslyn.* The caption under Sonny's photo that accompanied the story asked, *Losing his touch?*

The charges, like so many others, went nowhere.

Barely three weeks later, Queens DA Nat Hentel indicted Sonny and four codefendants for the Rupolo homicide. The Hawk's history of ratting on mob bigwig Genovese, his pride in being a hit man, and his murder being ordered by a debonair mobster, such as Sonny, made irresistible fodder for the press. Reporters chased the story, churning out column inches, day after day.

After hearing that police had put out an alarm for him, Sonny avoided the spectacle of being chased and turned himself in at around 11 a.m. With his instinctive understanding of the press, he controlled the story in his own way. Dressed in a gray suit with a silk black-and-white tie and matching lapel handkerchief, he stood impassively before the court, with his black cashmere topcoat folded over his hands, once again hiding his handcuffs. Prosecutors said that although Sonny was not at the scene of the homicide, he had ordered it and therefore was just as guilty.

This time, however, he did not get released on bail. Word had leaked out that there was a witness being held under heavy guard in a secret location. Authorities could not risk letting Sonny out on the street, where he could find a way to kill the witness.

The witness was Richard Parks, one of the robbers arrested in the bank robbery case. He told detectives that Sonny told him to steal a car and deliver it at a prearranged time to a motel not far from John F. Kennedy International Airport. Switch cars were a favorite tactic of Sonny's. He often used them when trying to evade police surveillance.

Parks didn't feel like making the effort to steal a car and instead borrowed one from a friend. When he arrived where he had been told to bring the car, he saw four men lifting what appeared to be a body out of a car. They placed the body on the ground, while they prepared to open the trunk of another car. The body, however, turned out to be a live person, the Hawk, who suddenly began fighting for his life.

Three of the men cursed the fourth man, the one who had shot the Hawk, because he had screwed up—how could you not kill him? He took out his gun to shoot him again, but the others stopped him, yelling that it would make too much noise.

Improvising, one of the men pulled out a knife. He knelt on the wounded Hawk and plunged the knife into him until he stopped wriggling. It was a grisly scene, blood spurting as the Hawk gasped his last breaths. His eye patch fell off in the struggle. Not wanting to leave any evidence behind, one of the men picked it up and threw it into the witness's car.

Parks saved it as a souvenir.

The Rupolo homicide would be a career-making case for the Queens prosecutors, and they were determined to keep Sonny locked away. That didn't stop the headlines about Sonny, however. A day after the homicide indictment, the State Liquor Authority announced that it would hold hearings on mob connections to two Long Island discotheques where a murdered go-go dancer named Irene Brandt had worked. Local police files indicated that Sonny and one of his underlings, loan shark Philly Vizzari, had been spotted at the Left Bank, one of the two discos. The SLA authorities believed Sonny was the real owner, and the murder of a young woman who worked there got their attention.

Brandt, a pretty bleached blonde from Massapequa, was twenty years old when her body—hands and feet tied and throat slashed—was found in Blue Point, then a largely rural area about an hour and a half east of New York City. Brandt danced at night but worked as a bank teller during the day. She disappeared September 26, 1966, along with $21,109 she allegedly embezzled from the bank. Police theorized that she stole the money to bail a boyfriend out of jail.

Another theory was that she was the paramour of Julius "Julie" Klein, a square-jawed ex-convict who also was part owner of the other disco, the Shore Club. They also believed that Klein was involved in Brandt's murder, something Klein brushed off dismissively: "I wouldn't do such a sloppy job."

Klein had set up his own bookmaking operation in the Deer Park/North Babylon area in Suffolk County. Though it was in the sticks, the operation competed with one that had already been set up by Vizzari. An unhappy Vizzari set up a meeting with Klein to sort things out. Just beforehand, however, Vizzari learned that Klein planned to resolve the dispute by sending a gunman his way. Vizzari sent his own gunman in response. The two gunmen faced off in the streets of Wyandanch, but peacemakers intervened and bloodshed was averted.

It was a serious offense for Klein to go after one of Sonny's guys. A sit-down was called. Sonny listened to the two sides, and Klein persuaded Sonny to let him keep operating after agreeing to pay Sonny rent. For Sonny, it made good business sense. He now had two men competing to make him money. Vizzari had no choice but to eat his losses.

Klein had his own mob connections, and Sonny admired him. Years later, he said approvingly, "Yeah, I know Julie. Julie was tough."

The SLA hearings didn't yield much. Witnesses tied Klein to the Shore Club, but no one produced solid evidence linking Sonny to the other club. (A couple years later, a close friend of Brandt's was found shot to death. After his murder, a letter he had written showed up in prosecutors' offices; Klein was charged and then convicted of her murder.)

The constant barrage of investigations into Sonny made for great headlines. However, to the public, Sonny appeared untouchable. Behind the scenes, however, the bank robbers were talking. For the entire month in September, they were held secretly in the Nassau County Jail under tight security. Then their names surfaced as they were transported in an armed two-van caravan from the jail to appear before a Nassau County grand jury. In an unprecedented show of force, between twenty-five and thirty cops and detectives, carrying riot guns and shotguns, guarded the prisoners as they were ushered through a special entrance.

The bank robbers who were talking were none other than John Cordero, James Smith, and Richard Parks. They were questioned about a $30 million-a-year bookmaking operation in New York City and Nassau County run by Paul Vario Sr., then a rising power in the Luchese family. While Sonny was fending off the charges against him, Vario was making a move on Sonny's territory.

There seemed to be no limit to what Cordero, Smith and Parks—all low-level street hoods—knew about the upper reaches of the Mafia. It was Parks who told authorities he had witnessed the Hawk's murder. And the men also claimed to have information about the shocking home invasion in Oceanside.

Just two months later, in December, the bank robbers' testimony about that home invasion yielded the fourth major indictment against Sonny that year. The Nassau District Attorney charged that Sonny had ordered his crew to rob the home of jukebox executive Abraham "Al" Ezrati. Al wasn't home, but his two teenage sons were. The crew robbed the house and gagged the two teenagers with adhesive tape and handcuffed them to a pole in the cellar.

At the time, jukeboxes were big business for the mob. The scam was simple. They would lease jukeboxes to restaurant owners and charge them a hefty commission. They created a monopoly by setting up a sham union of workers to service the machines. Any restaurant owner who tried to save money by buying his own machine could expect union pickets to show up. And if that wasn't enough, the seller of the jukebox would get a threatening phone call, or worse. It was a simple shakedown racket, all the more appealing because it was an all-cash business.

For Nassau County prosecutors, the home invasion case was

momentous, their first shot at a big-time mobster. When Sonny was transported from the Queens House of Detention, where he was being held on the Rupolo homicide charge, to the arraignment, six uniformed cops and six detectives, all armed and ready, flanked him.

They took him to the identification bureau, where he was fingerprinted and had his mug shot taken. A desk sergeant asked his name. Sonny just smiled.

"As if I didn't know," the desk sergeant muttered.

Then he was taken to the courthouse, where armed policemen stood on the roof and patrolled the corridors. Police allowed Tina to briefly talk to him. They kissed and smiled at each other for all of three minutes before he was taken away.

For Tina, Sonny's jailing was galling. She decided to go public— violating the long-standing norm of Mafia wives remaining quietly in the background. She invited reporter Greene to her home.

"The only reason my husband was arrested was because his name made a nice headline in a political campaign," she said, accusing Queens DA Hentel of capitalizing on Sonny's notoriety for his own reelection campaign.

"Christmas is coming, and I want my husband home, and my children want their father. I don't care what anyone thinks about my husband, this is America, and you have to have legal proof before you put a man in a cell, throw away the key, and forget about it."

Greene asked her about the Cosa Nostra code that required wives to stay at home and be quiet. Tina laughed.

"The first time I ever heard the word [Cosa Nostra] was when I saw Joe Valachi on TV. My husband makes his money in real estate, dry cleaning, and theatrical management. I know how much we have in the bank. The papers say Cosa Nostra people are rich. So, why am I counting every penny for legal fees?"

Greene, like many men, was taken by her poise and beauty. And it was clear that her devotion to Sonny was fierce. "Every woman should only have a husband as fine as the man I married," she told him. "I love him and every day without him is like dying a little."

Just days after the home invasion indictment, Sonny's mother, Maria Carvola Franzese, died at her home on Leonard Street in Brooklyn. Sonny blamed her death on a broken heart.

"That's what killed my mother, when she heard I got locked up for murder," he said years later.

The court allowed him to pay his respects to her. Corrections officers took Sonny—with one handcuffed to each arm—there in a plain black station wagon under heavy security via an undisclosed route. He walked to her bier, then bowed his head and cried.

He was not allowed to attend her funeral Mass.

Back in the Queens Detention Center, things weren't any better. He got an ominous warning from a fellow inmate, Morris Spokane.

Spokane and two of Sonny's codefendants in the bank robbery case, John "Johnny Irish" Matera and William "Red" Crabbe, had gotten jammed up for receiving $125,000 in rare stolen coins. Matera and Crabbe got long prison sentences, but Spokane's sentencing was mysteriously postponed.

One day, he approached Sonny in jail.

"He was a Jewish guy who hung out with me . . . He came to county jail in New York . . . I'm in there. Who comes in? Morris Spokane and myself. And I got scared. I said, 'What's going on here? Something is wrong.'"

"Look, Sonny," Spokane said, "a couple of detectives come and see me. They told me to tell you to plead guilty to five years. That if you would plead guilty, they'll leave you alone."

"How could I plead guilty?" Sonny replied. "I'm innocent. I never did it."

"I know, Sonny," Spokane said. "But the government can do what they want. If it was me, I'd take it. If you lose the case, you're going to get ten times more than five years."

The conversation unnerved Sonny. He suspected a setup. He knew the government was out to get him. Still, as he ruminated about his conversation with Spokane, he began to think that something more was at play, something closer to home.

Not much later, word leaked out that mob big shots, particularly Carlo Gambino, were upset about all the publicity Sonny generated, and that he was running some unsanctioned operations, one with unproven muscle, and a robbery ring.

Orders went out that the bank robbers should cooperate with the government.

CHAPTER 9

Sonny Goes on Trial

"I'll meet him in Hell."

WHEN SONNY STRODE into the federal courthouse in Brooklyn for his bank robbery trial in January 1967, he felt confident. His lawyer, Maurice Edelbaum, a rumpled and brilliant criminal defense attorney who represented entire syndicates of mobsters, had assured him that he had everything under control. But he hadn't factored in the iron will of U.S. District Court Judge Jacob Mishler.

Mishler, a no-nonsense jurist, ran a strict courtroom, starting every day at 9 a.m. and ending at 5 p.m. Attorneys knew better than to show up late. He had no hobbies; his life was the law. Friends told him he looked like the comedian George Burns, though he thought he was better-looking. Like Sonny, Mishler was revered by the men who worked under him.

Sonny would come to hate him with a passion he reserved for no one else in his life.

The trial got off to a false start. Journalists had reported Sonny's mob connections, and Edelbaum pounced. He complained vociferously that the national media coverage had destroyed any chance Sonny had of getting a fair trial. He demanded a change of venue.

Sonny, who rarely traveled outside the confines of New York City and Long Island, was alarmed. "What are you doing?" he demanded.

"Leave it to me, leave it to me," Edelbaum assured him. "I've got friends there."

Mishler agreed with Edelbaum. Declaring the press coverage overheated, he moved the trial to Albany, more than three hours north of Brooklyn. Albany, the state capital, had a small-town feel and was heavily populated by government workers. As changes of venue go, Edelbaum couldn't have gotten anything more starkly different from New York City.

Sonny went along with the move—"He's my lawyer. I believed him"—but was uneasy. "Why'd they even make that move?" he said years later. "They had no right to move to Albany. Albany is a strait-laced country. Telephone workers. Who they going to vote for?"

Albany can be an inhospitable place in the winter, and that particular winter was bitterly cold, with temperatures settling at zero degrees or less for days at a time. Sonny, out on $230,000 bail, stayed with Tina in the relative comfort of the Sheraton Inn Towne Motel, while his codefendants languished in jail under heavy security. Mishler stayed at the same hotel. Sonny, walking to court in a pile-lined car coat made of beige suede, made an impression. When talking to each other, reporters, who had been admonished not to write about his mob connections, nicknamed him the "Handsome Don."

The trial opened on January 30, 1967, with lawyers from both sides picking a jury in under six hours. It was easy because virtually all the prospective jurors swore that they hadn't read anything about the case or Sonny and his codefendants, Crabbe, Matera, Florio, and Nicholas "Nick" Potere. Among the spectators was James C. Mosley, the assistant district attorney for Queens, who was preparing for his upcoming case against Sonny: the homicide of Ernest "the Hawk" Rupolo.

The bank robbery indictment laid out a relatively simple case: Sonny had selected the banks to be robbed, supplied street maps and floor plans, and shared in the proceeds for the robbery spree—seven banks in forty-four days. Prosecutors planned to argue that Sonny's decision to take over direct planning of the robberies came at an underworld sit-down convened to iron out hostilities. Assistant U.S. Attorney Michael Gillen, a slim and shaggy-haired man, and two staffers were seated on the prosecution's side.

A battery of lawyers sat at the defense table, with Edelbaum, the leader. Edelbaum—bombastic, loud, and described by one reporter as "lionlike"—was famous for his courtroom theatrics, so much so that other lawyers eagerly tried to snag a seat whenever he was involved with a trial. The defense's case was equally simple: The key witnesses were bank robbers and liars and were testifying in exchange for reduced sentences.

First up on the witness stand: James Smith, one of the four bank robbers who had turned. Balding and wiry at thirty-one, he seemed to be perpetually squinting behind thick glasses. He had been the one designated to jump over the counter and scoop up the money. During one of the heists, he hurdled the counter. However, his eyesight was so bad that he missed the big stuff and grabbed only one-dollar bills. After that, he wore glasses all the time.

Gillen put the Mafia itself on trial. He had Smith describe the Mafia hierarchy—from boss to soldier—in detail. Sonny was the underboss, number two in command, and Whitey was the lieutenant. Red and Nick were soldiers at the bottom of the pecking order. The soldiers, he said, were the "ones who do the dirty work."

Asked if he had ever heard Sonny discuss assaults and killings, Smith said, "Well, he had told Mr. Parks in front of me, he says, 'When I tell you to do something, you do it. If I tell you to pipe somebody, you pipe them. If I tell you to kill somebody, you kill somebody.'"

"What does 'pipe' mean?" Gillen asked.

Smith responded carefully. "That is to hit somebody over the head with a pipe."

Gillen methodically walked Smith through the planning and the commission of the bank robberies. At the core of his case was a meeting that, he said, happened in July 1965 in which Sonny met with the robbers and took over the operation.

*   *   *

Defense attorneys countered that Smith had cut a deal in exchange for special treatment in prison and a lighter sentence. To buttress their contention, they produced a letter Smith had written from prison. It turned out that Smith and the other bank robbers were avid letter writers. They had been held under tight security to ensure their safety, and they were stir-crazy. They also knew well the value of their testimony in the highest-profile federal mob trial in the country.

In one letter, Smith wrote: *We are pretty steamed up about us being shanghaied to this place. We want out . . . It is real bad here . . . Everybody feels the same way I do, if something ain't done soon, the deal is off.*

Edelbaum cross-examined him about making a deal, but Smith insisted no deal was made. Anxious to undermine his credibility, Edelbaum asked, "Would you hesitate to lie on the stand to save yourself from going to jail?"

Smith replied that he wouldn't hesitate to lie to save himself: "No, I wouldn't."

It was a solid blow, but not quite enough. Edelbaum wanted the jury to know that Smith and the others were the dangerous criminals, not his client. He asked Smith why the bank robbery gang had been armed during the heists.

"In the event they had to be used for whatever purpose," Smith replied evenly.

"Does that mean you would kill if you had to?" Edelbaum bellowed.

"Probably," Smith answered.

Then Edelbaum made perhaps the most significant strike in terms of the evidence: He got Smith to admit that he had originally implicated Sonny's associate Anthony Polisi as the mastermind. But Smith was ready with an explanation for that. He said he had been too afraid at first to name Sonny.

"I'm in jail a long time, and I seen what happened to others who testified against their partners," he told the court. "There's no place you can hide in jail."

That early omission by the bank robbers was a problem for Gillen. They had waited until some months after they were arrested to implicate Sonny. He countered that by invoking the bloody backdrop of the Mafia at every opportunity. Smith's fears, as well as those by his fellow bank robbers, hung in the air as they testified about receiving death threats from Sonny's emissaries.

In a hearing without jurors present, Gillen quizzed Smith about murders. He argued that he needed to demonstrate that Smith was absolutely terrified for his life.

He asked whether Sonny had ever talked about Eleanor, Ernest Rupolo's widow, who had married John Cordero after the Hawk's death.

"Well, he wanted to know about Mr. Cordero's wife, that she was doing a little talking in the neighborhood about her husband that was killed, and he was concerned about it. And there was talk that if she didn't stop it, she would be the next one to go."

Gillen asked whether Smith had ever heard Sonny talk about the Hawk. He said he had, at a bar at the Aqueduct Motor Inn in Queens—the same place where the sit-down was allegedly held. Smith didn't waste any time getting to the point.

"Well, Mr. Franzese let it be known that everybody in the room was concerned about the talk that was going around concerning this guy, Rupolo. He said that he had ordered his hit, and that everybody here had something to worry about," Smith testified.

"What do you mean, a 'hit'?" Gillen asked.

"To kill him," Smith replied.

Gillen tried to grill him further about the Hawk, but Mishler cut him off. Gillen pivoted to other murders.

"Did you know a man by the name of Joe 'the Fish' Vitelli?" he asked.

"Yes," Smith replied.

"What happened to him?" Gillen asked.

"He was shot dead in a park in Brooklyn because they thought he was an informant for the narcotics bureau."

"Did you know of a man, Artie Rupolo, not Ernie?"

"I heard of him," Smith said.

"What happened to him?" Gillen asked.

"He was shot dead, too, because they thought he was giving information to the local police," Smith said.

"Did you ever hear of a man by the name of Arnold Schuster?" Gillen asked.

"Yeah," Smith replied.

"What did you hear about Schuster?" Gillen asked.

"Well, he was a legitimate citizen, and he put the finger on Willie Sutton, and a couple of days later, the man was shot dead a couple of blocks from his house," Smith replied.

Schuster, a twenty-four-year-old Brooklyn clothing salesman, had spotted Sutton, a famed bank robber on the lam, on a New York subway. He alerted the police and later got his own few minutes of fame on television, where he bragged about aiding in Sutton's arrest. Unfortunately for Schuster, mobsters watch television, too.

Gillen asked Smith about more murders, until Mishler cut him off again, asking him to present evidence of a direct threat made against Smith. Gillen was only too happy to oblige. He asked Smith what happened while he was being held in the Nassau County Jail.

"Well, my girlfriend came out to the jail to visit me, and she told me that Nick Potere told her that the other guys had signed statements against [the other defendants] . . . and that Sonny realized that I was in a bad position, and that if I was going to jump on the bandwagon against [those defendants], that would be all right, but if I went any further, to stop and think of the consequences."

"What would be the consequences, in your mind?" Gillen asked.

"To have me snuffed," Smith replied.

Careful to ensure that people in the Albany courtroom understood the language of the New York streets, Gillen asked, "What's 'snuffed'?"

"Killed," Smith replied.

Even one of the defense attorneys seemed caught off guard by the lingo. "What's the word?" he asked.

Gillen, delighted at the opportunity to underscore it, said, "'Snuffed.'"

Something else came out in that hearing. Gillen said the prosecution had been given information by a secret informant who had been working with the government for the past ten years. He said he couldn't reveal the informant's name, because it would be an immediate death sentence.

When the jurors returned to the courtroom, Charles "Blackie" Zaher, the getaway driver in two of the robberies, took the stand. Tall and thin, with a thick head of black hair—hence his nickname—he was the youngest of the bank robbery gang, at twenty-four years old. He also was an admitted drug addict and it showed. He was jumpy. FBI agents and Gillen had pegged him as the weak link and worried about his ability to weather a grilling on the stand.

Gillen turned that to his advantage. He asked Zaher about a death threat against him at the Federal House of Detention on West Street in New York City. Zaher explained that the prison chef approached him and told him Sonny knew he was going to testify against the other defendants: "But if you go any further, you're dead."

Terrified, Zaher decided his only option was suicide. He slashed his arm with a razor blade: "I didn't have the nerve to cut deep enough. So I talked Cordero into cutting me. He cut the artery."

Zaher was taken to the hospital and survived.

Richard Parks was next up. A husky, sleepy-eyed man, with a black crewcut, he was a difficult witness. He complained about prison, saying he was treated like "an unwanted animal," held in isolation and given cold food. He said it affected his mind. But he also said that two other inmates threatened him if he mentioned Sonny.

*   *   *

Finally John "Blue Boy" Cordero took the stand. In his own way, he was disarming. He admitted to being a drug addict and said he spent $75 to $80 a day on drugs, but he linked Sonny directly to the bank robberies. He testified about specific conversations he had with Sonny about them.

In one, Cordero described Sonny's consternation over their mistakes. When they tried to rob the bank in Massachusetts, the robbers failed to get to the vault, and Sonny wanted to know why. "I told him that two men were standing across the street, and he said, 'You have guns. I don't like this running out of banks.'"

They agreed to move past that hiccup, and Cordero went on to say that Sonny gave him the floor plans for a bank in Denver. "He told me, 'I want this bank taken Friday because President Johnson's wife is in Denver and she will be there giving a speech or something, and all the security will be drawn downtown, and also there was a Shriners' convention going on that will cause a lot of confusion, too, so make sure you hit this bank on Friday.'"

Sonny went on, according to Cordero: "And take your wives along with you. It wouldn't look good if you three guys traveled alone. You take your wife, and have Mr. Smith take his wife, too."

But they didn't hit the bank on Friday. They missed their flight and had to rob it on Saturday, when it had no money. Sonny was furious at the stupidity of their mistake, Cordero said.

It was effective testimony.

Next Gillen needed to establish a link between Nick Potere, an electrical contractor, and the others. He argued that the defendants' legal fees were paid through Potere's company. His bookkeeper took the stand, but parried Gillen with ease. She testified that the money was merely a loan. Then she got off the stand, walked over to the defense table, and kissed Potere on the lips.

Years later, Sonny blamed Potere for the indictment. "He gave the DA the idea," he said. "Because he didn't know how to carry himself and he tried to come on like something he wasn't."

* * *

After five weeks of testimony, both sides presented their closing arguments. Sonny never testified.

Edelbaum indignantly pointed out the witnesses' unsavory pasts and their histories of lies. His co-counsel compared the prosecution's case to a "grade-B movie" played by "four characters in search of a stage."

Gillen, in his summation, argued that while Sonny hadn't personally held up the banks, he had planned the robberies and claimed half the proceeds. Then he played his trump card—the stark, naked terror of his witnesses. "You could smell the fear!" he shouted. "These men knew that death could follow them into jail."

Two days later, the jury foreman, his hands trembling, read the verdict on March 3, just after midnight: guilty.

Sonny appeared to turn pale, but remained composed with his hands clasped. Inwardly, he focused his rage on Mishler. He saw the judge as on the prosecution's side "all the way." Tina permitted herself one choked cry before regaining her composure.

The day after the verdict, the *New York Times* reported gruesome allegations that prosecutors had filed in court, but that the jurors had never heard: Authorities believed Sonny had killed "thirty or forty or fifty" people and that his codefendants Crabbe and Florio had killed on his orders.

For decades, Sonny had thwarted prosecutors at every turn. The impact of this first guilty verdict became clear when Judge Mishler later handed down his astonishing sentence: fifty years. It would be the longest sentence Mishler ever imposed.

Sonny sat frozen-faced. Tina was not there.

"You watch," he told Mishler, "I'll do the whole bid."

Mishler also imposed a $20,000 fine—which Sonny never paid—and made the sentence indeterminate, meaning that authorities could grant him parole if he agreed to squeal on other mobsters. FBI agents had been trying to get him to do that for years. With a virtually lifelong prison sentence hanging over his head, they hoped he'd change his mind.

Sonny was freed on $150,000 bail, pending appeal.

* * *

A week later, on April 21, 1967, Judge Mishler sentenced the bank robbers. Gillen argued for no time, but Mishler gave them five years each. He said he didn't think they would be unsafe in prison, because Sonny—knowing that authorities had the discretion to determine how much time he would actually serve—wouldn't let anything happen to them.

"The last person who would want anything to happen to you is Franzese," Mishler said. "He should be on his knees every night praying that nothing happens to you."

Edelbaum insisted he would win on appeal. Sonny believed him, so much so that he didn't put plans in place for a trusted hand to succeed him. He had beaten every other rap; he would beat this one. Besides, he said, he wasn't guilty.

Sonny insisted he never even met the bank robbers. "Never happened. I'll take a truth serum today. Not even a lie detector, but truth serum. Never happened. I never had a meeting with them. Why would I want to have a meeting with them? I don't know them."

Asked why he thought Mishler gave him such a long prison sentence, Sonny smiled and said, "Maybe I had an affair with his second wife."

Mishler "hated me for what reason, I'll never know. I'd always felt that he thought I had an affair with one of his wives."

The verdict and sentence didn't end the drama, which extended through three more cases and nine appeals—all presided over by Mishler, who refused to be intimidated by the threats he would face in the years to come.

When Mishler died in 2004 at the age of ninety-two, Sonny spoke of wanting to find his grave, once he got out from under the prying eyes of his parole officer. "If I get off of parole, I'll go there. I'll find it," he said, "and I'll go pee on it."

Sonny also said of Mishler, "I'll meet him in Hell."

CHAPTER 10

On Trial for Homicide

"How could I hate a guy I don't know?"

CROWDS BUSTLED around the Queens courthouse on November 2, 1967, an unseasonably warm day for that time of year. Word had spread about the trial that was about to open. News reporters and camera crews had come from across the country to cover it. Bystanders who couldn't get into the courthouse craned their necks to see witnesses come and go. It was an event.

It was the opening of the Ernie "the Hawk" Rupolo homicide trial. The case had it all—a one-eyed hit man whose body was found in Jamaica Bay, a streetwise widow with secrets of her own, and a handsome mobster who allegedly ordered the hit to avenge Vito Genovese.

New York police had pulled out all the stops on security. They transported Sonny to the courthouse in a fortified police van, with plainclothes detectives and cops armed with shotguns flanking him on both sides. When they opened the doors of the van, Sonny emerged in a tailored suit, looking slightly bemused by all the cameras snapping his photo. He looked like a matinee idol, and the throngs were electrified.

Coverage of the trial dominated the local TV newscasts, and photographers eagerly tracked the comings and goings of every witness. Inside the courthouse in Kew Gardens, there were no spare seats. You had to know somebody to get a seat. Everyone was prepared for a show, and they got one.

The Hawk's murder was as grisly as his life; he once bragged that he made his living by "stabbing, killing, burglary, or any other crime I get paid for."

The case consumed the Queens district attorney's office, particularly prosecutor Mosley, a cerebral, resolute man utterly convinced of Sonny's guilt. He and his lead detective, Joe Price, spent virtually every waking hour discussing trial strategy and trying to calm their restive witnesses. They also indulged in a bit of macabre humor typical in prosecutors' offices: They used one of the concrete blocks that had been tied to the Hawk's body as a doorstop.

The Hawk's widow, Eleanor, who also had the dubious distinction of having married bank robber Cordero after her husband's murder, camped out in DA's offices. Her particular status gave her a certain leverage over the harried prosecutors because Cordero was the first bank robber to turn. She leveraged her status to the hilt, airily directing people to bring her soda and sandwiches. She reveled in the attention, and she had a way of making sure she was the center of it. Any man who encountered her was not likely to forget her.

When newspapers reported that Alice Crimmins, accused of killing her own children in Queens, had a police guard, Eleanor charged into Mosley's office, curlers in her hair, screaming.

"How come some bitch who killed her two kids gets police protection, and I can't even get a lousy detective to take me to Brooklyn? I'm going to get dynamited out of my car someday, and a lot any of you will care!" she shouted.

"She didn't get protection. Only for a few hours, it's been withdrawn. Leave me alone," Mosley responded.

The scene was typical of Eleanor. She knew that her husband was key to Mosley's case. She and prosecutors also knew that Cordero was besotted with her. He was adamant about keeping her safe and had insisted that she not testify. It wasn't a hard deal to make, as prosecutors had no idea if they could control her on the stand. Knowing she wouldn't have to appear publicly,

Eleanor treated the Queens district attorney's office as her own personal province, sometimes marching in with her own pillows and sheets for conjugal visits with her husband. The attorneys were irritated, even a little aghast at her brazenness, but felt stuck. They knew that if she was happy, her husband would be happy.

While Eleanor lapped up the attention from the DA's office, she wasn't stupid. Every time she walked through the bedlam outside the courthouse or rode by in a car, she hid her face from photographers with a large hat or gloved hands.

In addition to Cordero, Zaher and Parks were queued up to testify, and they weren't happy. They had been moved from jail to jail and kept in virtual solitary confinement to keep them safe, and they were breaking down mentally. The trial had been delayed for months by pretrial legal maneuvering. During that delay, they sent word that Sonny had offered them $20,000 each if they dropped the case.

Then Zaher, who had been whining for months that he wanted to get out on bail—"I don't like jail, you know. You seem to have the impression I like jail"—made news when he escaped from Manhattan Civil Jail. He used a blade to saw through the lock on the mesh window gate and fled through a fourth-floor window and down a fire escape.

Detectives, not wanting to alert the Mafia that their high-profile witness was on the lam, quietly searched for him for five days. They finally issued an alarm, and the New York Daily News picked it up: POLICE RACING MAFIA FOR ESCAPED INFORMER.

A month later, a couple of New York City patrolmen saw Zaher hanging around a Queens bank. He had a gun, stocking cap, and a rented car idling up the block; he insisted, however, that he wasn't planning on robbing the bank. He was after the bookmaker who made deposits there. Police locked him up anyway.

Finally, by November, the trial was under way. Mosley's first witness was the police photographer, so he could introduce the grisly photos of the Hawk's body. As the man wrapped up his testimony, Mosley dragged out a pair of concrete blocks and asked him if those were the blocks tied to the victim's body. The witness got off the stand, bent over them, and affirmed, "Those are the blocks."

Point made.

Next up was Ernest's brother William, a short, jowly, middle-aged man who had been closer to his brother than anyone else. For a street guy like William to even get up on the stand was tantamount to suicide. (Years later, the mob's vengeance would become apparent when he was murdered.) He talked about the last time he saw his brother.

"Well, he was with his friend, someone by the name of Roy Roy. He came to my house about eleven-thirty, after I closed my place of business. He changed his clothes. I gave him a pair of my pants and a shirt. It was a warm night, and he left with his friend on his way, and that was the last I saw of my brother."

Mosley pulled a pair of torn pants out of a box, holding them at arm's length to avoid the odor. He asked William if he had seen those pants before.

William stiffened. "Yes, they are my pants," he said.

Charles Zaher—his black hair long because the jail barber refused to cut the hair of a stool pigeon—took the stand. For all his threats not to testify, he came through for Mosley. There were four men on trial—Whitey Florio, Red Crabbe, Sonny Franzese, and Thomas Matteo—but Sonny was the one the prosecutors wanted to be sure was tied to the homicide. Mosley asked Zaher what Sonny had said at the sit-down at the Aqueduct, and Zaher replied, "Mr. Franzese said he ordered the Hawk's hit."

The defense pushed back, prodding Zaher to tell jurors his history as a bank robber, car thief, and drug addict. They even got him to admit that he shot up a few hours before the sit-down.

John Cordero was next and said he, too, heard Sonny say he ordered the hit. As he testified, Tina, who was sitting in the audience, put her right hand to her temple and extended her forefinger as if it were a gun. Cordero saw it, paused, and took a sip of water.

Tina wasn't alone in her show of support for her husband. Sonny's henchmen filled the courtroom and hooted with laughter at Mosley's objections and muttered insults under their breath. Their tactics weren't confined to the courthouse gallery. Someone threatened Judge Albert Bosch, as well as Mosley and his family. Just what the threats were, and how they came in, were never made public, but Mosley's wife abruptly packed up her four young children and moved them into a hotel under police guard. When they returned home, the children were told to never answer the phone. Their parents, in trying to shield them, couldn't hide their fear. The children knew something very bad was going on.

Back in the courtroom, the trial ground on. Cordero remained composed on the stand, parrying defense questions with relative ease. Then one of the defense attorneys saw a way to get under his skin—through Eleanor. Everyone knew how crazy he was about her. Anytime he got sprung from jail to talk to the prosecutors, he called her. If she didn't answer immediately, his mood would go dark. It wasn't just his jealousy. Cordero saw it as his duty to protect his wife from Sonny's hoods, who would have liked nothing more than to shut her up permanently. The DA's office believed there was a hit out on her.

The attorney asked him where Eleanor was. "Is your wife here?"

"You can call her," Cordero said, warily eyeing the hoods in the audience.

"Is your wife here?" the attorney demanded again.

"Where, here?" Cordero said, trying to deflect the question. "What are you talking about?"

"In the courthouse," the attorney replied.

"I don't know," Cordero responded.

In a voice dripping with sarcasm, the attorney said, "Do you know where she is?"

Cordero, offended, took the bait. "Yes, I know where my wife is."

Mosley objected, but was overruled. The defense attorney pressed on a bit more, then moved on. The message had been sent.

Bob Greene briefly testified about the conversation he had with Florio about the night Cordero took a few shots at him outside the Kew Motor Inn, after Eleanor had accused Florio of killing her husband. Greene, like Sonny, could take command of a room and was deeply respected by his peers, but he didn't have much effect on reporters in the gallery.

Reporters attended court daily and had developed a certain camaraderie common to newsmen covering big stories. They compared notes and found they mostly felt the same way: They thought the prosecution's case was pretty flimsy.

Mosley knew his witnesses had credibility problems, and he tried mightily to maintain focus and corral them into doing what he needed them to do.

Richard Parks was up next. He told the story of the night he happened upon the defendants who were wrestling with the half-dead Hawk.

"They were carrying him. He made an outburst. He said, he screamed the words 'No! No!'"

The men dropped Ernie to the ground. "And Crabbe pulled out the gun, and then he went to go over to the body and he took a few steps, and Florio grabbed him by the arm and he says, 'Not with the gun.' And he had a knife, and he had his knife in his hand, and Crabbe grabbed . . . the knife out of Florio's hand. And he bent down, like on one knee, and he stabbed the body about three or four times in the chest."

Parks told the story without any emotion, making it all the more spellbinding. The jury hung on every word.

Defense attorney Maurice Edelbaum then stepped up. He had a letter Parks had written from jail in a fit of anger. Parks had filled it with outlandish lies in order to force the prosecution to drop him as a witness. Edelbaum went through the letter, line by line, asking him if they were lies, each one more outrageous. Parks stayed cool under fire, but finally he blew, screaming that he had wanted to discredit himself as a witness.

Though he hadn't won the exchange with Edelbaum, Parks had made a bigger point: He had written the letter out of pure terror.

All of the witnesses had done what Mosley needed them to do, but he knew that he needed someone outside this clique for corroboration.

James Mosley called on John Rapacki, in jail for assault and robbery, but not one of the mobsters' circle. Nervous and intense, he testified that Crabbe had told him while they were in jail that Sonny's crew had killed Rupolo: "We took care of him. The boss ordered it."

Rapacki came across well. He seemed to desperately want the jurors to believe him.

In his summation, Mosley began with how police solved the case—with four strokes of luck. First, the corpse floated to the surface, despite the concrete blocks, and second, the body was identifiable. Third, Eleanor had accused Florio of murdering her Hawk. And fourth, when police solved the bank robberies, they arrested the men who would become their witnesses.

Then Mosley conceded the obvious—his problematic witnesses: "This case came out of the gutter and out of the sewer. Where does the district attorney have to go for witnesses, whether we like it or not? To the gutter and the sewer . . . I don't vouch for the character of these witnesses, but I submit that they did not lie here."

Sonny had remained resolutely composed throughout the trial. But in one photo snapped of him walking alone outside the courthouse, his face was drawn and he appeared thinner. The strain on him was evident.

In his defense attorney's summation, Edelbaum cajoled and flattered the jury, waving his hands and banging on the defense table. He attacked the witnesses' credibility and pointed out the concessions—like Blue Boy Cordero's conjugal visits with Eleanor—that they had wrung from prosecutors in exchange for their testimony. "Doesn't it make your stomach turn to think that scum like that can dictate to elected officials?" he shouted.

It was a good show, but Mosley still felt confident as the case wrapped up.

Then Parks, familiar with the ways of the Mafia, warned him: "They're gonna come up with a story."

It came in a last-minute letter to Judge Bosch, literally minutes before the jury was to begin deliberations.

The letter had been written by Walter Sher, an inmate on Sing Sing's death row. He was there because, at the age of twenty-three, he had killed a watchmaker in Manhasset, a wealthy community on Long Island's North Shore. He and a friend had burst into the store in 1962, intending to rob it, but the watchmaker fought back. Sher shot him twice, and they fled; Nassau County police quickly apprehended them. In court, Sher, an intelligent and wily man, said he heard voices and that people were trying to poison his food. That, plus the fact that his mother had committed suicide, persuaded the judge that he was incapable of understanding the charges against him. He was committed to the Matteawan State Hospital for the Criminally Insane.

When the trial for the watchmaker's murder opened, Sher was brought back from the hospital. One night, a woman called six of the jurors on the case and told them he was a vicious killer and not at all insane. The jurors reported the calls to the court, but the case continued anyway. Sher was found guilty of felony murder and sentenced to death. He was to be executed by January 27, 1964.

Sher managed to stave off the execution by filing legal appeals, based in part on the anonymous woman's calls to jurors. By the time he wrote the letter to the judge in the Rupolo case, he had nothing to lose.

Sher had gotten to know Rapacki when they were both in the

Nassau County Jail. He wrote that Rapacki hated the Hawk because he had swindled him out of money. He said Rapacki had
told him he killed Ernie Rupolo. There was just enough detail in
the letter to establish that Sher really knew Rapacki. For the prosecution, it was the equivalent of a neutron bomb.

Bosch delayed jury deliberations for a day as Mosley and Price
scrambled to find out what they could about Sher. Before they
walked into the prison to meet with him, a guard warned Price,
"Look out for this one. He's very, very sharp. Watch yourself.
He's made up his mind what he's gonna do, and he's gonna do it."

Upon hearing the news, John Rapacki was both furious and
frantic. "What a jerk I am! I'm getting nothing out of this, and
now I'm being framed for murder!"

He demanded truth serum and screamed at the prosecution
team, "I thought they'd kill me! But I never thought they'd do
this. If Sonny hits the street, he'll kill my wife. I know they'll
kill her!"

The next day, Bosch agreed to allow Sher's testimony, which
meant Rapacki had to go back on the stand to be questioned by
defense lawyers.

Near tears, he shouted, "They're going to kill me. They're
going to poison me. They're going to poison me in prison. You
don't know how powerful they are. They're more powerful
than you . . . If Sonny beats this, he's gonna figure no one can
touch him!"

Rapacki glumly confirmed that he knew Sher from the jail, but
screamed, "That's a lie!" every time defense attorneys asked him
about talking to Sher about the Hawk.

Sher, who came to the courthouse in handcuffs and leg irons, was
up next. He glanced suspiciously around him, like a feral animal,
but managed an oily grin for photographers. On the stand,
though, he looked absolutely terrified.

The defense attorney set the stage. "Mr. Sher, you said before
that you are in the condemned cells of Sing Sing prison?"

"Yes, sir," he said quietly.

"Is that what is commonly known as the death house?"

"Yes, it is," Sher replied.

Courtroom spectators were rapt. Sher clearly was the star of the day.

After walking him through his murder conviction and incarceration, the defense attorney had him lay out what he knew of Rapacki's relationship with the Hawk. Then he went in for the kill: "And did John Rapacki tell you, in words or substance, that he killed the Hawk?"

"Yes, sir, he did," Sher replied.

Mosley was furious. In his cross-examination, he got Sher to admit that he had been committed as legally insane, but later had been found to have faked it. He was unable to shake Sher from his story, however.

Summing up his case afterward, Mosley was red-faced with anger and shouting that Sher's testimony was the obvious lie of "an admitted psychopath."

Within hours, the all-male jury returned with a verdict: not guilty.

Spectators applauded, until Judge Bosch ordered them to stop. Sonny smiled for photographers as a younger man helped him on with his silk-lined overcoat. Tina, her hair cut short and coiffed, highlighting her cheekbones, looked lovely as she sobbed hoarsely, saying, "He did it, he did it," meaning he beat the charge. Then she collapsed in Sonny's arms.

Years later, Sonny denied ordering the hit on the Hawk. "Look, I beat that case. If I did it, I would tell you. I didn't even know the guy. I never met the guy. May God strike me dead this minute if I'm lying. I never met the man."

Told that Eleanor was quoted as saying they hated each other, he said, "How could I hate a guy I don't know?"

He didn't deny knowing Eleanor, however. "She was no good. She's a rat. She was everything you want to call her. She was an—excuse the expression, she was a whore. I never touched her, I'll be honest with you. But she was no good."

And he was sure she was motivated by jealousy: "She was mad because she wanted what my wife had."

None of that mattered with his acquittal. That night, he celebrated at the Copa.

Mosley and Price drowned their sorrows at a neighborhood bar in Queens.

CHAPTER 11

Peep Shows, Porn, and Pop Music

"You make money, it translates into power."

AFTER SUCCESSFULLY shaking off the homicide case, Sonny decided to do what he always did: He went back out on the street. One day, he was walking through Times Square with a couple of associates when something caught his eye. It wasn't the silhouettes of nude women plastered on the storefronts or the signs advertising every kind of sexual fetish for sale. It was the long lines of male customers waiting to get in to view the peep shows. He made a few quick mental calculations and realized that someone was making a fortune off porn.

By the mid-1960s, massage parlors and peep shows—where coins in a slot would reveal a few minutes of sex films or live sex acts—exploded in Times Square in New York City. There wasn't a block or corner without an XXX or LIVE GIRLS sign. Nothing was hidden behind brown paper bags. It was all out there, for the world to see, thanks to a landmark U.S. Supreme Court decision in 1964 that held that all but the most extreme pornography was protected under the First Amendment.

Dressed in paisley shirts, bell-bottoms, and a walrus mustache, Marty Hodas was in the middle of it all. A coarse and cocky man, Hodas figured he knew what guys liked, and that he could make a lot of money off it. He had started out in jukeboxes—long the province of the Mafia—and moved on to peep shows, where men could satisfy their fantasies by feeding an endless stream of quarters into the machines. Figuring more was better, he started to offer live sex acts performed on a stage. (He was so proud of his acumen that he decided to show it off to his twelve-year-old daughter, Romola, inviting her to sit in the audience as a couple, dressed in black leather, performed in a sadomasochistic show complete with whips and chains. She fainted.)

The cash poured in, literally clogging his machines if he didn't clear them out regularly. In one year, one of his peep show emporiums brought in $1.52 million, the equivalent of $10.7 million today. In all, he had 350 machines, plus adult bookstores and massage parlors.

Hodas leased some of his peep show machines to Robert Genova, regarded by some as Sonny's man in Times Square, who had several adult stores on Broadway. Genova and Lawrence Abbandando, another associate of Sonny's, immediately saw the income potential and decided to cut out Hodas by starting their own peep show business with 120 machines of their own. Hodas, understandably, was not happy about the competition. Hodas was no pushover, but given their connection to Sonny, there was little he could do about it.

Hodas tried to befriend Sonny, and Sonny let him think that was possible. Hodas invited him to a family party at his home in Lawrence, a predominantly Jewish suburb not far from the Brooklyn border, but light-years away from the sleaze of Times Square. Many of Hodas's parties were bacchanals, literally orgies with drunk and high prostitutes copulating in full view of his young children. Sonny avoided those. As much as Hodas's revenues impressed him, Sonny would never deign to attend something like that.

Before long, it became clear that Sonny and Hodas would not be friends, but partners. "A guy came," he said years later. "He told me he wanted half of my store."

It was classic Sonny: Establish a relationship, provide an incentive, and then lay out the terms. But Hodas wouldn't budge.

He had built the business, and it was his. He refused to give in. At night, he'd pace around his house, muttering, "They're not going to get a fucking penny from me."

Hodas might have been defiant, but he couldn't have been more wrong. A little while later, an intruder surprised him at his home. He fired off some shots, prompting the intruder to make a hasty retreat, but Hodas wound up getting arrested for possession of an unregistered and loaded firearm.

Then some thugs grabbed Marty's youngest son, Jarrett. They picked up the six-year-old as he walked home from his school bus. They didn't hurt him. They bought him ice cream and dropped him off at home with a note pinned to his shirt: *Hi, Marty, just to let you know we're thinking very seriously of you.*

Marty got the message, but made a show of shrugging it off to his frantic wife. Then as twelve-year-old Romola was walking to school, three men drove up next to her in a black limo. "Hey, Romola, come over here. Your mom told us to pick you up."

Though she wasn't yet a teenager, Romola was already battle-hardened. "My mother told you what?" she shouted. "You think I would go with you and miss school? It's eight o'clock in the damn morning. There's no way my mother told you that!"

They backed off that day. But there was another attempt, when Romola was away at summer camp. A dark-suited man approached her in the hallway of her dormitory. She screamed, and he fled.

None of those incidents were ever tied directly to Sonny, but Marty Hodas knew all too well that the mob wanted a piece of his very lucrative business. Exactly who broke into his home or tried to kidnap his children was never clear. What is clear is that Sonny came out on top. Authorities concluded that Sonny swooped in and did what he had become known for: He negotiated a truce, memorialized in a handwritten note, in which Sonny was referred to by his given name: *John gets $4,000 a week until $100,000 is received. Thereafter he receives $1,000 a week for the rest of the year. All new stores, Marty puts up to 50% cash with John, and we are partners. Marty assumes all responsibility for running the stores.*

It was just the kind of arrangement Sonny liked, except for one thing. It was embarrassing for a man like him to be making money off a woman. It might have been fine for the Gambinos, who made a fortune off pornography, but not the Colombos. That kind of business was strictly beneath them. He kept his association with Hodas very quiet.

Years later, when Hodas was charged with tax evasion, he offered the novel defense that he hadn't actually underreported his income. His tax filing was accurate, he said, because he deducted his $100,000 annual payoff to organized crime. The government didn't regard that as an allowable exemption. After four days of trial, he was convicted and sentenced to a year in jail.

One of the actresses in Hodas's hard-core loops was Linda Lovelace, who went on to star in the mainstream porn hit *Deep Throat*. Sonny helped finance it with his friend Louis Peraino, more commonly known as "Lou Perry," the son of Colombo capo Anthony Peraino. Songwriter Tony Bruno, Sonny's old friend, wrote the musical score. It went on to become the most profitable porn film of all time.

Lou Perry was "a schemer, he was a smart guy," Sonny recalled. As for Lovelace, Sonny's recollection is unprintable.

Always an active earner, Sonny continued to branch out in business. He kept up a frenetic pace and expanded seemingly everywhere. It was almost as if the bank robbery conviction had never happened, or perhaps it was his attempt to line up as much revenue-producing business as he could before he went away. He raked in money through a hot credit card racket, loan-sharking on Wall Street, and a sophisticated robbery racket that brought in millions. Sonny told Michael: "You make money, it translates into power."

The stolen credit card racket was simple. A couple of guys under Sonny's loyal loan shark Philly Vizzari would get cards from a Queens fence, who got them from pickpockets or burglars. Then they'd use the cards for airline flights, hotel stays, expensive meals, running up thousands. The twist Sonny's crew put on it was innovative. Vizzari would allow his loan shark customers to pay off their debt out of cash receipts and then make out bills for that amount on the stolen credit card he provided. The bills would then be submitted to the credit card company for reimbursement, and Vizzari would be paid an additional "service charge" for his trouble.

They concentrated on major national credit card companies, bank cards, and airline cards, because they were able to run up very large bills in a short period of time. Restaurants and clubs were among Sonny's favorite targets, because nobody ever remembered who signed the bill. Chances of getting caught were virtually nil, and the reward was high.

Wall Street proved to be fertile ground as well. Gamblers, so often the best customers of Sonny's loan-sharking operations, didn't limit themselves to horse races or card games. A Wall Street clerk named Jerry had a habit of picking bad stocks and ended up $5,000 short. He went to a dry-cleaning store in Greenwich Village run by Nathan Sackin, one of Sonny's loan sharks. Sackin loaned him $5,000, which came from Sonny, with a vig of 5 percent, or interest of $250 a week.

Jerry couldn't pay it. Sackin, ever accommodating, told him that he could work it off if he found him three other customers. Jerry did just that, but it turned out that the three new customers didn't pay, either. That couldn't be tolerated, and the inevitable resulted: Sonny had Jerry beaten.

Jerry survived the beating, but he was in deep and terror-stricken. He wasn't a street guy. Desperate, he went to the Manhattan District Attorney, who outfitted him with a tape recorder. Jerry called Sackin and told him that his girlfriend's uncle or his uncle's wife might lend him $400. "I know she can get it, but she won't do it for me," he said, adding helpfully, "Maybe you could bust her head a little bit."

Sackin demurred, apparently uncomfortable with beating a

woman, but suggested that Sackin could come out "smelling rosebuds" if he could find a buyer for $100,000 in stolen stock certificates.

Jerry agreed and got another phone call, which he taped. "Anything slips, you're the one who gets the beating," the man told him.

"I know this," Jerry replied, cowed.

"You are dead—dead," the caller said.

The DA sent in an undercover detective, who offered to pay Sackin $10,000 for the stolen stocks. Sackin agreed and was arrested. He cooperated with the DA's investigation, but Sonny was never charged. It was enough, however, to prompt the New York State Senate to open an investigation into the Mafia's influence on Wall Street—more unwelcome publicity for the Mafia that some guys blamed on Sonny.

The robbery ring was in its own way more troublesome for Sonny's standing in the organization. Sonny was said to have a large crew of men, who were regarded as unproven toughs by the bosses. Sonny's men were robbing banks, post offices, and supermarket payrolls in Queens, Long Island, and Tarrytown, north of New York City. They worked in teams of four or five, were always armed, and always wore either Halloween masks or ski masks to hide their faces. They were more sophisticated than most robbers; they used hypodermic needles and nitroglycerin to crack safes and walkie-talkies to communicate.

They brought in a lot of money, but also a lot of heat. Worse, the men seemed more loyal to Sonny than to anyone else. The commission had bypassed Sonny for Joe Colombo to head the family because some bosses thought Sonny was "high-handed," but any attempt on the commission's part to do anything else would have led to a rebellion among his men. More than other mob bosses, Sonny inspired genuine loyalty on the street.

As the money rolled in, Sonny decided to invest it in a variety of legitimate businesses. He favored bars, cocktail lounges, and motels, and had a stake in clubs patronized by homosexuals. Homosexuality was still a shameful secret for many men in the 1960s, so it also provided the added benefit of blackmail—another crime with a high return and little risk of being prosecuted.

Sonny loved the nightlife and entertainment businesses. Unlike many street guys, who didn't know how to carry themselves in legitimate places, Sonny knew how to act. He was just a natural and never came on too strong. He became friendly with Norby Walters, a Brooklyn-born show biz impresario who opened Norby Walters's Supper Club, near the Copacabana. Walters was profane, animated, and always a lot of fun. He loved being around celebrities, and they loved being around him. Jackie Mason and Stiller & Meara worked out their material there. His supper club was the perfect place for late-night drinks after a night at the Copa. There was just the right mix of celebrities and tough guys.

One night, a Playboy Club employee named Anthony Lewis was having a drink at the supper club's bar. Two street guys, Oresto Bruni and Rosario Parisi, were also there, talking to two women. Bruni and Parisi weren't exactly upstanding citizens— Bruni had been arrested for assaulting a cop and drunk driving, and Parisi had been arrested for the kidnapping and rape of a fifteen-year-old girl. One of them asked Lewis to move so they could get a better view. As he turned away, he felt an ice cube down his back. Insulted, he confronted the men, but they didn't back down. "Wait here," Lewis snarled. "I'll be back."

The men shrugged it off and resumed chatting up the women, but Lewis was as good as his word. At 1:05 a.m., he returned to the club with a .32 automatic and fired five rounds at Bruni and Parisi, as other customers dove under tables. Three bullets hit the bar; the other two hit Bruni and Parisi. They were pronounced DOA at Roosevelt Hospital. An off-duty cop, who happened to be at the bar, pointed his gun to Lewis's head and placed him under arrest.

When the commotion died down, a chef emerged from the kitchen and asked, "What happened?"

"I just blew my joint," a sullen Walters replied.

The State Liquor Authority had already suspended the club's liquor license for other infractions, and the shoot-out sealed the club's fate. The state shut it down.

But Walters, like Sonny, was an agile entrepreneur. He opened up a talent agency and focused on booking Black artists, figuring other agencies wouldn't devote much time to them. Sonny said years later that he was partners with Norby in the talent agency—something Walters denied—but regardless of the specific business arrangements, both men agreed that Sonny stopped by frequently. He loved being around the artists. They had a dazzling roster of talent: Dionne Warwick, Rick James, the Commodores, the Spinners, the Four Tops, Patti LaBelle, and Ben Vereen. As with his music labels, Sonny never interfered with the artists' creative process, and they appreciated that. He and Dionne Warwick, in particular, hit it off.

"I knew them all," Sonny said years later.

Sonny's tentacles seemed to be everywhere. He was pulling in money, but had to pay out tens of thousands of dollars to fund the appeals of his bank robbery conviction. Maurice Edelbaum, like most experienced defense attorneys, did not work unless he was paid up front. Sonny hated paying him anything, but Edelbaum assured him they had a good chance of winning on appeal.

Years later, Sonny sounded bitter about how much money he paid his lawyer: "I paid him a lot of money and he never got me an investigator or nothing. I had to get everything myself all the time, myself, he never did nothing. After I paid him and all, he still wouldn't put up a dime."

Asked how much he paid Edelbaum, Sonny said, "I don't wanna remember. They'll lock me up for income tax evasion."

Edelbaum took the case to the U.S. Court of Appeals and hit them with a battery of arguments, among them: judicial misconduct, the fact that none of the men convicted of the conspiracy were actually present at the bank robberies, that the defense was denied the name of an informant, that the jury instructions were flawed, and that evidence had been obtained through illegal wiretaps.

The illegal bugs rankled Sonny. He seethed at the indignity of FBI agents listening in on intimate arguments with his wife. "I didn't know. Had an idea, but they denied it," he said.

Edelbaum urged the court to require the Justice Department to search its records for evidence of unconstitutional eavesdropping. It was not a bad argument, as average citizens had no idea how often the federal government was installing illegal eavesdropping devices in people's homes.

The U.S. Court of Appeals was not swayed, however. Judge Henry J. Friendly wrote: *We see no reason for embarking on what, so far as we can see, would be a policy of requiring such an investigation in every criminal case, even when there is not the slightest reason to suspect offensive conduct by the government.*

On March 25, 1968, the court upheld Sonny's bank robbery conviction. It was a setback, but Edelbaum insisted it wasn't over. He planned to take the case all the way to the U.S. Supreme Court.

Sonny figured he had a shot and stayed focused on making money.

That December, his old pal Joe Colombo had a Christmas party at the home of Mike Savino, his brother-in-law. He invited his top men and gave everyone ties as gifts. In keeping with his new role as family boss, he pulled out a piece of paper and made a speech, giving his own version of the history of the Cosa Nostra.

He also disclosed some sobering news: A longtime member of another family was in daily contact with the FBI.

It was both a festive and solemn event—an important meeting—attended by the key players in the Colombo family.

Sonny was not invited.

CHAPTER 12

A Home Invasion

"I don't want your kids to identify anybody."

THE HOUSE on Links Drive in Oceanside on the South Shore of Long Island wasn't an imposing affair. It looked like an average suburban high-ranch set on a small lot close to homes next to it with a simple concrete strip for a driveway. Nothing about it suggested that its occupants had a lot of money, which is why the brazen daytime home invasion—in which two clean-cut teens were bound and gagged—set off alarms among local law enforcement officials in Nassau County.

The owner of the house was Abraham "Al" Ezrati. He had a vending-machine business and some jukeboxes, a profitable all-cash business. He happened to have a machine at a Queens bar called Sonny's, which also happened to be a bar Sonny occasionally patronized.

In June 1965, Ezrati's car was stolen. A week later, a man called his home to say that he had insurance forms to sign. Al's eighteen-year-old son, Milton, who was home with his fourteen-year-old brother, Lester, answered the phone.

"My parents won't be home until five o'clock," Milton explained to the caller.

"That's okay," the man said. "You're old enough to sign."

Not long after that phone call, three men showed up at the Ezratis' house. Milton answered the door. The men wore black stocking caps, sunglasses, and gloves—not the typical wardrobe for a warm summer day—and mustaches that had been drawn on with an eyebrow pencil. But what caught Milton's attention was the gun.

Al Ezrati had always told his sons, who often helped their father roll coins from his business, that their lives were far more important than money. In the event of a robbery, he told them, "Don't be brave. Don't fight."

With his father's words reverberating in his head, Milton stepped aside as the men pushed their way in. There was a sack of coins from the vending machines on the floor, and they quickly scooped that up. They also grabbed $3,000 in cash and a pair of his father's expensive cuff links. Authorities later said the thieves stole a total of about $10,000.

The men took Milton and Lester down to the basement, which served as their den, and handcuffed them to a pillar. Lester, an avid TV watcher, asked them if they could leave the television on, but they denied his request. Then they slapped adhesive tape over their mouths and left.

The teens were stuck in the basement until their seventy-year-old grandmother happened to stop by the house. Milton's high-school graduation rehearsal was that day, and his grandma was planning to attend. Instead, she heard her grandsons' muffled screams and went down to the basement to find them handcuffed. She called police, who had to use a hacksaw to free the boys. Milton missed his graduation rehearsal.

A little later that day, Ezrati got a phone call from an unidentified man: "Hello, Al? You know who this is. I heard about what happened today. I don't like it any more than you do, but we've got our differences to straighten out. I don't want those kids to identify any [police] pictures."

"Go to Hell!" Ezrati shouted, hanging up the phone.

The case puzzled authorities. Abraham Ezrati was a law-abiding citizen, with no known ties to criminals, and he could give them no reason why anyone would target him for a robbery. Despite his jukebox business, there certainly didn't seem to be any connection to organized crime. Then several witnesses came forward and cracked the case.

The witnesses were none other than James Smith, Richard Parks, and John Cordero—the very same men who had testified against Sonny in the bank robbery and homicide trials. They said they knew all about the strange home invasion in Oceanside because they had been directed to do it by Sonny.

Based on their information, authorities made a case against Sonny and his driver, Johnny Irish Matera. They said Sonny planned it and Matera carried it out. They charged the men with seven counts of conspiracy, robbery, grand larceny, and assault. If convicted, they would face up to sixty-five years in prison.

Of all the cases against Sonny, the crime of robbing a respectable businessman and handcuffing his two innocent teenage sons to a pillar in the basement of their suburban home was perhaps the most chilling. It was one thing to kill another mobster or rob banks, but to rough up civilians was another matter. It showed police and the public just how far Sonny and the Mafia were willing to go to make a point.

When Sonny's trial on the home invasion opened in March 1969, Smith, Parks, and Cordero were queued up to testify. Sonny showed up on the first day in a conservative glen-plaid suit, looking relaxed and smiling as he spoke to his lawyer, Maurice Edelbaum again. Occasionally he'd step out into the courthouse hallway and talk to other men, who gathered around and listened to him respectfully. There was nothing about Sonny that came across like a hardened criminal. The only thing that seemed a bit out of place was the unusual number of expensive Cadillacs pulling up to the courthouse.

The trial got off to a false start after Edelbaum, as he had in the bank robbery case, successfully pushed for a mistrial. Judge Paul Kelly granted it, as they had only spent two days picking a jury. He ordered new jury selection to begin. Then Edelbaum, arguing that the national coverage of the Hawk homicide trial made it impossible for Sonny to get a fair trial in Nassau County, tried to get the case moved off Long Island. Kelly denied the change of venue. The case would be heard in Mineola, the county seat.

The story behind the bold daytime robbery, according to prosecutor Donald Clavin, went like this: Sonny knew Al Ezrati from the Queens bar called Sonny's. He wanted to put his own vending machines in the bar; Ezrati resisted, wanting to keep that territory for himself. Unhappy with Ezrati's refusal, Sonny called a meeting with Matera, Smith, Parks, and Cordero. He sketched out a plan to rob him. Matera, Sonny's trusted aide, would be the leader. Sonny told Smith and Parks to go along with him and do whatever he told them to do. The point of the robbery was not so much to steal a lot of money—the actual take was relatively small by any estimation—but to intimidate Al Ezrati into going along with Sonny's plans.

As in the bank robbery trial, Smith was first up on the stand. Perhaps because he had already testified so many times before, he answered questions in a seemingly bored monotone, coming across almost as mechanical.

"Franzese spoke directly to me and Parks," he told the court. "He said we were to go with Johnny tomorrow, that he's got all you'll need and do exactly what he says. He said there's one thing he wanted understood, and that's that there are two kids involved and he didn't want them hurt."

He went on to describe how Matera picked them up and was carrying an attaché case with him. Inside the case were three pairs of gloves, three pairs of sunglasses, three black hats, three loaded pistols, two pairs of handcuffs, adhesive tape, and eyebrow pencil to draw on fake mustaches. Matera was the one who called the Ezrati home with the phony story about insurance papers for the stolen car.

After the robbery, Smith said, he complained to Sonny that the teens might identify him. "Don't worry," Sonny told him. "I'm going to call that cocksucker and straighten things out."

He then described the phone call, which he said he overheard because he was in a Queens motel room with Sonny when he made it.

Edelbaum again attracted his own gaggle of admirers in the courtroom gallery. He approached his cross-examination with the same zeal as before and followed the same tack he had used in the earlier trials—he attacked Smith's character. He brought up Smith's role in the bank robberies and asked, "Were you prepared to kill to get away [in the bank robberies]?"

Smith paused, gave a slight shrug, and said, "I believe I would."

His matter-of-fact response sent a ripple of muffled gasps through the courtroom.

Cordero was up next. He testified that after the robbery of Ezrati's home, he heard Sonny call Al Ezrati.

"He said to Al, 'We have our differences that I don't understand, but I don't want your kids to identify anybody,'" Cordero said.

He also said he saw Sonny pay off Smith and Parks after the robbery.

Parks, just as sullen as he had been in the earlier trials, was the last bank robber to take the stand. He, too, said he heard Sonny make the call to tell Ezrati to make sure his sons didn't identify anyone.

They didn't.

Milton, twenty-two at the time of the trial, took the stand. Court officers had Matera stand up. Asked if he recognized him, Milton said, "No, I don't recognize him."

He said the same of the other robbers.

Lester, too, testified that he couldn't pick anyone out. It had been years since the robbery—four to be exact—and he insisted he really didn't remember.

Their father made for an even less satisfying witness for the prosecution. Al said he didn't know Sonny; and although he confirmed getting the phone call—that was easily documented in phone records—he said he didn't know who had called him.

The Ezratis' testimony dealt a serious blow to the prosecution's case, but the defense wasn't taking any chances. Edelbaum ripped apart Smith, Cordero, and Parks as liars in his cross-examination; but by then, their third trial testifying against Sonny, it was almost routine for them.

Then, just as both sides were readying their summations, the surprise arrived. It was eerily identical to the one that had severely undercut the Queens DA's homicide case against Sonny. It came in a letter to the judge from an inmate who had been in the Nassau County Jail at the same time Smith and Cordero were held there.

His name was Edward Winkle. He wrote to the judge that he had important information about the key witnesses. Kelly had little choice but to listen to what he had to say. Winkle would be the defense's only witness.

Winkle testified that while he was cleaning the bank robbers' cell area, he overheard Smith telling Cordero, "Cahn (Nassau District Attorney) knows we did it and wants to know if we want to get out of here." His testimony made the point: The robbers were pinning the blame on Sonny to get out from under the charge.

Clavin, in a last-ditch effort to save his case, produced six corrections officers who worked at the jail to discredit Winkle. They testified that they had no work records showing that Winkle had been assigned to Smith and Cordero's area. As rebuttals go, it wasn't a bad one. However, by that point, the damage was done.

The case wrapped up after eighteen days. On April 17, 1969, it went to the all-male jury. They deliberated for four hours and returned with a verdict at 11:30 p.m.: not guilty.

The courtroom erupted in a chorus of gleeful shouts and back-slapping as Sonny's family and friends rushed to embrace him. Judge Kelly thanked the jury for their service; Sonny, breaking into a wide grin, thanked the jury as well. Then he turned and thanked the judge. He left without taking reporters' questions.

An embittered Clavin, however, did take reporters' questions, telling them, "I'm a very unhappy man. The only people who lose are the people in this county."

He blamed the loss squarely on Al Ezrati. "The victim wouldn't cooperate with law enforcement officials . . . That makes it difficult for the prosecuting attorney to get a conviction."

Tina was ecstatic over the victory. Her husband had beaten a serious case and also had gotten great news on his bank robbery case: In March, as the home invasion case was going on, the U.S. Supreme Court granted a writ of certiorari in the bank robbery case, ordering the lower court to review the eavesdropping in Sonny's case. He was the only one of the petitioners to be granted the writ. Edelbaum had been right.

It seemed as if their lives would finally get back on track. The Manhattan DA's bookmaking case was still out there, but Sonny was confident about winning that one, too. Tina and Sonny felt optimistic and closer than ever. That year, a song, "More Today Than Yesterday," burst through the Billboard charts, rising to number 12. It had a memorable refrain that resonated with romantics everywhere: *Oh, I love you more today than yesterday, but not as much as tomorrow.*

It became their song.

Back at home, Tina was determined to put on a show of normalcy. She threw a huge party in her backyard for Michael's graduation from high school in June 1969 with more than five hundred guests. It was a lavish affair, with top-tier entertainment, and everybody was enjoying themselves. John, then all of nine years old, and his best friend from across the street, were allowed to stay out late in the front yard that night. They got bored with all the adults and decided to walk all the way down the block to the stop sign. It really wasn't far from the house, but they weren't allowed to venture that far.

At the stop sign, there was a car with two men sitting in it. Tina had told John many times not to talk to any of the men in cars who seemed to be in the neighborhood all the time. "Don't bother them, ever!" she had warned him.

But the boys were curious. They couldn't resist. They walked by the car. The men, it turned out, were FBI agents. One of them rolled down his window and called them over. He pulled out his gun and said, "This is for your father."

They backed away slowly and then ran back to the house. Worried they'd get in trouble with their parents, they didn't tell anyone. Later that night, however, John's friend confessed all to his mother. She told Sonny and Tina. They were furious, not at the boys, but at the agents. What kind of men would terrorize a couple of nine-year-olds like that?

It was the first of several ominous signs that their lives might not get back on track.

In the ensuing days, Michael started to hear from his high-school friends that their parents had been subpoenaed to testify about the party. A happy celebration of a rite of passage had been turned into a bitter humiliation for the entire family.

The rumors spread. "Kids used to tell my children that I murdered people," Sonny recalled. "It was bad, terrible."

Six months later, in December, Joe Colombo's son Anthony got married and held his reception at the Queens Terrace, a popular venue for mob family gatherings at the time. Scarpa, the FBI's well-paid informant, loved passing on the family gossip and noted that even the Gallo brothers were there.

But not Sonny. "He's under a lot of heat" because of his recent trial. For Sonny to miss such an important family social event was notable, he said.

He was right. It was a sign that Sonny's standing in the family was slipping. Even though he beat the home invasion case, the bank robbery conviction was still hanging over his head. Besides, his criminal trials were attracting far too much attention. There was no rallying around a man who insisted he was wrongfully convicted, even one who had produced so consistently for the family. Mafia men talk about honor and loyalty, but that dissipates quickly when there's a sense that one of their own might be losing his power. Nobody wants to be around a loser.

Sonny's friend Dominick "Mimi" Scialo was named acting capo to take over Sonny's affairs if he went away, but little else had been done to ensure that Sonny's rackets continued to run smoothly. Law enforcement worried about that, fearing that an all-out war might break out as different Colombo factions tried to claim Sonny's rackets. But Sonny was convinced that he wasn't going anywhere. He had already won a favorable ruling from no less than the U.S. Supreme Court. He was just waiting for the lower court to act on that order.

The order went to the lower court—back to Sonny's old nemesis Jacob Mishler. In January 1970, he ruled that because the illegal recordings from Sonny's house were not used in the bank robbery case, the conviction stood. The recordings didn't have evidentiary value, since they only picked up the day-to-day routines of a suburban family. In a small concession, Judge Mishler also ruled that the recordings would not be made public.

It was a devastating blow. After three years and hundreds of thousands of dollars spent, the appeals failed. They were out of options. Sonny, always so adept at evading authorities, had run out of luck. His family and friends had thought he was invincible, but he wasn't.

Two months later, on March 26, Mishler entered a final judgment of conviction. He denied Sonny's plea for bail and reimposed his sentence of two consecutive twenty-five-year sentences, plus ten-year and a five-year concurrent terms for receiving stolen money and property. Tellingly, he never set a minimum sentence, meaning that the amount of time Sonny served would be dependent on his actions. It was a way of protecting the lives of the witnesses, but it was also clear that Mishler was trying to give Sonny an incentive to rat.

And the FBI tried, many times, to turn him, Sonny recalled. One day, two agents approached him and said, "Why don't you join us?

What the hell do you got going for you? You're going to die in jail. You're never going to come out. Why don't you join us?"

"Nah," Sonny said. "I can't join you. I don't believe in that stuff."

And he turned around and walked away.

A few days after Judge Mishler's ruling, the inevitable moment arrived. Sonny had to enter prison to start doing his bid. And, as was typical for the Franzese family, Sonny and Tina never sat the children down and told them what was about to happen.

He walked out of the house that morning and didn't come back.

CHAPTER 13

Sonny Goes Away

"I wouldn't let a dog go to prison."

BY EASTER 1970, it was over. Sonny entered the U.S. Penitentiary at Leavenworth, Kansas, an imposing structure built by prisoners in the late 1800s. Its reputation was well-known. It was where the worst of the worst were incarcerated, where prison guards weren't afraid to assert their authority. "If inmates had it coming, they got it," said one former Leavenworth guard.

Sonny took up residence in a ten-by-six-foot cell, where others told him what to do, where to go, what to eat. He hated every minute of it.

"You can't do nothing," he said. "Whatever you see in the movies is the truth. You can't do nothin'. You're, you're watched. You're told what to do. You're told how to walk. You're told how to go to your cell, everything."

FBI agents again approached him to try to get him to cooperate. It was part of their playbook to approach potential witnesses repeatedly, hoping that they might just hit the person when he was in the right frame of mind—in other words, depressed and miserable about the prospect of years of incarceration. But Sonny would have none of it.

"I wouldn't let a dog go to prison. I could never, that's why I could never be a rat. I hated prison so much, how could I ever give a guy up?"

Agents reminded him—and he knew they were right—that he

could shave years off his sentence just by talking to them. He knew, too, that a rat—one who had never been disclosed in court—had helped make the bank robbery case against him, and that rat was on the outside while he rotted in prison. But he brushed off the agents. The very thought of talking to them disgusted him.

"Never happened. I'd go to the electric chair before I'd do that. I'd rather go and die in the electric chair," he said.

Prisons are gossipy places, and word spread about Sonny's refusal to talk to the agents, burnishing his reputation. Even prison guards made admiring comments to him about it. Behind bars, Sonny managed to attract his own kind of fame.

"Officials come up to me," he said, "telling me, 'You know something? I went through your whole case. You don't rat out on cops. You don't rat on nobody.'

"He said, 'If I'd have committed a crime, I'd come and look for you.'"

But Leavenworth was still prison. Against the odds, Sonny managed to build his own determined, unbowed existence. He immediately sent word out through other men to see what other wiseguys were incarcerated there. He summoned the ones he wanted to speak to and heard about their internecine feuds. Afterward, he ate with a guy he trusted and told him: "When we're done eating, I want everybody down at the handball court tonight."

The messenger passed the word, and the men assembled at the court that night. Sonny told them their feuds were over. "From now on, we all sit together because we can't let the niggers think we're weak."

And they did.

By then, Sonny was in his fifties. Still athletic and disciplined, he ran daily and worked out. He had always liked handball, and he took it up again in prison. Before long, he was the prison champion.

"Make up your mind to do something, you do it," he said. "It's nice to have, believe it or not, when I was in Kansas, Leavenworth, the whole office at lunchtime used to come down and watch me play handball. Everybody—the whole, even women— everybody used to come down. I used to see them and they used to sneak in. I play a pretty good game."

Bocce was another popular game in prison. Although it origi- nated in Italy, Sonny hadn't played it before. One day, he noticed some younger men playing it.

He watched the other players, sizing up the best ones. Always interested in competition, he approached one of the better players and asked him if he'd partner with him. The man agreed.

"So we play, so now they shoot the ball. Now we're losing the game by one point. So now it's my time to shoot. So now to get it in there, the ball has to go like this. This way, this way, this way. I said, 'How the hell am I going to get it in there? Jeez, I don't know.'

"So I took the ball and I whooshed it in there. The ball comes next to me, the last ball, and you think it's going to stop. It goes right in. I take the point away from the guy, and I win the game. So it started to feel good. So I go down the next day and play again, unbeaten."

"I was so good that they were talking about me from prison to prison."

The other inmates were confounded by his skill and demanded to know where he had taken bocce lessons. He couldn't have picked up that game that quickly without lessons, they insisted.

"Where am I going to take lessons?" Sonny scoffed. "Just throw the ball, that's all."

Back at home, Tina insisted on maintaining the fiction that Sonny was away at college. Everybody in the family knew that was what they were supposed to say. But her fiction did little to ease the pain of Sonny being away, and visits to the prison were ago- nizing for the entire family. They were allowed one day a month, so they tried to go at the end of the month to get two days in a row to justify the long trip from New York to Kansas. Each time, Tina admonished the children not to cry; she was determined that her children remain strong and proud.

"Don't make one bad remark," she told them. "You stand at attention."

John was ten years old when his father entered Leavenworth. As they walked up the forty-three steps to the entrance, the sight of the forbidding prison looming in front of them overwhelmed him. He burst into tears. Somehow Sonny saw him from a window. When they walked into the visiting room, John held his head down in an effort to hide his tears. Sonny walked over to him and gently smacked him on the face.

"Hey, son," he told him softly. "I just want you to know if you're going to cry, cry with your head up. You don't ever have to be ashamed for crying."

That his father could see his pain and try to help him with it while he was stuck in prison stayed with John for the rest of his life, and he loved him for it.

Sonny's brother Carmine and close friend Joseph "Little Joey" Brancato were on the visitors list. They passed on messages from him and kept him apprised of what was happening on the outside. Sonny, as always, listened carefully, a trait that set him apart from other street guys. Just a month after Sonny entered Leavenworth, they told him with some bemusement that his old pal Colombo had come up with a crazy idea.

The FBI arrested Joe Colombo Jr. in a bizarre plot to take $200,000 in silver coins and melt them down into silver ingots, which were more valuable. His father was incensed by the arrest, which he said was bogus. He decided to fight back with a publicity campaign. He started the Italian-American Civil Rights League, an organization he said he created to defend the rights of downtrodden Italian Americans. He then called newspaper reporters to press his case that Italian Americans were discriminated against and that there was no such thing as the Mafia. But he didn't stop there. He had his men picket the FBI's offices in Manhattan. The pickets went on for weeks.

The picketers weren't limited to Manhattan. More than two hundred showed up at the Nassau County Courthouse in Mineola after Tina was subpoenaed to a grand jury there in October 1970. The district attorney's office said she was under surveillance because the rackets squad wanted to know the source of her income. Tina, predictably, accused the authorities of harassing her.

The spectacle of the pickets embarrassed guys like Scarpa. He complained to his FBI handlers that the league was idiotic and that Colombo was turning the family into a laughingstock.

But the league had its uses, which Sonny recognized. Mario Puzo's bestselling book *The Godfather* was being turned into a motion picture. Producers planned to shoot scenes on the streets of New York. Colombo used the league to protest that the movie production was ethnically biased. Suddenly, producers found themselves blocked from working at locations that had already been approved. And they started to get threatening phone calls.

The pressure escalated until the producers agreed to a meeting with Colombo. A compromise was reached: In exchange for hiring some Colombo associates as extras and striking the words "Cosa Nostra" from the film, their problems would disappear. One of the extras was Lenny Montana, a three-hundred-pound Colombo enforcer who played the loyal hit man Luca Brasi. Producers also quietly made some payments to ensure labor peace, and Sonny, according to some associates, got a piece of that action while in prison.

Years later, Sonny deemed *The Godfather* to be one of his favorite films. "Terrific movie. I think it's one of the best movies ever made."

The details and nuances of life in the Mafia portrayed in the movie were too accurate to have sprung solely from Puzo's imagination, Sonny said. "He had to get it from a mob guy. Puzo couldn't get that information himself. He had to get it from somebody."

That person, he said, was Bonanno, the disgraced mob boss Sonny referred to as "Joe Bananas." Sonny believed Bananas persuaded Puzo to name the character in the book Sonny—Don

Corleone's libidinous and hot-tempered oldest son—after him in an attempt to make him look bad.

Bananas had always been jealous of him, he said. "He wanted to be like me, but he couldn't."

Colombo delighted in the success of the pressure campaign against *The Godfather*, but his picketing strategy didn't work as well when Nassau police arrested him in March 1971 for mediating a dispute between gangsters over the take from a $750,000 jewelry heist. As Colombo spent the night in the Nassau County Jail, there was another league protest, this time led by women in bouffant hairdos and coats with mink collars. The effect was comical.

A couple of months later, over Memorial Day weekend, there was an incident that led to another arrest, one that was never publicized, but one that had far more significance to Sonny. It would become a turning point in the bank robbery saga, and it happened at the home of John and Eleanor Cordero.

Eleanor had come home from grocery shopping and jumped in the shower because it was a hot day. John was home, and he had been stewing. He watched Eleanor's comings and goings obsessively and was convinced she was cheating on him. As she showered, he confronted her.

Eleanor, sick of his possessiveness, shot back: "Yeah, I fucked a guy in our bed last night!"

That kind of sarcastic comeback might not have any effect on a guy like the Hawk, but it sent Cordero into a rage. He lunged at her with an ax, slicing her repeatedly. She went down.

He dragged her out of the shower and began a bizarre ritual that lasted over the next two days. He fed her Valium, raped her, and cut her some more. When he was finally tired of it, he told her he was going down to the basement to sharpen the ax so that he could finish her off by cutting her body up into little pieces.

While he was in the basement, Eleanor found the strength to pull herself into the kitchen, where there was a phone. As she lay bleeding on the kitchen floor, her daughter Stephanie came home.

Stephanie immediately called 911. John Cordero fled before police got there.

Rescuers took Eleanor to the hospital, where she had more than one thousand stitches for her wounds. Doctors told her that the tranquilizers had actually saved her life because they prevented her from bleeding to death. While she recovered, Stephanie lived with Eleanor's relatives.

Eleanor survived, but was left with ugly scars all over her body. Terrified that her husband would follow through on his promise to finish her off, she went into hiding. Police from the New York Police Department kept watch over Eleanor and Stephanie. A month later, police arrested Cordero and charged him with assault with an ax, but the charge went nowhere. Eleanor became convinced that they let him go because of his testimony against Sonny. He had been too valuable a witness, and it would be far easier for something bad to happen to him if he was in jail.

John had gotten away with attacking her, a fact Eleanor blamed on Sonny. But she had a daughter to take care of, and she decided to get her life on track. She changed her name and got a job as a barmaid. One night in September, when she came home from work, Stephanie told her that two men had come to the apartment wanting to talk to her. Stephanie told them she was working, and one of them left a card with a phone number.

Eleanor called the number and reached an investigator named Nick Conti. They agreed to meet at a bar. Nervous about what she would be walking into, Eleanor called a cop she knew at the New York Police Department. He told her to go ahead with the meeting and said that a detective would be there watching.

When she got to the bar, there were two men waiting for her. Conti, who was about thirty-five years old and balding, introduced himself. The younger man who was with him had curly black hair and a wrestler's physique. He said only that his name was Carmine.

Conti took the lead. "We don't want you to lie, but would you be willing to go into court and tell how your husband lied when he testified against Sonny?" he asked her.

Eleanor, wary, said, "Did my husband lie?"

Conti pressed her. "Didn't your husband talk to you about this case?"

"No," Eleanor replied.

Conti tried a different tack. "Do you think fifty thousand dollars is a lot of money?" he asked.

Eleanor parried again. "When my father died, he left me $186,000 and eleven months later, I was working for sixty-five dollars a week," she said.

Conti switched gears again. "Do you know where any of the other witnesses are?"

This time, Eleanor threw him a bone. "No, but I may be able to locate one of their girlfriends."

She agreed to call him back with any information she could find on the other witnesses.

When she got back home, she decided she needed as much protection as possible. She reached out to a Nassau County detective, Edward Quinn, whom she and John had gotten to know during the home invasion trial. She told him everything that had transpired and gave him the phone number she had been told to call.

Quinn called the number. It went to the law office of one of Sonny's lawyers.

He then alerted an FBI agent, who summarized the entire incident in an Airtel memo sent straight to Director Hoover.

Eleanor, meanwhile, began to consider her options. She was hiding out from a homicidal husband and trying to support herself and her daughter in a low-wage job. She told Quinn that as long as Sonny stayed in jail, she'd probably be safe—at least from him or his henchmen—because he wouldn't do anything to jeopardize his chances of getting paroled. But she also understood that she had some very valuable information. If Cordero's attack on her had persuaded her of anything, it was that she needed to change her life.

* * *

Meanwhile, Colombo was pushing ahead with his Italian-American Civil Rights League, which, by now, had garnered national attention. He gave television interviews and held fundraisers for the league, much to the chagrin of his associates, particularly Gambino.

On June 28, 1971, Colombo held his second annual league rally at Columbus Circle in Manhattan. More than ten thousand people attended. Colombo shook hands and posed for pictures like a politician running for office. Suddenly shots rang out, and he went down. He was shot three times in the head and neck.

His bodyguards immediately shot and killed the shooter, identified as Jerome Johnson, a Black ex-convict. Colombo was rushed to the hospital, where he underwent five hours of brain surgery. He survived, but was left paralyzed. Scarpa and other Colombo family members kept guard over him at Roosevelt Hospital in New York City.

Johnson didn't have any known reason to kill Colombo. Authorities theorized that the hit had been organized by Joe Gallo, who had built ties with Black gangsters while he was in prison. Others thought Carlo Gambino hired Johnson.

Regardless of who was behind it, the shooting set off a scramble for who would be the next boss of the Colombo family. Had Sonny been out of prison, he would have been on the short list of people considered by the commission.

But Sonny was behind bars, doing a fifty-year bid. To the commission, he was as good as dead.

CHAPTER 14

Family Fights to Survive Without Sonny

"The money I gave guys. Not one of them
sent me a dime."

WITH HER HUSBAND AWAY, Tina went to work. She started at the top, going into Manhattan to work in couturier designer show-rooms. She was a natural saleswoman and had the style and aplomb that put her very exclusive customers at ease. She had the ability to suss out people's wants and desires, and assured them that she was the only one who could meet them. The customers loved her.

Tina loved being around the beautiful clothing. She loved them so much that she helped herself to jackets, dresses, and blouses. She accumulated racks and racks of clothing, some of which she never even wore. Her last name ensured that payment wouldn't be an issue.

She missed Sonny terribly. She was the only single mother on her block, and everybody knew why she was on her own. She decided her children would have as normal a life as possible, and never spared any expense on their birthday and holiday celebrations. She also did some gambling.

Like Sonny, Tina was good at keeping things hidden. And like most gamblers, she frequently lost. She didn't think she should have to pay bills or debts; and she became increasingly reliant on old friends, like Dominick "Mimi" Scialo, the acting capo who had stepped in to fill Sonny's shoes with his crew while he was away, to bail her out. Mimi was by her side frequently.

Sonny kept tabs on her through people like his nephew Tutti, who would come by the house to give her money. Before going to prison, Sonny had hidden cash at his sisters' houses. Initially he had done it to keep it away from Tina, fearing she would spend it. Now it was there to help pay household expenses. There is a myth that the Mafia takes care of families while its members are in prison. For the Franzese family, that turned out to be just that, a myth.

"It hurt," Sonny said. "I would go to sleep nights and talk to myself. I couldn't believe it. The money I gave guys. Not one of them sent me a dime."

The money Sonny sent through Tutti was also his way of keeping Tina dependent on him. He hated having his very attractive wife on her own, and her spending still grated.

"She didn't miss nothin'," Sonny said. "For all the months, she used up all the money I had. Used up a lot of money. I told her, I said, 'You know, honey, you've got to understand something. I'm getting old. I'm not going to make this kind of money all the time. Save it for your old age.'

"I says, 'You know, our old age when we can't move. You're going to be like me. You're going to get old, too.'

"She never cared. She thought I was going to live forever. I think she was nearly right."

Then in July 1973, the family got alarming news. There had been a riot at Leavenworth. Five inmates held four prison employees hostage in the prison laundry for hours, and one guard was killed. The riot ostensibly had started over complaints about religious freedom, but Sonny's friends and family were sure that it was a cover for an attempt on Sonny's life.

Sonny had turned increasingly to Michael, the oldest son still at home, who was taking premed courses at Hofstra University, a private university on Long Island. Michael tried to step up and be the man of the family. He coached John's Little League games, and all the boys looked up to him because he was a great athlete. He'd take them to batting cages and kept all the stats. His girlfriend, Maria, a fellow Hofstra student, was the scorekeeper. He didn't just coach them, he gave them pep talks about how to carry themselves and live their lives.

All the kids admired Michael. He was smart, good-looking, and took the time to be around his younger siblings. John idolized Michael. He talked about him constantly to his friends. He desperately wanted to be like his brother. One day, John ran home, having fallen on a fence, nearly taking his eye out. It was Michael who rushed him to the hospital.

Tina worried about the effect Sonny's absence had on her youngest three children, John, Gia, and Little Tina. They were very conscious that when they went out for a pizza or to a diner, other people were staring at them. At school, the other kids stopped talking to John, even the girls. He had always been a happy-go-lucky kid, but after his father went away, he felt angry. He figured if everyone thought he was a bad kid, he might as well be one.

Tina poured her energies into getting her husband out of prison. She pushed his lawyers to file motion after motion. She was sure they could come up with a legal stratagem that would prove her husband's innocence. And she reassured Sonny that she knew he had been framed.

"Sonny," she told him, "you don't have to tell me you're innocent. I know you're innocent."

"What makes you say that?" Sonny asked.

"Sonny, if they (the bank robbers) were your friends, I would know them. You introduce me to everybody you know."

Years later, as Sonny recalled that conversation, he said Tina was right. "She was a good woman. She was very, very stern about things. And she didn't care. Because she was savvy."

Each time, the motions went to Mishler, the very judge who had sentenced Sonny to fifty years. Each time, he rejected them.

In December 1973, Michael and Philly Vizzari were indicted with two other men on charges of extortion and conspiracy for

strong-arming an auto mechanic. Michael had opened an auto
leasing business with Sonny's help. He wanted a $2 million line
of credit from a bank. To get it, he agreed to buy the banker's fur
coat, which he promised to Tina. The auto mechanic had a different plan for the coat—he took it and sold it. Michael, under pressure from Tina, told him to get the coat back. He held on to the
mechanic's Camaro as insurance.

The next day, the mechanic called him and said he couldn't
find the coat, but needed his car. Michael refused. Unfortunately
for Michael, the call was being recorded.

Michael regarded the case as a nuisance, but the charges were
serious felonies. If he went away, Tina would lose her rock.

Tina redoubled her efforts to get her husband out of prison. She
wrote letters to Mishler, harangued prosecutors, and proclaimed
Sonny's innocence to anyone who would listen. She wrote to
President Richard Nixon, senators, congressmen, and state legis-
lators. She went to John Malone, then the head of the FBI office
in New York. She spent time in libraries and found a clipping
that placed Sonny in a different location on the date he was accused of planning the bank robbery conspiracy. She read law
books.

"She was a fighter," Sonny said. "Listen, I've seen her, I've
seen her fight like a maniac for me."

She hired two private detectives at $1,100 a day to prove
Sonny's innocence. They set out to find police surveillance reports that would prove that Sonny was somewhere else on the
night of the infamous sit-down. Michael later claimed that a detective showed him the surveillance reports, but they were never
presented to the court.

Undaunted, Tina turned to Jerry Zimmerman, a big, fast-talking
car salesman who worked for Michael and was close to the family. A special state prosecutor had charged New York State Supreme Court justice Dominick Rinaldi with perjury. Zimmerman
told Tina he knew an IRS agent who was working on the case and

that the agent happened to have documents that would exonerate Sonny in the bank robbery case.

She taped a body recorder to his chest, with an on/off switch activated from his front pants pocket. She sent him to meet with the agent at a Holiday Inn restaurant in Westbury as she and a friend sat at a nearby table. Zimmerman pressed the agent to talk about giving him documents that would exonerate Sonny in exchange for Zimmerman testifying against Rinaldi.

Tina turned the tape over to federal prosecutors, who opened up an investigation. But she wanted insurance. She reached out to Manny Topol, a courts reporter at *Newsday*. Though the family had always harbored a deep distrust of reporters, particularly *Newsday* reporter Greene, Tina had read Topol's coverage of high-profile murder trials. She decided she'd take a chance on him. She invited him and his wife, Sydell, to lunch at her home. Her parents were there, along with her very well-behaved children. Tina was a gracious hostess.

She told the Topols that Sonny had been framed and that she was sure the feds had placed illegal bugs in their bedroom. Topol had no illusions about who Sonny was, but he believed deeply in fairness. He listened to Tina and was struck by her intelligence. He wrote the story about Zimmerman, complete with photos of him decked out with the body recorder.

As the Zimmerman case worked its way through the system, a new lead on proving Sonny's innocence emerged: Eleanor Cordero.

A bartender who knew Michael told him that a woman named "Rusty" had been at his bar talking about how Sonny Franzese had been framed. He set up a midnight meeting with her in the parking lot of a diner in Lindenhurst. Friends wanted Michael to wear a wire, but he decided against it.

Rusty pulled up in a red Mustang, and she was prepared. She pointed a .32 at his groin and said, "If you're wired, you're dead."

Rusty was Eleanor. She patted Michael down; once she was

convinced Michael had nothing on him, she said, "What do you want?"

Michael told her his family needed her help.

"Your father's innocent," she told him. "They set him up. I know everything. I can get him out. But I want money, and I want protection from my husband and the government."

Michael, by then a pretty savvy business negotiator in his own right, took care not to be too specific, but he assured her they could work something out.

Eleanor was in bad shape. She was drinking heavily, looked rough and talked tough. It was also clear that she was still terrified for her life. Michael and a friend stashed Eleanor and her daughter in a motel next to a topless joint wedged in between strip malls on a busy street in East Northport. Michael babysat her, but was miserable because she kept coming on to him and took offense when he demurred.

One night, as he sat on the couch watching the Super Bowl, she came out wearing only a negligee. He ignored her. Insulted, she whipped out a knife and held it to his throat. "You don't think I'm attractive enough to sleep with?" she growled.

Michael managed to talk his way out of it and decided he needed to find someone to keep her company. He turned to the ever-reliable Jerry Zimmerman. When Eleanor and Jerry met, they clicked; he stayed with her every night for the next six weeks.

When Tina found out about Eleanor, she insisted on meeting her. Michael was reluctant, knowing that the two of them would hate each other, but Tina would not be denied. He brought Eleanor and Stephanie over to the house, and Tina sized her up. Eleanor sized up the house, Tina's clothes, her Cadillac.

"She was mad because she wanted what my wife had," Sonny said.

Eleanor decided that she hadn't asked for enough in exchange for her information and upped her demands. She wanted $50,000—money for Stephanie's college education and a house in Massapequa.

Tina rented her a house and tried to placate her; however, Michael was right—the two women couldn't stand each other. They couldn't have been more different. Tina, petite and lovely, always wore designer clothes and still turned men's heads. Eleanor, scarred and big-boned, favored cheap clothing, and no amount of makeup could hide her scars.

Michael and Tina, united in purpose, got what they wanted after weeks of meetings with Sonny's attorneys. Eleanor came through with an affidavit. It hadn't been easy, as she kept insisting there were errors in it and she wouldn't sign it until the lawyers' secretaries retyped it. They did, over and over and over. Finally, they produced an affidavit in which she affirmed Sonny's innocence in language only the lawyers could have written:

> *To my knowledge, all the testimony involving John "Sonny" Franzese and implicating him in a conspiracy to commit the above-mentioned bank robberies is false.*
>
> *He did not aid in the planning or execution of any of them, nor did he share in the proceeds. This story was devised by John Cordero, James Smith, Richard Parks and Charles Zaher to secure favorable treatment from the government on the sentencing for the bank robberies that they planned, committed and pleaded guilty to.*

The lawyers needed that affidavit in order to file a motion to win Sonny a new trial. Tina, by then pretty canny about leveraging her husband's notoriety for well-timed news stories, made sure the affidavit got to Topol.

He read it, but he wanted his own insurance that he wasn't getting had. Before doing any stories about it, he arranged for Eleanor to take a lie detector test. She passed.

Authorities countered that she was making these new disclosures only after the statute of limitations had passed and she could no longer be charged.

Eleanor told Topol that Sonny had been framed.

"The only reason they threw him into it was to get a lesser sentence. They first came up with his name three months after they were arrested. It was a frame, pure and simple."

She told them it was a stupid idea. "I told them it wouldn't work. Nobody was going to believe that bullshit. But they did. I couldn't believe they got away with it."

Topol asked her if anyone in the Franzese family had put her up to telling this story. She said they hadn't and that she had tried to contact them through others, but failed—conveniently leaving out how she had met Michael and Tina more than once.

Topol's stories about Eleanor's new information enraged the authorities. Police investigators, and even other reporters, demanded to know how he could write stories suggesting that Sonny was innocent.

"The guy's an animal. We gotta get him off the streets," law enforcement told him.

"But no one really faced up to the fact: Did he really do this?" he told an interviewer years later. "They kept telling me it didn't matter."

But to Topol, it did matter. "I felt very strongly that if you are going to get him, you should get him for what he did, and not for this."

Eleanor's affidavit, and the attendant publicity, bolstered Sonny's motion for a new hearing. The motion would be decided by none other than Judge Mishler. It would take several months before they got a ruling.

Meanwhile, FBI agents scrambled to track down John Cordero, who was very helpfully available in prison in Fayetteville, North Carolina, after violating his probation. They confronted him with the facts laid out in Eleanor's affidavit. He insisted she was lying because she was still angry about the ax attack and that she had been paid off by the Franzeses. He insisted that his testimony had been truthful.

"I wouldn't change a word," he told them.

As the family waited for Mishler's decision, a few loose ends got tied up. In October 1974, FBI agents, acting on a tip, found Mimi

Scialo, the capo who had been so attentive to Tina, buried in a Brooklyn social club cellar encased in concrete with a garrote around his neck and his genitals stuffed in his mouth. Scialo had a habit of making enemies because he had a vicious temper and mouthed off when he was drunk. But those close to Sonny knew that he didn't like how much attention Scialo paid to Tina. They heard that Brancato had taken care of the problem with the help of a few soldiers. To Sonny's friends, the message was clear.

Sometime after that, Frankie Blue Eyes, a longtime and loyal friend of Sonny, saw Tina at the Miracle Mile in Manhasset, the very exclusive shopping strip on Long Island's Gold Coast, where she was working by then. He was careful not to acknowledge her. She saw him, however, and called out, "What? Frankie! You don't say hello to an old friend?"

"Ah, Tina, you know my eyesight is bad," he lied.

He would have liked to take her out for a drink as a friend, but he worried about how it would look and, worse, the consequences of something being misconstrued. He left quickly.

Meanwhile, Michael was making money and friends in the auto business, and premed classes seemed like a waste of time. He visited his father at Leavenworth, and they agreed: He would get straightened out, become a goodfella. He would begin a yearlong pledge period and be assigned to Andrew "Mush" Russo, a Colombo capo and Persico's cousin.

It was a significant step for Michael, and he took his new role seriously. Around that time, he was driving Eleanor to a meeting with his father's lawyer to discuss the progress of the motion to get Sonny a new hearing. Their conversation is described in an FBI memo: *"If this doesn't work," he told Eleanor, "we'll kidnap Judge Mishler's daughter and hold her for ransom."*

The ransom would be Sonny's release from prison.

Eleanor told the FBI about the threat, and Mishler's family was alerted. Years later, when Michael heard about what Eleanor had told the FBI, he denied it.

The government filed documents to counter Eleanor's. One FBI report contained particularly significant information countering her claims of Sonny's innocence, as it laid out a scheme to bribe Eleanor for her testimony. It was by an FBI agent who recounted Eleanor's September 1971 meeting with investigator Nick Conti and another man to talk "about getting Sonny Franzese out of jail" and their offer of $50,000 to change her story.

On March 12, 1975, Judge Mishler turned down the motion for a new hearing.

Sonny's lawyers immediately filed an appeal.

John "Sonny" Franzese leaves the Nassau County Courthouse in Mineola with his lawyer
Abraham Sereysky on August 22, 1963, after being questioned by Nassau DA William Cahn.
"I was a pretty good dresser," Sonny said. *(Photo courtesy Newsday, LLC)*

Christina "Tina" Franzese, wife of John "Sonny" Franzese, is interviewed at home in Roslyn on December 17, 1970. "She had class, she had class," Sonny said.
(Photo courtesy Newsday, LLC)

John "Sonny" Franzese is escorted down a staircase by armed officers at the
Nassau County Police Headquarters in Mineola on January 5, 1966, on his way to an arraignment.
"You thought it was easy being a tough guy? It ain't easy, pal!" Sonny said.
(Photo courtesy Newsday, LLC)

John "Sonny" Franzese (center) is led back to a police car on December 29, 1966, after visiting
the funeral parlor in Brooklyn where his mother, Mrs. Maria Carvola Franzese, was laid out.
He was not allowed to attend her funeral. His mother died "when she heard I got locked up for
murder," Sonny said. *(Photo courtesy Newsday, LLC)*

Carmine Persico leaving the Nassau County District Attorney's office after a mob round-up in 1963. Like other gangsters, Persico covered his face. Sonny never did. "I wasn't a guy that was afraid, you know," Sonny said. *(Photo courtesy Newsday, LLC)*

John "Sonny" Franzese at 102 in a nursing home in Queens, New York. "I'm still alive. Ain't that something?" *(Photo courtesy Newsday, LLC)*

Newsday investigative reporter Bob Greene in front of the newspaper building on Long Island. Sonny hated his stories. "Kids used to tell my children that I murdered people . . . terrible," Sonny said. *(Photo courtesy Newsday, LLC)*

John "Sonny" Franzese walking to court in Queens, New York, to attend his trial for the homicide of Ernest "the Hawk" Rupolo, a one-eyed hitman who had crossed Sonny's ally, Vito Genovese. "Look, I beat that case. If I did it, I would tell you. I didn't even know the guy," Sonny said. *(Photo courtesy Bob Peterson)*

John "Sonny" Franzese's homicide trial in Queens, New York, attracted reporters from all over the world in 1967. Eleanor Cordero (center), wife of the state's key witness, reveled in the attention but always hid her face from potential hit men. "She was no good. She's a rat," Sonny said.
(Photo courtesy Bob Peterson)

Two detectives carry the concrete blocks that were tied to Ernest "the Hawk" Rupolo's body, which was found in Jamaica Bay, New York, in August 1964. "I never killed this guy," Sonny said.
(Photo courtesy Bob Peterson)

After John "Sonny" Franzese's acquittal in the homicide of Ernest "the Hawk" Rupolo, Franzese's wife, Tina, collapsed in his arms, crying tears of relief. "She was a good woman," Sonny said. *(Photo courtesy of Bob Peterson)*

Prosecutor James Mosley (second from left) and detectives drown their sorrows at Luigi's Bar in Queens after losing the Ernest "the Hawk" Rupolo homicide case. John "Sonny" Franzese and his friends had other plans. "After I beat the homicide, we had a party at the Copa," Sonny said. *(Photo courtesy Bob Peterson)*

Mob boss Vito Genovese, longtime friend and champion of John "Sonny" Franzese, was the "toughest cocksucker I ever knew," Sonny said. *(Photo courtesy U.S. Library of Congress)*

A typical jail cell at Leavenworth Penitentiary in Leavenworth, Kansas, where John "Sonny" Franzese was incarcerated, beginning in 1970, after his conviction for conspiring to rob banks. "People wonder how I did the time. I say simple . . . one day at a time," Sonny said. *(Photo courtesy Kenneth LaMaster)*

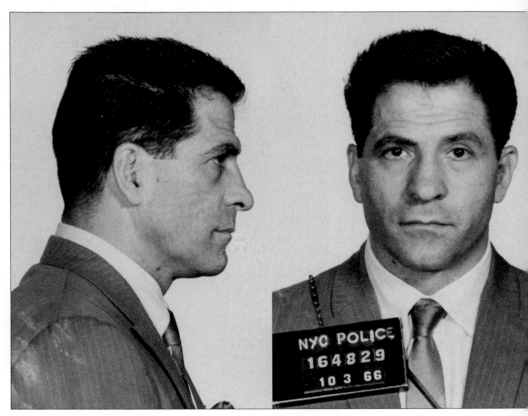

Mugshot of John "Sonny" Franzese in 1966. "I was a good-looking guy," Sonny said.
(Photo courtesy New York Police Department)

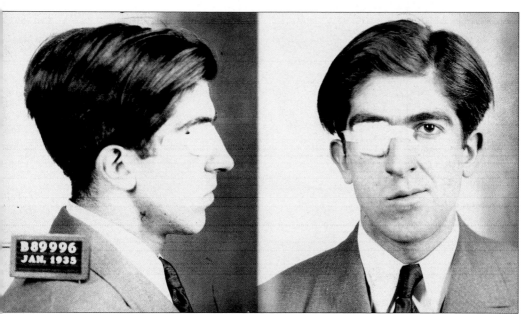

Mugshot of Ernest "the Hawk" Rupolo in 1935. "Why would I deal with garbage like that?" Sonny said.

Mugshot of John Franzese Jr.
in 1996. The favorite child of
Sonny and Tina Franzese,
he later testified against his father.
"I don't know what happened to him.
Maybe all the drugs he took screwed
his mind up," Sonny said.
*(Photo courtesy Nassau County
Police Department)*

FBI agent Robert Lewicki,
who was John Franzese Jr.'s
handler, at his desk in 2004.
"He [John] would be the last
guy I thought would do that.
But he did it," Sonny said.
(Photo courtesy Robert Lewicki)

Newsday

FINAL EDITION, 5 CENTS, ©1966 NEWSDAY INC., LONG ISLAND, VOL. 26, NO. 187, WEDNESDAY, APR. 13, 1966

FBI NABS FRANZESE AS SUPER-DILLINGER

Say Ring Hit 5 Banks in 44 Days

Story on Page 3

AP Wirephoto

WAKE OF TERROR. A U.S. Army ambulance hurries past a burning oil storage tank yesterday as it arrives at Tan Son Nhut Air Base in Saigon shortly after the base was shattered by a Viet Cong mortar attack which killed seven Americans and wounded more than 100 American and South Vietnamese servicemen. The barrage also destroyed four planes. (Story, other photos on Page 5.)

China Says U.S.'Attack Plane' Downed

Story on Page 5

The front page of *Newsday* on April 13, 1966, when John "Sonny" Franzese was arrested for conspiring to rob banks, the case that would be his downfall. He insisted he was innocent. "They had me down as the biggest bookmaker and some other things that made me very, very rich. How could I go and rob banks?" Sonny said. *(Headline courtesy Newsday, LLC)*

Milton (left) and Lester (right) were handcuffed to a pole in their basement and their mouths duct-taped in a bizarre home invasion robbery in Oceanside, New York. John "Sonny" Franzese was charged with masterminding the robbery but was acquitted. "I don't want these kids to identify any pictures," Sonny allegedly told their father. *(Photo courtesy Lester Ezrati)*

Street view of the Copacabana nightclub, a favorite hangout of John "Sonny" Franzese. Mob boss Frank Costello was said to have been a silent partner in the club. "All the top entertainers in the country, in the world, they all wanted to work there. That was the Madison Square Garden of show business," Sonny said.
(Photo courtesy New York City Municipal Archives)

John Franzese Jr. (left, in the striped shirt) talks with Joe DiGorga (center) and his father, Sonny Franzese. Unbeknownst to DiGorga and Sonny Franzese, John was wearing a wire. This surveillance photo was part of the evidence entered in the 2008 federal case against Sonny Franzese, DiGorga, and others, who were convicted at trial. *(Courtesy of the U.S. Attorney)*

CHAPTER 15

Business Behind Bars

"I don't care if I lose, as long as I fight them."

ONE DAY, SONNY was in the prison visiting room when a woman approached him. She was the mother of John "Sonny" Wojtowicz, who had tried to rob a bank in Brooklyn in 1972 to get money for sex-change surgery for his partner. The robbery went awry, and the story became the subject of a magazine article and, later, a hit movie, *Dog Day Afternoon*. Wojtowicz had his brief moment of fame when he was portrayed by Al Pacino in the movie, but he still had to deal with a twenty-year prison sentence.

The day his mother approached Sonny and grabbed his arm, she was worried.

"Sonny, do me a favor and look after my son," she told him.

"I've been looking after him anyway," Sonny replied.

Wojtowicz was a misfit, an amateur bank robber who was so inept he robbed the bank after the daily cash pickup. He also had a slightly effeminate manner that made him a prime target in prison. Seeing that, Sonny made sure the other inmates didn't hurt him.

He found himself making unlikely friendships in prison, like with the leader of the Black Muslims. "There were nice people in prison, I met a lot of nice guys in prison. Even though they were bad, they were nice," he said.

But there was never any forgetting who Sonny was. When he spoke, other men paid attention.

"Oh, they listened to me . . . Hey, listen, I'm more worried about being afraid to fight again than to fight 'em. I don't care if I lose, as long as I fight them. Because if you fight them, they ain't going to fight you again. I fought a guy, when I was in, four times. He beat me three times, and the fourth time, I knocked him out. I would never give up."

Without even trying, he exuded a powerful physical presence. He would walk into a room and take command with a single look, even in prison.

"They all respected me because they knew that I wasn't a guy that would walk away from it, you know."

Harlem drug lord Nicky Barnes sent word that he wanted to meet Sonny. Sonny refused.

"The guy that was putting all the drugs in the guys' bellies. I wouldn't meet him," he said.

As his family and lawyers fought to get him out of prison, Sonny made the most of his time. In addition to daily workouts, he read everything he could get his hands on, Machiavelli, the Bible, Shakespeare—"Shakespeare was a crook. He robbed all his stories from the Italian stories."

And he kept an eye on his money. Sonny always kept a close circle of friends around him who could pass on important messages. He was always careful when speaking to outside visitors, like Michael or Brancato. They spoke in their own code. Other inmates, eager to make a good impression, were available for sundry tasks. And prison officials were barred from listening in on any conversations he had with his lawyers.

So despite the day-to-day restrictions of prison life that Sonny chafed against, he managed to keep some of his businesses running on the outside. Michael had taken over his legitimate car dealerships on Long Island, which were useful for laundering money, and trusted associates handled other rackets. Sonny liked to keep his own hand in the music business, however.

In the early 1970s, he heard about a prolific Black singer/songwriter named Van McCoy, who had his own recording company. McCoy needed money to produce a new song he had written that he was sure would be a hit. Black artists didn't have an easy time getting financial backers. Through a contact, he turned to Sonny for help. He gave him the money and told McCoy, "From now on, I'm in whatever you do."

The song was "Do the Hustle," a surprise hit in the summer of 1975.

That same summer, Michael and his girlfriend, Maria, were planning their wedding. Tina desperately wanted Sonny to attend. She wrote the court, begging for the judge to grant him a furlough: *Over the past ten years, the length of involvement with my family with this court and this case, much has been said about my husband. All of these words taken together tend to paint a picture of a man larger than life. But this is not the case. He is a man, a husband and a father. He is the head of a family who has endured much agony and pain alone and now asks in the name of dignity and humanity that he be allowed to be present at a moment of great happiness for his family.*

Mishler denied the request.

Michael and Maria were married on June 22, 1975, at the Queens Terrace, the mainstay for mob social events. Tina, who was thrilled about Michael marrying a nice girl, made sure it was a grand affair, with more than six hundred guests. Nonetheless, Sonny's absence stung.

Sonny worried about what his incarceration was doing to his family, particularly John, who missed his father terribly. After one visit from young John, Sonny sat down and wrote him a letter:

Thursday I had a sneaky suspicion you weren't feeling good. When you told me about it today, I was relieved, but I did seem a little bit disappointed because I felt you would have so much to talk about with me. After all, I am your

*Dad. I wanted to be able to help you in any advice you
might need. I hope our little talk about education sunk in
your head. From experience there is no substitute for learning. You heard my words to Michael there is no money in
the world to make a man want to spend one day in jail.*

*Why are you so bashful when I put my arms around you
and kiss you. I'll tell you this. I am proud when I do this!*

Of all his children, friends thought John was the most like
Sonny. They looked strikingly alike. John had his father's build
and walk and the same broad grin. He also had an easy charm, a
certain gallantry that girls loved. John had no problem meeting
girls; just like his father, he cheated on his girlfriends. In his
mind, that's just what the men in his family did.

Once his father went away, John felt shunned by other kids at
school. Having a father who was a mobster in prison didn't win
him any social cachet in his soft suburban school district. He decided he'd act like a tough. It became his protective barrier, an
emotional shield against the judgment of others.

At home, the mood was often tense. Tina was a perfectionist and
fastidious housekeeper; no one dared walk on the white carpeting
in the living room. She combed it with a rug rake so that no foot-
prints would show. Tina was obsessed with cleaning. Even after
the children had cleaned their rooms, she'd declare that they didn't
do a good enough job. Then she'd sweep through their bedrooms,
throwing out mementos and personal diaries that they had stored
in their rooms for safekeeping. Though all the children were accustomed to her arbitrary dictates, John knew, even as a teenager,
that there was something more to her obsession with cleaning.

He thought it might have been her way of dealing with her own
inner turmoil. That might have been true, but there was something
else going on. Tina knew that Sonny had his children, particularly
Little Tina, hide money in their rooms to keep it away from their
mother. During her cleaning sweeps, she'd always find it.

Money was the way Tina tried to make up for Sonny's absence in her children's lives. She made sure that they appeared rich and successful to the outside world. She dressed her daughters in designer clothing and wore vibrant Versace dresses even while cooking at home. When John was old enough to drive, she gifted him with a new car and would give him a new car every year after that. The money her husband carefully put away in savings and AT&T stock rapidly dwindled.

It drove Sonny crazy. "I had a wife, no matter what they asked her, she done for them," Sonny said. "Never thought of tomorrow. Don't forget I had a lot of money. I went away. The money, it's all gone. It ain't easy to be without a father. I told her, 'Tina, look, I'm in jail. Wise up. Worry about tomorrow. I won't be around to help you.'

"It didn't make any difference. She just loved to spend. I had a hell of an experience, I'll tell you. But I don't mind her spending the money. What I minded was her not being smart enough to teach her children not to spend money."

She didn't just spend money on her house and the children. She spent a fortune on lawyers. When the legal avenues seemed to be going nowhere, she and Michael turned again to Eleanor, urging her to testify in court that Cordero had lied. Eleanor, by now fed up with promises of money and nothing coming through, upped her demands. Michael and Tina told her they couldn't do more until a new trial was granted and Sonny got out. A tense dance played out between the two sides, as each tried to keep the other side in line.

Then by October 31, 1975, Michael took the step he had been preparing for the past year. He was formally inducted into the Cosa Nostra. He became a goodfella, a wiseguy, a made man. He had already demonstrated a knack for business, and word was circulating among the families that he was a comer. Plus, he had the backing of a highly respected made guy, his father.

Michael's timing was good. The commission had decided to

"open the books" to fill their ranks, which had been depleted by deaths and old age. His assigned capo was Andrew Russo, his father's friend and Persico's cousin.

That Halloween night, Michael was told to pick up his sponsor, Joseph "Jo Jo" Vitacco, and to drive him to Colombo's catering hall in Bensonhurst, Brooklyn. Once they entered the hall, he saw five other recruits. Around midnight, they were called into the dimly lit banquet hall, one by one, where solemn-faced family capos were seated on folding chairs shaped in a U.

Michael walked in and stood in front of Thomas DiBella, the family boss, who asked, "Are you ready to take the oath of the Cosa Nostra?"

"Yes," Michael responded.

"Cup your hands," he told him.

Michael did as he was told. DiBella dropped a piece of paper, lit on fire, into his hands. "If you ever violate the oath of the Cosa Nostra, may you burn in Hell like the fire burning in your hand."

Then he pricked Michael's thumb with a pin, squeezing out a drop of blood. "This is a blood tie. Your allegiance to the Cosa Nostra is bound by blood. Should you violate the oath, your blood will be shed."

Afterward, they all sat down for a banquet of veal, pasta, and chicken. Vitacco came in with a brown paper bag and asked DiBella, "Should I give them their bag of money now?"

The recruits looked up, rapt. The older men howled. It was a joke. In fact, it was up to the recruits to make *them* money. A portion of everything they did would be kicked up through the ranks to the top men. No bags of money were handed out.

Michael decided then that he would separate himself. In every family, there were earners—the men who brought in a lot of money—and the workers—the men who delivered the brutal beatings and did the murders that kept the businesses running. Michael decided he would become an earner. Instinctively, he knew how to leverage his newfound power to increase his income.

The news of his new status spread, and Michael was treated

with a certain respect. In keeping with his role as the de facto patriarch of his immediate family, he decided to take teenage John to dinner and fill him in on his new life. He took him to a Chinese restaurant in New Hyde Park, not far from their home, and explained it to him. He laid out the rules, the hierarchy, the way they did business.

To John, it was a revelation. He had always known his family was different from other families but didn't know why. Sometimes he'd ask his father about it, why other parents seemed to be warm and loving toward their children, while Tina was harsh and often punished her children for the smallest infractions. Sonny would simply say, "They're not like us." After Michael explained everything to him, he felt a wave of relief. He knew, finally, that he wasn't crazy.

It was a turning point for John, who was still a teenager. He desperately wanted to be like Michael and his father. Michael started bringing him around with him, and it was amazing to John. Everybody treated them with respect. John was in awe.

In late 1975, Mishler held a hearing on Sonny's lawyers' latest motion for a new trial. He talked about all the disturbances Tina had created in court and warned her, "This is on the merits. No amount of threats is going to make a difference to me."

For the first time, Sonny testified in court. His testimony was terse and to the point. He said he was not involved in the bank robberies and that he had never met the four bank robbers who testified against him, until he saw them at his arraignment.

Sonny's testimony, while noteworthy, wasn't enough. They had a new witness—one of the bank robbers, Zaher. He submitted an affidavit vividly describing how the bank robbers got the idea of pinning the crime on Sonny—from an FBI agent.

"Later that night, when we were returned to West Street (jail), Cordero got very excited. 'Did you hear what Thatcher (an FBI agent) said? Hoover would give his left nut for Sonny! We would get a suspended sentence if we could get something on Franzese.'"

Smith and Parks responded, "Are you crazy? You'll get us all killed if we put Sonny on something."

But as they spoke, they formed an idea. They decided to implicate Sonny in something they knew about—the bank robberies. At the hearing, Zaher laid out their thinking in his testimony:

"We were looking for incidents to bring a man like Sonny Franzese's reputed character to a meeting with us; and at one time, Cordero shot at Whitey Florio in the Kew Motel or in the parking lot. This is what took place, what I was told, because I was not there. I said I was there, but I wasn't. Eleanor and John Cordero were in the John Doe Room drinking when Whitey Florio came in. And Eleanor said to John, 'That's the guy who killed my husband, Ernie the Hawk.' And she said it loud because she was drinking, and there were a few words between Cordero and Whitey.

"Anyway, John walked her out to the car, and Whitey came out into the parking lot. John seen Whitey come into the parking lot and thought he was going to hurt him, I guess, and he pulled out his gun and threw a shot—he shot a few times at Mr. Florio.

"So from that incident, we knew that it was—we thought it was reported because FBI agents knew about the incident. So we figured that we would use that as the plot to get Mr. Franzese at the meeting because it was reputed that this guy Red Crabbe did have something to do with his murder."

Zaher said he discussed the risk of a perjury charge with Cordero. However, Cordero, who was something of a jailhouse lawyer, batted it away.

"Don't worry about it," Cordero told him, "a guy like Sonny, with his reputation, will never take the stand and try to refute what we were saying."

Besides, Zaher testified, they were angry that Sonny and the family weren't stepping up to pay their legal expenses.

"That was part of the reason why we were turning against him, because he wouldn't—they weren't doing the right thing," he said.

It was compelling, but the prosecution had its own ammunition. They had interviewed Zaher's wife, Ann, who told them that her husband had assaulted her to get her to agree to testify that he had lied at the original trial. She told them that she didn't know whether he had lied or told the truth at trial. She also told them Michael Franzese had offered to pay her $10,000 for her testimony.

And they produced another witness who said Eleanor had bragged about selling her testimony.

In the end, Judge Mishler was unpersuaded by Zaher's recantation. The other bank robbers hadn't changed their testimony, and he picked apart inconsistencies in the new information. At one o'clock in the afternoon, on January 21, 1976, he issued his ruling: "The motion is in all respects denied."

Four hours later, Mishler's law clerk received a phone call from an anonymous caller: "Just tell the judge he made a fatal mistake in the Franzese motion today."

The call set off a scramble among FBI agents as they tried to find out where it came from, while at the same time increasing security for the judge and his family. The ruling had been tightly held and not released to the public. The list of suspects was short. Mishler told Sonny's lawyer that he believed Tina was behind the threat.

FBI agents questioned her, but she adamantly denied having anything to do with it. She told them she had been too depressed when she heard about the ruling to do anything. She said she had cried into the evening.

A month later, Tina wrote Mishler a seven-page letter in which she protested her innocence, but she also made clear her feelings toward the judge: *That is not to say that my feelings for you are warm, or that thoughts of such conduct have never entered my mind, to be perfectly honest and candid. However, I am not a fool.*

She chided him for rebuking her for having an angry outburst in court: *What protects you from not being pointed out?*

She went through the evidence, point by point, insisting that

Mishler had not given her husband a fair shake. But she also provided an insight into the toll Sonny's incarceration had taken on her: *The last six years have been a long and lonely vigil for my family and myself. It has just been myself against a whole administration.*

But she carried on.

CHAPTER 16

Easy Betrayals

*"I am in the winter of my life where every
year counts . . ."*

AFTER THE OMINOUS phone call to Judge Mishler's chambers, prison authorities were notified and took action. Whenever they thought an inmate was too comfortable in prison, they transferred him to another prison. Inmates called it "diesel therapy." Sonny was moved to the federal penitentiary in Atlanta, a prison known for housing the toughest men. He settled in quickly.

In March 1977, Gina Lynch, a twenty-seven-year-old model, went to Atlanta to visit her husband, Vinny, a member of the Westies gang who was doing a twenty-year stretch for murder. Sonny was standing at the prison window and saw her. He went over to Vinny and asked who she was.

"That's my wife," he proudly told him.

Vinny introduced them. "Meet my best friend and racquetball partner, Sonny," he said.

The name meant nothing to Gina. She went back to visit her husband again that night, and he excitedly told her, "I had dinner with Sonny!"

At dinner, Sonny had mentioned that he knew Gina from her modeling spreads. Vinny got jealous, snapping, "That's my wife!"

"Take it easy," Sonny reassured him. "Doesn't she have a brother?"

"Yeah, Billy," Vinny said.

"I want him with me," Sonny told Vinny. He gave him a phone

number. It was the number for Michael, who was running Sonny's crew. "When you see her tonight, tell her to call her brother and give him this number to call."

Gina did as her husband told her. Because it was a long trip from New York, she was staying in Atlanta for two weeks so she could get in as many visits as possible. Before she even got back home, her brother, Bill Ferrante, met Michael and was switched to his crew. "It's like IBM," her brother told her, laughing, "the switch to Michael's crew."

Michael and Ferrante clicked. Sonny sent instructions from prison, through phone calls to Gina. For months, he kept in touch with her. She thought his attentions were solely to use her to pass on messages to her brother. He was, after all, sixty years old, old enough to be her father.

In their phone calls, they talked about everything and became close friends. She thought Sonny felt sorry for her because her husband was in prison. She had no idea that Sonny actually had other plans for her.

Michael had resolved the extortion case against him—the auto mechanic changed his testimony and cleared Michael and his codefendants. Though Michael had gotten out from under it by paying a $250 fine and pleading guilty to disorderly conduct, the publicity about the case had hurt his businesses. He needed to come up with another way of making money, and Sonny decided Ferrante could help.

Michael was good at business. Other guys in his crew, like Ferrante, took care of the problems that required a stronger hand. Michael moved in on a flea market and found plenty of loan-sharking opportunities among the vendors and began making money again.

Behind bars, Sonny was making plans. He had reason to— Junior Persico was locked up in Atlanta with him, and they discussed the future of the Colombo family. The family had been in disarray since Colombo's shooting, with leadership changes and feuding factions. They wanted their people in place.

Sonny made a full-court press to get out of prison. Michael and Tina were still trying to get evidence that he had been framed, but their efforts had gone nowhere. In November 1977, Sonny did the unthinkable: He decided to plead his case to Mishler, a man he loathed, in a carefully typed letter:

> *Dear Judge Mishler,*
>
> *I realize you are a very busy man and have no time for answering foolish letters. On the other hand, I feel certain you will not mind taking a few minutes out to ease the mind of a confused man serving fifty years in prison. Therefore I trust you will be able to unravel a few things for me that have caused me to stay awake many nights in the near eight years I have been incarcerated. This is not the first letter I have written regarding my confusion, but I always seem to get more or less the same answer: "My conscience is clear, it was the jury who found him guilty." The latter is the attitude everyone seems to take when my conviction is mentioned, but it is little relief to my anguished heart and mind. It is I who must serve the fifty year sentence, and all I ask is the answer to a few questions when I ask, "Why?"*

He went on to say that he had offered to take a lie detector test, to no avail, and that no one was listening to the witnesses Tina had produced. Then he talked about how he had become the fall guy:

> *Your Honor, isn't it a fact that only the guilty are in fear of the truth? Why, then, is the F.B.I. afraid of the truth? I am in the need of help, but no one wants to bring out the truth; that the F.B.I. needed a "fall guy" and I was the chosen one! If you doubt my word, Your Honor, off the record, just between you and the agents, take them aside and ask them confidentially if they would be willing to take a lie detector test in regard to the Franzese case. I will bet my life not one of them will agree to the test.*

With all due respect to most law enforcement agencies, since Watergate, we now know that even some of our highest officials will resort to steps outside the law if it helps their need. In my case it was simply suppression of evidence on [the] part of the F.B.I. and the Assistant U.S. Prosecutor in order not to admit that [he] had made a mistake in indicting me.

He concluded with a heartfelt plea that made clear that at sixty years old, he was wondering how many years he had left:

Your Honor, I am asking you to assist me in my probe to get at the truth. Is that such a terrible thing to ask. It isn't as though I were a young man and could say, "To hell with it," and let it go at that. I am in the winter of my life where every year counts and already I have spent almost eight years in prison needlessly for a crime I am innocent of. My wife continues to turn up facts that prove beyond a doubt that only lies were told against me and I will never stop trying to prove my innocence.

It was an extraordinary letter, both elegantly written and strikingly deferential. Sonny had little hope that Mishler would change his position, particularly since the judge had notified the parole board of the threat against him. Still, it was important to have his feelings on the record, as another parole hearing was coming up. The timing was especially important because if Sonny got out, Persico would still be in prison and Sonny would be the Colombo family boss.

The timing was significant for another reason. At the time, the United States Parole Commission made all decisions regarding parole for federal prisoners. The U.S. president appointed commissioners, and the Mafia, even with its reach, had little hope of getting to a federal parole commissioner. Then in November 1977, President Jimmy Carter appointed a New Yorker, Benjamin

Malcolm, New York City's corrections commissioner, to the U.S. Parole Commission. The mob saw that as an opening, according to an informant, who tipped off the FBI.

The informant said Michael hoped to bribe Malcolm to win his father's release. In fact, Malcolm wanted nothing to do with anything of the kind. Then the FBI learned of a plan to cook up a $50,000 book deal about Sonny's case with a writer in order to funnel that money to a witness for Sonny. The writer they planned to approach was *Newsday*'s Manny Topol, who had written articles questioning Sonny's conviction. Topol, when he learned that they would just be using him to pass on a bribe, rejected it out of hand.

But when the U.S. Parole Commission summoned Topol to testify at Sonny's parole hearing in August 1978, he agreed to do it. He knew about Sonny's past, but he believed strongly that he was not guilty of the bank robbery conspiracy.

When Topol went to Atlanta to appear before the parole commission, a commissioner asked him, "Did the Franzese family put pressure on you?"

"No," Topol replied.

"Did they offer you any money or threats?" the commissioner asked.

"No," Topol answered, "the only threats I got were from the government."

The commissioner tensed.

Topol wasn't being flippant. When he was checking out Sonny's claims of innocence, he called various law enforcement agencies to see if they had surveillance reports on Sonny because those reports were critical in determining whether or not Sonny attended the sit-down with the bank robbers—a key piece in the case against Sonny.

He made a call to the IRS, and the agent told him, "You may be asking one question too many."

Topol shot back, "Are you threatening me?"

"Whoa," the agent replied. "Did you hear a threat? Just saying."

Not long afterward, Topol was audited for the first time in his life. It didn't turn out particularly well for the IRS, however. The government actually owed him money.

After Topol finished his testimony, Sonny called him over. "Thanks," he said. Nothing more.

Topol's testimony made an impression on the commissioners. More important, Sonny had been a good prisoner and would remain on parole for the rest of his fifty-year sentence—meaning he would be subject to the ever-watchful eyes of law enforcement for years to come. Concluding that Sonny's release would not jeopardize public welfare, the commission agreed to release him.

Sonny was released on November 14, 1978. Tina and the rest of his family were jubilant. They celebrated with a coming-out party at a Manhattan nightclub, where champagne flowed as Tony Bennett performed.

Michael was especially excited. That year, Sonny had filed the paperwork to formally adopt him; he would no longer be the stepson. Michael was up-and-coming, and Sonny was there already. "And we were really going to start to make some noise in the [Colombo] family," he recalled.

The commission had other ideas, however. When Sonny, still a capo, asked that his soldiers be transferred back to him, the commission refused. Michael, furious, wanted to wage war. Sonny quieted him. He believed strongly in deferring to the edicts of the commission. He saw himself as a member of an army, who would die with his boots on.

Sonny's stature on the street was assured, but tensions and jealousies within the family abounded—and he knew it. Not long after his release, two FBI agents showed up at his house on Shrub Hollow Road. Surprised, even a little amused, Sonny ushered them into his living room as Tina looked on warily.

They explained that there was a credible threat to his life. Under the law, they were obligated to inform him.

Sonny laughed out loud. "What do you care?" he told them. "They'd be doing you a favor."

The agents left. Sonny never explained to his family why or who had made the threat against him.

Instead, he did what he always did—he got down to business. One of the first stops he made was a visit to his old friend Norby Walters, meeting him at the Stage Deli in Manhattan. After the unfortunate shooting at his old club years earlier, Walters's talent agency had taken off. He broke through when a singer in one of his acts, Gloria Gaynor, made the record "Never Can Say Good-bye," which made the top 10 in the music charts and helped usher in the disco era. Walters was making money. He also was a long-time Franzese family friend. Michael and John called him "the ticket guy" because he always was able to comp them tickets to the hottest concerts.

The day of the visit, Sonny brought Michael and John along. After some time joking, laughing, and reminiscing about old times, Sonny took over the conversation, shifting it in a dramatically different direction.

"Let's get to business," Sonny said with an edge in his voice. "I hear you're doing very well all them years I've been gone. Nobody bothered you because of me."

Walters stopped smiling.

"How much do you think we should get paid?" Sonny said, his jaw set.

Walters started to hem and haw and threw up his arms, suggesting that he and Sonny weren't really partners.

Sonny pressed on. "How much do you think? Three thousand? Thirty-eight hundred a week?"

Walters stammered. Then Sonny moved in for the kill: "Hey, Norby, how much is your life worth?"

Walters turned white.

"Done!" he exclaimed, throwing up his hands. Not another word was said.

Sonny, Michael, and John left shortly afterward, pleased with the way the meeting had gone. John, who then was just eighteen years old, and hadn't attended such meetings before, felt a surge of pride. *That's what it means to be a Franzese,* he thought.

That they were shaking down a longtime family friend—and they genuinely liked him—wasn't a concern. As they were in their car driving home to Long Island, Michael said, "John, we've got something to tell you."

Sonny chimed in, "Me and your brother been talking—"

Michael continued, "Look, we're going to give you the music business. We're going to give you Norby."

It would be John's job to pick up the money from Norby. He couldn't have been prouder. He was thrilled to be included, but he was also aware that his father and brother weren't telling him everything. That grated, but he would faithfully pick up the money from Norby for the next eight years, hoping that someday he would be treated as an equal partner.

Sonny went to work for Michael's Mazda dealership, Lynn Imports, in Hempstead. It was a sufficiently legitimate business to satisfy his parole officer. Sonny's office was across the street from the dealership and very private. One day, Sebastian "Buddy" Lombardo went to see Sonny about a problem. He said his boss, Lawrence "Fat Larry" Iorizzo, was being shaken down by wiseguys from Brooklyn. He said Iorizzo had gone to the federal Organized Crime Strike Force for help, but they did nothing. Frustrated and frightened, he reached out to Sonny, whom he knew from a previous deal.

Iorizzo was a behemoth of a man with huge appetites for food and drink—he weighed 450 pounds. He was just as rapacious when it came to women—he was a bigamist. But for all his personal quirks, he was a very smart businessman. He had developed a highly lucrative gasoline bootleg scam as the president of Vantage Petroleum, which supplied gas stations all over Long Island.

Iorizzo's scam was deceptively simple. At the time, New York made taxes due when the distributor sold gas to a retailer. The tax was based on the amount of gas sold—the difference between the opening inventory and closing inventory. Iorizzo merely inflated his closing inventories. In other words, his books showed that he sold less gas than he actually did, reducing his tax. And whenever possible, he had the retailers pay him cash, which, of course, was easy to hide. It made sense for retailers because they were getting cheaper gas.

Distributors could trade gasoline among themselves tax-free, and Iorizzo used that to confuse investigators. He created a daisy chain of paperwork, with phony shell companies, making it appear that the gasoline had moved from company to company. When the state tried to collect taxes on the gas, investigators would find that the last distributor in the chain, which appeared to owe the money, was nothing more than a shell company. Anyone trying to track whether the taxes were paid would have to go through multiple, deliberately obscure transactions to figure it out. The scheme left government investigators flummoxed and kept Iorizzo fat and happy.

Iorizzo was pocketing $1 million a month, and people started to notice—street guys always pay attention to who's making money. That's why he sought out Sonny. "And he told me that I might be able to do some things with his son Michael if I needed his help," he later told investigators.

In other words, Sonny's price for his help was for Iorizzo to make Michael a partner. Initially Michael was skeptical, until Iorizzo walked into his office with a paper bag filled with $400,000 in cash. Michael wanted in.

The low-level wiseguys moving in on Iorizzo were easy to dispatch. Michael sent his crew to talk to them, and they backed off. Michael and Iorizzo agreed that 20 percent of the profits would go to the Colombo family and they would split the rest fifty-fifty.

Meanwhile, Sonny was taking care of other matters. He sent Gina a note: *You have to come and see me.*

When Gina showed up at Sonny's office, what she thought had been merely a friendship turned into a full-blown love affair. Although he would bed scores of other women over the years, his relationship with Gina would last the next forty years.

It was as settled as Sonny had felt for a long time. Business within the tumultuous Colombo family was being resolved, as well. Junior Persico had been released from prison and named family boss, but he never commanded the respect on the street that Sonny did. Some people believed that it infuriated him.

In July 1981, Persico summoned Johnny Irish Matera, who by now was a capo, to a meeting in his basement, ostensibly to discuss a drug deal Matera had on the side. Matera was never heard from again.

His transgression? Michael believed it was because FBI agents had followed Matera to a meeting with Persico with some hoods in Brooklyn, causing Persico to violate his parole.

Sonny, however, was sure that there was another reason: Persico's long-simmering jealousy. Not long after Matera's disappearance, Sonny sat in the kitchen of Bill Ferrante's Miller Place home, eating eggplant Parmesan with Gina and her mother.

Suddenly, Sonny broke down. "He killed Johnny Irish," he said as tears streamed down his face. "He had my driver killed."

CHAPTER 17

Michael Flying High

"I can't be Sonny in sunny Florida."

ON MONDAY NIGHTS, Michael hosted a private dinner party at the Casablanca, a nightclub in Huntington that he partly owned. These were not quiet affairs. Food and drink flowed freely and scores of guys would show up to have fun, talk business, and pay their respects to Michael, who told people he was a Colombo capo. They treated him like a don, and he loved it.

At the time, crushed velvet jogging suits and gold chains were the rage in that set. One night, a hood showed up wearing the same burgundy jogging suit as his host. Michael took him aside and said, "I'm not going to send you home tonight, but next time you're going to have to change."

Michael could afford to be imperious. Money was pouring in from the gas tax scam. He and Iorrizo were splitting a take of $2 million a week, some weeks, $4 million. Every week, he would drive into Brooklyn and give the Colombo bosses between $250,000 and $500,000 in cash. Michael was a popular guy.

He didn't deny himself, either. He had a private Learjet, a helicopter, and a selection of flashy cars to get around in. He had condos and a house in Delray Beach, Florida, where he docked his speedboat and a forty-foot yacht. He installed his wife and their young children in a mansion in Old Brookville, a community of mansions. Michael had an indoor racquetball court, and not one, but two, dining rooms, one with a $90,000 dining-room set. Though it was opulent, there was a slight odor of gasoline in the air from the bags of money Michael brought home.

Michael was riding high, and Sonny didn't like it.

"We don't need that," Sonny told him. "How much money do you want? You're going to get us all pinched. You're stealing all the freakin' money, what are you doing that for? How much do you want to make?"

Michael paid him no heed. He was coming into his own.

Sonny was worried about the attention Michael was attracting. However, he was more upset about the money from the gas tax scam that Michael wasn't giving him. He was convinced that Michael was holding out on him. Tina was sure of that, too, and she nagged Sonny about it constantly. Sonny, in turn, complained, "I don't know what the hell this kid makes" to Gina, his mistress.

Sonny questioned guys in Michael's crew about the money, but they had little information to offer. Michael was always cagey, like Sonny. A deep rift developed between the two of them.

Eight years behind bars, plus legal battles, had cost Sonny a fortune. He needed to make money. He turned his attention to other business.

A man named Walter Fiveson had the distributorship for Polyglycoat, a sealant for car paint that was marketed as a substitute for car wax. His brother-in-law, who also happened to know Michael, was his partner. One day, Fiveson noticed that warranties he offered for his sealant had been altered to give customers an inferior product for the same price. It wasn't long before he decided he knew who was responsible—his brother-in-law. He confronted him and told him he was cutting him out of the distributorship. Not long afterward, Fiveson received a very specific threat that if he fired him, he'd be killed.

Badly shaken, Fiveson turned to one of his salesmen, Orlando "Ori" Spado, who knew people he thought might be able to help. Through a friend, Lou Perry, Spado set up a meeting with Sonny. They met at La Trattoria Siciliana on Second Avenue in Manhattan. It was a comfortable meeting place for Sonny, as it was owned by his son-in-law, the husband of his daughter Lorraine. Sonny was there with Tina and the children and had Spado sit right next to him.

Sonny was cordial and quietly asked Spado what the problem was before turning away for a bit to confer on what to serve the table. Spado dug in, but a short while later, he felt violently ill and rushed to the restroom, vomiting. His dish had been served with a fish sauce, and Spado, as he had casually mentioned earlier, was allergic to fish. Sonny had two of his men take Spado to the hospital. Spado survived.

Sonny later told his family how much he disliked Spado and that he had told Lorraine's husband to serve him the fish sauce. But knowing Spado could help him make money, he had his men take him to the hospital and allowed him to live. That, family members said, showed what a good guy Sonny was.

Spado never knew.

A couple of weeks after their first meeting, an associate of Sonny's summoned Spado to a meeting at the Russian Tea Room, on West 57th Street in Manhattan, at 10:30 a.m. Spado was puzzled, as the restaurant didn't open until noon, but he went anyway. He walked in and Sonny was in the first booth on the left, his regular booth. He was sitting with Perry and Michael. It turned out that Michael had been a key player in the phony warranties.

Spado wasn't sure Sonny understood exactly what had happened, so he started to explain it to him. Sonny stopped him with a cold stare that terrified him: "Do not think for one moment that I don't understand what is going on here. Keep your mouth shut and listen."

Sonny resolved the problem and told Spado that he could use his name in the future, which meant, of course, that Spado would have to give him a piece of the action any time he did.

Meanwhile, Iorizzo, who had been an enthusiastic guest at Michael's Monday-night parties, started noticing a problem in the gas scam books in the spring of 1982. Checks were bouncing and product was being pulled. A lot of money had disappeared—$3 million, in fact. He confronted Michael.

"I don't know what happened," Michael told him.

That answer didn't satisfy Iorizzo, who was convinced Michael had stolen it. Then one day, a member of Michael's crew, Frank Castagnaro, nicknamed "G" for gangster, showed up. He put a gun to Iorizzo's voluminous belly and said, "Shut up, or you're dead."

Iorizzo shut up. He wanted to appeal to Sonny, but by then, it was too late. Sonny was back in prison in June 1982 for violating his parole.

Gregory Scarpa, the Colombo capo who was also an FBI informant, had tipped off the feds that Sonny used the Georgetown Inn in Mill Basin, Brooklyn, as a cover for meetings. The feds took note and watched as Sonny met with Gambino capo Carmine "Alberto" Lombardozzi and Colombo associate Robert Cordice. Both men were convicted felons, a violation of Sonny's parole.

At Sonny's parole commission hearing, it quickly became obvious that there was little chance of Sonny staving off a return to prison. A furious Michael berated Sonny's parole officer, James Stein. Two days later, Stein received an anonymous call from a man who said simply, "You're dead."

At the time, Michael had a former NYPD cop on retainer as his private investigator, who he used for, among other things, finding addresses. Stein wisely erased any traces of his home address or family. As far as a paper trail went, he became invisible.

Sonny was sent to Otisville penitentiary, a medium-security facility located about seventy miles northwest of New York City, near the Pennsylvania border. Junior Persico was there, as well, having violated his parole around the same time. When Gina visited Sonny at Otisville, she saw the two of them together and noticed a palpable tension between them.

By then, Sonny had become convinced that Persico—who had been so close to his own family that they had each other's children over for dinner—was the top-secret informant he believed had set him up in the bank robbery case. He told Gina that he was sure Persico was the guy who persuaded the four bank robbers that they could testify against Sonny and survive. The reason for his perfidy was simple, in Sonny's mind—Persico needed Sonny out of the way so that he could become boss. Except for the bank robbery conviction, Sonny would have been boss.

Just what persuaded him that Persico had turned on him was never clear.

With the family boss and Sonny in prison, the Colombo family leadership was in disarray. Michael redoubled his efforts to get his father out. He was careful to use an intermediary so that it could never come back on him. The intermediary was a man named Luigi Vizzini.

Michael would meet Vizzini for breakfast and dinner at the Atrium, an airy restaurant across the street from the World Trade Center in New York City. Before each meeting, everyone would go into the men's room and take off their clothing to ensure that no one was wearing a wire. Michael never arrived alone; he was always accompanied by two large and ugly men. And he never got into a car.

Michael, who got his marching orders from Sonny in prison, spoke obliquely, but made it clear he would do what he needed to get his father out. He emphasized that he could get his hands on a lot of money. Authorities had heard that the Franzese family had a standing offer of $50,000 to $100,000 to anyone who could get Sonny out of prison.

"I'll do almost anything, okay, to get him out," he told Vizzini. "And when a guy sits at a table and tells me, 'I got a direct contact into the parole board, I got direct info, I can definitely make a deal to get him out,' I listen."

Michael didn't know it, but Vizzini was a federal informant. Moreover, the FBI was watching and taping every meeting he had with him. Agents marveled at Michael's levelheaded approach and caution. He never implicated himself and never was charged.

Vizzini was not so fortunate. His body was found riddled with bullets and burned in a car. The murder has never been solved.

The gas tax scheme continued to generate millions. In the 1980s, gasoline bootlegging was organized crime's single-largest growth business. It was less risky than drug dealing and far more profitable. And the heavy car use on Long Island meant hundreds of thousands of drivers regularly bought gas at the pumps. Drivers who bought gas at the pumps paid the tax, and the bootleggers were pocketing it. Business was so good that bootleggers expanded into Connecticut and New Jersey and were eyeing Florida. Honest retailers had little choice but to participate in the scheme or they'd be forced out of business.

Word was spreading about bags of cash coming in. Genovese boss Anthony "Fat Tony" Salerno heard and called Michael down for a meeting. Chomping his ever-present cigar, he said, "I've got these five *mamalukes* who ain't earning me any money. Can you give them jobs?"

Michael readily agreed. "Sure, Tony, but you gotta guarantee they won't steal from me."

"Steal from you?" Salerno shouted. "If they steal from you, I'll cut off their hands, cut off their arms!"

Michael assured him that wouldn't be necessary.

"How much you want to pay them?" Salerno asked.

Not wanting to offend a boss, Michael said, "How about fifteen hundred a week?"

"Fifteen hundred a week!" Fat Tony shouted. "Give them five hundred dollars and me one thousand!"

Salerno was happy, but others were not. There was vicious infighting. Every guy in on the scheme became convinced that the other guys were holding out on him. The smart ones, like Michael, enforced an ironfisted discipline.

An accountant from Dix Hills owned some profitable gas companies. He had made the mistake of holding back $25,000. He got a beating and paid. Then someone figured out that he was selling gas at a price lower than what Michael authorized. Two members of Michael's crew were sent out with orders to machine-gun his offices. Another man tipped him off, and he got out before any bullets went his way.

It was the kind of activity that attracted even more attention than Michael's high-flying lifestyle. Organized-crime investigators created the Long Island Oil Industry Task Force and quietly opened an investigation. Their first meeting was held in the inauspicious setting of the basement of a courthouse in Uniondale, and that was by design. They wanted to keep their investigation under the radar.

Michael cloaked his business behind a veneer of legitimacy. He had corporate offices in Melville, a suburb about an hour east of New York City, and held meetings with his guys in a conference room. Wary of wiretaps, he had three noisemakers installed in boxes the size of transistor radios on the conference room walls. They made so much noise that the men at the meeting had to shout to be heard. But the point was clear: Michael was dragging the Mafia into the twentieth century.

Old-world rules kept intruding, however. In May 1983, authorities found the body of Lawrence "Champagne Larry" Carrozza with a bullet wound behind his right ear. Carrozza had been close to the Franzeses. Michael regarded him as one of his best friends, and he was the godfather to one of Carrozza's children. Michael's younger sister, Gia, the spitfire of the family, was even closer: She was having an affair with Carrozza, who was married. He and Gia, who was then just twenty, had told Sonny that he planned to leave his wife so he could marry her.

For a made man who was married to have an affair with another made man's daughter was a serious violation of Mafia code and a profound affront to a man as respected as Sonny. Michael has recalled being summoned to a meeting and being told what was going to happen to Carrozza. He went to Florida and was never implicated in the murder.

Michael attended Carrozza's funeral and comforted his widow and children, who had no idea that he, at the very least, knew all along what was going to happen.

Michael later portrayed Carrozza's murder as the inevitable and unfortunate result of violating his blood oath. Others close to the Franzeses thought there was a different motive for Carrozza's murder. They believed he was killed because he was getting too much of a cut from the gas tax scam. (Michael took over his operations after he died.) And Tina told friends that she was convinced Michael was behind Carrozza's murder.

There was more bad news in the spring of 1984, when Iorizzo was convicted of mail fraud in back-to-back trials in April and June. With more charges against him coming, Iorizzo jumped bail and fled to Panama. Still a bigamist juggling two families, he took just one of his wives and children, leaving the other family behind. Federal agents tracked him there, kidnapped him, and brought him back to the States. The stress of his new circumstances was too much. He started talking and entered the Witness Protection Program.

Michael wasn't overly worried, because he had kept himself well insulated. Besides, there was more important news for the Franzese family—Sonny got out on parole in June 1984.

The family held a coming-out party for Sonny. Less lavish than his first one, they had it at the Roslyn house. As a welcome-home gift, Michael gave his father a light blue Mercedes.

Sonny hated it.

Michael told Frank Castagnaro to buy Sonny a house near his home in Delray Beach, Florida. By now, Sonny was in his late sixties, and Michael told Castagnaro that he wanted to move him to Florida to keep him safe. Sonny, who had already been pushed aside by Persico, would have none of it.

"I can't be Sonny in sunny Florida," he said.

The rift between Michael and Sonny hadn't eased.

Then one day, Michael got a call from Vincent "Jimmy" Angelino, a Colombo capo who had been inducted into the family

the same night he was. Angelino was summoning him to a meeting with Mush Russo, the acting boss while Persico was in
prison. Sonny got the same call, only his meeting was at a different time.

There were rumors that Michael was hiding money—fueled by
Sonny—and he attracted publicity that irritated the family bosses.
Usually, Michael was adept at appeasing the bosses by throwing
more money their way, but this time was different. He was panicked. The stakes couldn't have been any higher: He was sure he
was being summoned to his own death. It was one thing for the
two of them to go in together to such a meeting; it was quite another to go in separately. He called Sonny, and they agreed to
meet at Michael's Old Brookville home.

"I have a bad feeling about this, Dad," Michael said. "I don't
like it, 'you in first, then me' stuff. This isn't right."

Sonny was stoic. "Michael, this is our life. We have been given
an order. We must obey."

Michael implored his father to fight, if not for themselves, for
their families. He told Sonny that it was his and Tina's fault for
asking around too much about the money.

Sonny was unmoved. "This is our way. Whatever happens
tonight happens," he said.

Michael was devastated. At the very least, he had thought the
two of them would go down in a blaze of glory like warriors. Instead, they each would go to their individual sit-downs, lambs to
the slaughter.

Sonny went to his sit-down first. He emerged from it very
much alive, but didn't tell Michael what transpired.

Michael went in to his sit-down, insisting he hadn't held back
any money. Always fast on his feet, he handled their interrogation
pretending to be confident.

Then Russo asked about Iorizzo, who had rolled. As such, he
was Michael's responsibility. If Iorizzo implicated a goodfella,
Michael would have to pay with his life.

"I've sheltered everyone in the family from Iorizzo," Michael
insisted.

Russo countered, "But your father said—"

Michael immediately batted that back. "Don't play that game with me!"

He swore that his father didn't know anything, that he had kept him in the dark as a way of protecting him.

After two hours, Russo gave a subtle signal. Michael would live to see another day. Later on, Angelino told him something disturbing. "You know," he said, "your father didn't do you any favors in there."

Michael was stunned, but kept it to himself. A few years after the sit-down, Angelino was found shot to death.

Michael summoned up the courage to confront his father about what Angelino had told him. Sonny flatly denied doing or saying anything that hurt Michael, adding, "If Jimmy Angelino was still alive, I'd kill him again."

But Michael knew.

CHAPTER 18

John Steps Up

*"Around here, there was some work done.
Now let's go."*

SONNY NEVER WENT to business meetings alone; he always had a driver. More and more, John Jr. did the driving.

Sonny was a notorious backseat driver—"Why don't you back up? There's a pothole you missed!"—but he also liked to dispense fatherly wisdom to his favorite child. One day, as they were driving across the Belt Parkway in Brooklyn, Sonny gestured as if he were putting a gun in his belt and grunted, "Over here, son."

At first, John didn't understand. "Whaddya talking about, Dad?"

His father erupted. "I gotta explain to you everything! That's why you'll never be like me! Around here, there was some work done. Now let's go."

Then he understood—"work" was his father's, the family's, euphemism for "murder." Sonny never talked about anyone he had murdered; he knew well that there was no statute of limitations on murder. However, he felt a certain pride about what he had done for the family. He had been efficient and effective, and his self-regard slipped into the most casual of conversations with his sons. For example, it showed in his musings about acid for dissolving bones—"That's good, remember that"—or pizza ovens for getting rid of body parts—"You never know when we might need one."

To John, a conversation like that was normal. He'd always known his family was different, and Sonny convinced him that they were special. Sonny had explained to him that they were like their own army, willing to die for one another because family was the most important thing. Police got to people after the fact. They got there before the police did. To John, it made sense. And now that Sonny was trusting him enough to take him along to meetings, he was no longer just the goofy younger brother to Michael, the rising star. He was moving up, too.

John, barely out of his teens, eagerly stepped into the breach left by the tension between Michael and Sonny. He was never as enamored of money as his father or brother, but he loved the prestige of the Franzese name on the street. It opened doors for him, and people treated him like a princeling because that's exactly what he was. These guys who catered to him because of his last name seemed to know everything and were themselves treated with massive respect. He was dazzled.

He developed a few side hustles of his own. Record distributors were willing to pay $25,000 to have their records played by hot disc jockeys. John knew a Black DJ known as Rosko who would play the records. John would pocket the bribe money, and Rosko would play the single because he was too scared of Sonny not to do so.

One day, John drove his father into Manhattan to have lunch with music executive Jules Rifkind. As John told the story, that day, he got a master class in how his father made money:

After lunch, they were in Rifkind's office, and they were bored. Sonny turned to Rifkind and said, "How's that other guy? The reverend?"

"I just spoke to him a couple of days ago," Rifkind replied.

"Where is he?" Sonny asked.

"I think I know where he is," Rifkind replied.

"Call him up," Sonny said.

Rifkind complied and called the Reverend Al Sharpton, a prominent and savvy Black activist in New York. Sharpton moved easily throughout the social strata of New York City, but he also could shut down a company with a well-timed civil rights protest.

Sharpton came over and they all had a convivial conversation, laughing and joking, until Sonny got down to business. He asked who did the promotion work for various Black artists, like James Brown, who recently had had a huge hit with "Living in America." Sonny wanted to know if Brown, and other Black artists, got any promotion money.

"No, we didn't get any money," Sharpton replied.

Sonny probed, dropped a few more names, and probed some more. Someone mentioned the name of a prominent Sony Music executive, Tommy Mottola.

Someone came up with the idea that these Black artists should get money for the promotions. It simply wasn't fair. Sonny turned to Rifkind and said, "Make a call to Tommy. See if he's in."

Rifkind called. Sonny told him: "You go tell him that Sonny just came here and that he's going to have trouble with Al Sharpton. And that I could help him. But before that happens, see, you go talk to him and see if you can come up with a number that will satisfy him. But tell him that I'm the one doing the favor, of course."

Rifkind and Sharpton left and returned with a $100,000 check.

On the way back home with John, Sonny was in a good mood. "See, this is how it is when you hang out. When I hang out with you, you cost me money. I've got to pay for lunch. I've got to buy you lunch, you go to all these fancy places. You hang out with me, and we make money. You see?"

John embraced his role as his father's messenger and bagman, which was important to his father because it provided him with essential insulation. "Don't let anyone hand me money," he told John Jr. "You always take the money."

John knew, however, that Sonny and Michael lied to him about money all the time, and he resented it. For all that he was doing for them, they still viewed him as nothing more than a gofer.

Then Sonny told him something that swept aside those feelings of resentment, at least for the time being. His father was proposing that John Jr. become a goodfella.

John was thrilled. It meant he was finally going to be somebody. He would be treated with the same respect as all the goodfellas he had met. He wanted that desperately.

Michael adamantly opposed it. He warned his father that John would get himself killed.

Michael saw what his father knew, but had hoped would be a passing phase: John had discovered cocaine. At first, it was just drinking, a lot. Then when he started cocaine, he'd chase it with alcohol. He loved the way coke made him feel. As much as he liked trading on his father's name, the cruelty of the life got to him at times. He needed to push those feelings down, and the cocaine helped.

Besides, it was a heady time. He and Michael were moving up, and his friends treated him accordingly. In the beginning, John's friends gave him the drugs. In the beginning, he was able to hide his dependence. He was a practiced liar; he had learned from the best.

John always had been neat, careful about his appearance, and punctual. That started to change as his appetite for drugs grew. Occasionally, he'd binge and disappear for a day or two. Tina, frantic with worry, would urge Michael to do something. He'd send a member of his crew to keep an eye on him. It became such a routine assignment that they called it "Dracula duty."

Before long, the coke parties weren't enough. He moved on to heroin, which was cheaper, but involved needles. Once, desperate for a fix, he washed his works in the water from a toilet bowl. More than once, his friends pulled him out of crack houses in Harlem.

Dealers stopped comping him. He had to pay his own way. He started stealing. He was smart, though. He stole from family and friends because he knew they wouldn't call the cops on him. He stole his sisters' jewelry, his brother Carmine's wedding rings, even his father's jewelry. Once, he stole Carmine's expensive work tools and even his truck.

When he scored enough cash, he'd binge on drugs and prostitutes. He'd go for days without showering and practically lived in the subways of New York, especially in the winter because they were a place to get warm. But he never stayed in one place for long. He became deeply paranoid, convinced that someone was going to kill him.

Eventually he'd run out of steam, so sick and exhausted he would return home to Roslyn, banging on his mother's door. He dreaded the return home because he knew she'd scream at him. But she always took him in. He'd manage to clean himself up and stay sober for a few days, only to go back out on the street and start it all over again.

Sonny, who had always been so self-disciplined about food and drink, hated drugs. He had taken care to counsel all his children against drugs, and he felt helpless as he watched addiction consume his son's life. He tried to get John interested in boxing. One day at the gym, he pulled aside the boxing trainer, pressing some bills into his hand, told him he was doing a good thing and that he should keep working with John. When Sonny left, the trainer looked at how much he had handed him—$5,000.

It was a sign of Sonny's desperation. Sonny, the man who never paid for anything, was paying the trainer an astonishing sum in the hope that he would help his son vanquish his demons.

But boxing wasn't enough. John continued to use. Because of who he was and because of Sonny's well-known feelings about drugs, anyone who sold drugs to him should have known better. That became evident to the FBI in 1985, when agents investigated the murder of one of John's dealers. The man's body was found rolled up in a rug in a Brooklyn social club. No one was charged, but agents were convinced he was killed because he sold drugs to the son of Sonny Franzese.

With all the attention on John, it seemed as if nobody really noticed what was going on with his younger sister Gia. She was attracted to bad boys, and she didn't care if she broke the unspoken rules of their life. Every Thursday night, men would go to Michael's club with their girlfriends. Unattached women were forbidden. Gia didn't care. She went, and she got away with it because of who she was. She also developed a taste for drugs.

It had started with Carrozza. She had fallen deeply in love with him. His murder shattered her. She was sure she was the reason he was killed, and the guilt she felt consumed her. Like John, she starting mixing cocaine and heroin. For a while, she was able to remain presentable at family gatherings, but a downward spiral began.

Michael, meanwhile, focused on expanding the gas tax scam. He went to Florida, ostensibly to produce a movie about break dancing called *Cry of the City*. The production attracted a lot of publicity—the perfect cover for the primary reason he was there—and a lot of acting hopefuls. One day, he was taking a break, relaxing poolside, and he noticed an eighteen-year-old dancer, Camille Garcia. Though he was married with children, and nearly twice Cammy's age, he was smitten. He didn't know it then, but that chance meeting would change the course of his life.

Back in New York, Sonny, as always, focused on business, which wasn't so easy to conduct while on parole. He was accustomed to surveillance, but law enforcement never let up.

In November 1985, two Nassau undercover detectives were at a restaurant-bar called Laina's in Jericho with a confidential informant. In walked Sonny and John, who recognized the CI. John walked over to say hello. Sonny and another man, John "Sideburns" Cerrella, a Genovese associate, disappeared into a back room for twenty minutes. John asked the informant to meet him in the men's room. He was looking to score cocaine, but he didn't have any money. A little later, outside the club, John hit up the informant for money. He gave him $80.

In the life of undercover detectives, it was a routine, unmemorable night, except for one thing—Sonny was associating with a known felon. They decided to keep an eye on that club.

Other organized-crime investigators were paying attention, as well. Gregory Scarpa, the FBI's longtime informant, gave agents detailed information about Tutti Franzese's loan-sharking and gambling operations, with addresses and phone numbers. Although Scarpa didn't have or didn't dare to give up information about Sonny, information about Tutti was nearly as good, given how close he was to his uncle. Information was shared, and detectives on the Long Island Oil Industry Task Force decided they had to make a move on Michael.

A specialized unit trained in electronic surveillance broke into Michael's professional suite of offices in Melville in the middle of the night. They had to go in through the ceiling because Michael had installed a very sophisticated lock on the conference room, one of their key targets. They also knew that Michael had his offices swept regularly for bugs.

At first, they were puzzled by the three small boxes on the wall. They had no idea what they were. They didn't want to disturb anything, but finally, after three middle-of-the-night break-ins, they took one down and figured out that the boxes were noisemakers. They placed tiny microphones throughout the office suite, mainly in the ceiling, their only point of entry because of the door lock.

They hoped the private detective sweeping the place for bugs would miss theirs, and he did. Investigators heard everything they needed. When police arrested Michael in December 1985, one detective told him wryly, "The guy you hired wasn't very good. Maybe you should think about hiring someone else."

Sonny was with Gina and her mother decorating their Christmas tree at her brother's house when he heard the news. He screamed with rage. Michael had been arrested and had beaten other cases before, but Sonny knew this one was bad. Gina was worried, too.

"Michael is very jealous of you," she told him. "He's very frightened of you. He'll never stand up. He'll never stand up."

The news got worse: Michael was indicted on sixty-five counts of racketeering, mail and wire fraud, extortion, kickbacks, embezzlement, and obstruction of justice. News stories about his indictment touted him as a "new breed" of mobster—young, aggressive, and more sophisticated than his predecessors. It was certainly not the kind of publicity the bosses appreciated.

They got more unwelcome news when they learned who the judge on the case would be—Jacob Mishler. Michael's lawyer quickly filed a motion to have Mishler recuse himself. He prevailed, and the case was assigned to another judge, Eugene Nickerson.

Fat Larry Iorizzo, the man behind the gas tax scam, testified at the pretrial hearing. He said Michael had threatened to kill his son and that he had talked about murdering a parole officer. Then FBI Agent Christopher Mattiace testified about his surveillance of Michael's meetings with Luigi Vizzini and their discussions of trying to bribe a parole commissioner, which were taped.

The testimony crushed Michael's hopes of getting out on bail, but in the courtroom an even more devastating personal betrayal was playing out. A coterie of friends and family sat in the courtroom, including Michael's wife Maria, to support him. Before the hearing, Michael had persuaded Maria to sign divorce papers, telling her it was the only way to protect their property from federal seizure. Their friends believed that she went along with it because she thought the divorce was a sham.

As she sat there, those same friends saw her face fall as she heard for the first time that Michael had married someone else—Cammy, the dancer from the movie set—and that Cammy was pregnant with their child.

Judge Nickerson was unpersuaded by Michael's claims that the FBI had set a trap for him and that he never threatened his father's parole officer. He ruled that Michael was a danger to the community and ordered him held without bail.

Years later, Sonny was measured while talking about Michael. "He's smart," he said, "but sometimes, you know, smart guys become dumb."

In January 1986, Sonny was back at Laina's with his friend Joseph Caridi, who had a long record for illegal gambling and assault, along with ties to the Colombos. Two Nassau undercover detectives—a man and a woman—were there, too. Their cover was that the male detective, Robert Colucci, was a degenerate gambler in hock to Caridi. They saw Caridi at Laina's often. Just the month before, Caridi had told them that he had a man badly beaten "because he mentioned Sonny's name on the street."

Around 1 a.m., Colucci and his partner got up to dance. That's when they saw Sonny and Caridi seated at a booth. Sonny and his companion glared at them.

As they were walking back to their table, Sonny and Caridi blocked their path. Caridi reached out and grabbed Colucci by the arm and said, "Do you have any money for me?"

Colucci reached into his pocket and took out $100 he had wrapped up in a rubber band and handed it to Caridi. As he did, Sonny said hello. Then as Colucci walked away, Caridi told him, "Don't be late with your next payment."

"Don't forget," Sonny chimed in menacingly.

When the detectives sat down, they saw a stream of men and women greeting Sonny with hugs and kisses. Around 2:15 a.m., Sonny left with another man.

The detectives wasted no time. They went straight to the D.A.'s Office. They had Sonny on another parole violation.

Sonny was called down to his parole office the next day. He insisted that the rumors that he was a silent owner of Laina's were not true and that he and Caridi were just old friends. And he insisted that he always made sure to check if someone had a criminal record before talking to him.

"I didn't know Joe had a prior record," he said.

It was almost laughable. It was as if Sonny couldn't help himself. Then, in March, when he returned to the parole office for his regular check-in, Cerrella was there waiting for his parole officer as well. Sonny extended his hand to greet him. It was a harmless gesture, but the parole officers noted it.

Pressure on Michael was mounting as well. In a pattern strikingly similar to Sonny's history, Michael had fended off five different indictments for crimes ranging from loan-sharking to extortion. Then the one case caught up with him. In March 1986, Michael pleaded guilty to racketeering and conspiracy.

He was sentenced to ten years in prison and ordered to pay $14.7 million in fines. For him, it was a pretty good deal, as it cleared up all the charges against him in both Florida and New York. Authorities also allowed him to remain free on bail with Cammy and their baby, Miquelle, until he had to surrender to prison.

A month later, federal agents showed up at the Franzese home on Shrub Hollow Road and arrested Sonny for the parole violations. Tina leapt to his defense, telling reporters that the only reason Sonny was at Laina's was to discuss an engagement party for their daughter, Little Tina. "What they call associating, we call planning the children's party," she said.

Tina's argument might have held sway with reporters, but not the parole board. Sonny returned to prison that November.

Once again, Tina was on her own.

CHAPTER 19

Family Spins out of Control

"She was a strong-headed woman. She wasn't afraid."

TINA WAS DONE. Sonny's return to prison for something he should have been more careful about infuriated her. He always put his life on the street above his own family. He always lied to her about other women. By now in her early fifties, she was smart and always elegant. Her model-like looks still turned heads. John Jr. and her girls were grown, and basically out of the house, and Michael wouldn't be around much longer. She decided to leave.

She got an apartment in Manhattan and approached a divorce attorney. It was a cataclysmic decision; women in her world did not leave their husbands.

"She was a strong-headed woman," Sonny said admiringly years later. "She wasn't afraid, you know. She wasn't afraid."

Nonetheless, Sonny could not allow her to leave. He remained deeply in love with her, or at least with the image of the woman he had met when she was just a teenager. More important, he was worried about what her leaving would look like on the street. He could not afford to be seen as a man who couldn't control his wife.

Far worse, though, was the idea that another man might be paying attention to her. It gnawed at him. Although he cheated on her constantly, he could not abide the notion of Tina with another man.

From prison, he gave Michael and John his instructions: They were to watch her apartment twenty-four hours a day. They couldn't delegate the task to one of Sonny's minions, as it was critical to keep this quiet. Even a whiff of a rumor could hurt Sonny's standing. They did as they were told, taking shifts. When they found out which attorney she was talking to, Michael approached him and said simply, "You don't want to do this."

He didn't.

She approached other attorneys, but John and Michael made sure they got the same message. Defeated, Tina returned home.

Home, however, was no sanctuary. Gia, like John, had become desperately addicted to drugs. She came home rarely. Some nights, family members had to scour the crack houses of New York City to find her. Gia, though sweet and caring to her friends, had always been the headstrong one of the children. Unlike her quieter sister, Little Tina, Gia resisted her mother's orders and they fought. More than once, John physically pulled them apart. It seemed that there was always some kind of emotional explosion in the house.

By then, John was basically living on the street, coming home only when the harsh New York winter made it too cold for him to sleep outside. Tina always took him in. One bitterly cold night, he came to her door, filthy from days of drugging and drinking. She made him strip outside before ordering him to go straight to a hot bath in hydrogen peroxide. John was offended, and saw it as another example of his mother's crazy obsession with cleaning. In fact, Tina was still angry and disgusted about the last time he had come home. He had slept on her couch and left it infested with insects.

After a day or two at home, John would leave again.

Tina kept up the front of normal family life, throwing big Sunday dinners and pool parties in the summer for her grandchildren.

She continued working, selling designer clothing, and forged her own friendships outside the family network.

One day, she found her friend Sharyn, who was going through a divorce and feeling overwhelmed by it, crying in the back room of the exclusive store where they both worked. "I can't handle it," Sharyn confided through sobs.

"You can handle it and you *will* handle it," Tina responded. "When you have to see him, you look him right in the eye and smile at the son of a bitch."

Sharyn was grateful for Tina's backbone. In Tina, she saw a woman who had to pick up the pieces every time Sonny went back to prison. Tina was determined not to let anyone see her falter, ever. "Present a strong front," she told Sharyn. "People will think twice."

Sonny, too, kept up appearances in prison. He would communicate his business instructions by phone through his nephew Jerry. Jerry had a copy of Greene's 1965 *Newsday* article, THE HOOD IN OUR NEIGHBORHOOD, framed on the wall of his office. That story might have upended Sonny's family life, but it was valuable marketing.

John and his friends would go to Jerry's printing business to get their marching orders. Often John's friend Dan Pearson joined them. Pearson was a boxer—muscular, tough, and smart. He had grown up a poor Black kid on the streets of East New York. He and John had met at the Queens Theatre, in which Sonny had a silent interest. The theater showed movies, many of them X-rated, and later hosted concerts. Performers who were booked there had little choice but to agree because of Sonny's ties to the place. Once, even the police patronized the place: The New York City Police Benevolent Association, a police union, held an exhibition boxing match between New York City police and firemen there.

Just a year apart in age, Pearson and John Jr. clicked. They started hanging out. Pearson knew who John's father was, but didn't fully understand what it meant to be associated with the Franzese name. After spending time with John, he started to understand. They never paid for a meal at a restaurant or for anything they wanted. It was intoxicating.

The first time Pearson met Sonny was via a phone call to Jerry's office from prison. Jerry put the phone on speaker. They talked for a while, and then Sonny spoke to Pearson: "Look out for him. Be a friend. If you see something, make sure I know about it. Tell Jerry, and he'll get the message to me."

Pearson took his words to heart, more than once pulling John out of crack houses in Harlem. He didn't do drugs himself or allow anyone around him to do them, but he became John's protector.

Sonny admired Pearson's street smarts and used him to take care of problems. Once, Pearson and a friend, Frank Rizzo, flew to Florida on Sonny's orders to collect a debt from a businessman. The man had African artifacts on the walls of his office, including a machete. Pearson grabbed it and smashed it against the man's desk.

The man wrote out a check, but Pearson wasn't done.

"I want you to book us a return ticket to New York and a return ticket back here in case it bounces," he said.

The businessman did as he was told.

Back at Jerry's office, Sonny called. Even though prison calls were monitored, he clearly had been filled in on the details. "Good work," he said.

Sonny continued to push his legal appeals, filing a habeas corpus motion claiming newly discovered evidence in his case. He based it on an affidavit from none other than John Cordero, one of the key witnesses against him in the bank robbery trial. Cordero now was saying that he had testified as part of a plot to frame Sonny, and that members of the Organized Crime Strike Force were in on it.

Sonny's plans went awry, however, when police found Cordero running down the street in his underwear. He was terrified, he told police. "Please call the FBI."

They did. Cordero said he had been kidnapped by Sonny's associates, including John Jr., and held captive until he agreed to sign the affidavit. They stripped him down to his underwear so he couldn't flee. He said he ran because he was sure they'd kill him even if he did change his testimony for Sonny. John Jr. remembered the time with Cordero differently. He said everything had been fine.

At the hearing on Sonny's motion, Cordero took the Fifth. Of more significance, the prosecution accused Sonny's lawyer of being one of the men who kidnapped Cordero. Speechless, Sonny's lawyer paled. He appeared terrified. Whether he was afraid of the legal consequences or something worse was unclear.

Judge Mishler denied the motion.

After the ruling, the prosecutor Patrick Cotter got a message on his answering machine: "Cotter, you're a fucking dead man, you motherfucking asshole. We're going to get you. We know where you live, you motherfucker."

There was a pause, and then the caller continued: "I mean it, motherfucker!"

Cotter found the threat laughable, but the FBI didn't. Agents tracked down the caller. The man worked with the Westies, an Irish gang the Mafia often used to contract out hits. The FBI brought him in. They didn't have enough to make the case, but an agent told him, "We know you freaking did this. If anything happens to Cotter, we're coming for you."

Six months later, the man was found dead in his Hell's Kitchen apartment. The door was locked from the inside, and investigators concluded he had been hit.

Michael, meanwhile, had reached his own turning point. He did something that no one in his family would have ever thought possible: He began cooperating. In exchange for a reduced sentence, he secretly agreed to testify against old family friend Norby Walters about a scheme of paying off college athletes to shave points in games.

Before long, the secret leaked out; Walters called John.

"John, look I don't know how to tell you this. There is an idea, there's something going on. It looks like your brother might testify against me," he told him.

John refused to believe it. "Norby, there's no way that can happen," he said. "I'm positive. I'll go see Michael."

Then Vincenzo "Vinny" Aloi, a Colombo capo whose lawyer was friendly with Walters's lawyer, called him. "You've got to find out what's going on, because things don't look right here."

Aloi stepped up the pressure even more—he called Michael's ex-wife, Maria, to find out what she knew.

John went to see his brother in jail. "Michael, I'm your brother," he said. "No matter what, why are these guys saying that? Look, if something's going on, please tell me. This way, when I go back there, I don't walk in saying that nothing's going on and then you end up testifying."

Michael looked him in the eye and said, "I ain't testifying. None of it's true, brother. You know I'd never do that."

John went back to Walters. "You don't have nothing to worry about," he told him.

Less than a month later, Michael went before the Norby Walters grand jury and testified.

John had passed on bad information, a potentially fatal mistake—something Michael knew. Aloi called John in. Worried, John went to see Sonny in Petersburg, the medium-security federal prison in eastern Virginia.

"Dad, what do I do here?"

"Well, never let anyone say your brother is a rat, no matter what," Sonny said. "If anyone approaches you or anything like that, we never let anyone tell us to kill our own family. But that dies here, with me and you.

"But here's how we can help that not happen. We start listening for anybody trying to imply that and seeing if you would be willing, if they're promising you things to get close to your brother.

You make believe that you would be willing to do that, so that we can find out where that's coming from. And we can take care of that."

Somewhat reassured, John met with Aloi and managed to convince him he had no idea Michael was testifying.

As tensions were simmering in New York, Michael was in Chicago for the Walters trial. Strike force prosecutor Edward McDonald flew to Chicago to meet with Michael and Chicago law enforcement. After meeting, they decided to break for lunch. An agent gave their deli order to Michael, who casually got up to get the food.

Shocked because Michael was supposed to be in custody, Ed McDonald said, "What's he doing?"

"He's getting our food," an agent replied.

It turned out that Michael had been living with Cammy and their baby in a condo in Chicago as he awaited trial, and all that time was to be counted toward his sentence.

Incredulous, McDonald decided that something needed to change. When Michael returned with the food, McDonald pressed him for information about other Mafia figures.

"I don't understand," Michael demurred, insisting that was not part of his cooperation deal.

"Let me explain the facts of life to you," McDonald responded. "You have to give up wiseguys."

Michael, confident that he had negotiated a good deal for himself, smiled and gestured toward the Chicago agents. "These guys will take care of me," he said.

"Take him," McDonald snapped.

The agents followed orders, and Michael spent the night in jail. The next day, he entertained the group with funny stories about his night in a holding cell with drunks and low-level street hoods.

But Michael also saw the light. That's when he began to cooperate in earnest with McDonald. Unlike the typical wiseguy who had never been out of Brooklyn, Michael knew how to handle himself in a variety of situations. Guys in his crew were familiar with his patter; they called it "Michael fever." He had been the Mafia's emissary to important meetings throughout the country. He knew who the bosses were and what their major operations were in Chicago, Los Angeles, Phoenix, and Washington, D.C.

McDonald, a veteran organized-crime prosecutor, was surprised to learn from Michael that there was even a Mafia presence in Denver—the Smaldone brothers, who operated out of an Italian restaurant there.

Michael also persuaded four codefendants to plead guilty, assuring them that he would cover their lawyers' fees. (He didn't.) As time went on, he provided information about other men close to Sonny, but never had to testify against them.

Prosecutors might have been impressed with Michael's deep knowledge of the workings of the Mafia, but street detectives saw a guy who used his father's name and the mob's backing to get what he wanted and then turned on his friends when they were no longer useful to him. Worse, they saw a man who seemed to be in love with himself. "I used to ask him, 'Do you have a lot of mirrors in your house?'" one detective said.

Michael later insisted that the only thing he did was testify against Walters—who was convicted, only to have his conviction overturned on appeal—and that it didn't matter, because Walters was not a goodfella. As such, he wasn't testifying against one of his own. Nobody cared about Norby, he insisted.

In fact, Michael had been lucky. The Organized Crime Strike Force was disbanded around that time, and he didn't have to testify in any other cases. He did, however, manage to get a time limit set on his cooperation deal—something that is unusual—so that he would not have to cooperate with other investigators coming his way.

Tina, though, was appalled. "That's not the way we were brought up," she said. "Why do that to people that didn't hurt you? I can love him till I die, but I can't forgive him. Because it's too huge. I'm hurting every day."

Michael's betrayal was so huge that Colombo boss Carmine

"the Snake" Persico ordered him killed. Persico was so angry that he "will go to any length to kill Franzese," informant Scarpa told FBI agents.

Sonny didn't challenge the order.

Michael wasn't just turning on everyone who had made him who he was—he was working on a potential movie deal about it and was scheduled to come back to New York to promote it. As deeply respected as Sonny was on the street, that was simply too much.

Persico ordered that Sonny's operations be distributed among other capos. Sonny didn't threaten to go to war or publicly object, knowing his crew remained loyal to him. But he didn't take it lightly. He refused to give up the big moneymakers. Persico, who was having his own problems with criminal indictments at the time, didn't push back.

Michael got out of prison in May 1989, after serving only a fraction of his ten-year sentence, and was placed on five years' probation. He moved to California with Cammy and bought her family members houses, drove around in a Porsche or sometimes a Mercedes, and began work on his memoir. Back on Long Island, his ex-wife lost the Old Brookville mansion.

New York investigators said that it was just a matter of time before he would be killed. But men closer to Sonny were convinced that Sonny persuaded Michael, who had millions squirreled away from the gas tax scheme, to make a multimillion-dollar payment to the commission. He also agreed to stay out of New York.

Tina knew something more about that arrangement. She told friends: "When Sonny dies, then Michael."

Tina's life followed a similar downward spiral. A few months after Michael got out of prison and left, she was sentenced to five years' probation in connection with a credit card fraud case. She got off easy. Prosecutors described her as one of eight people involved in a pattern of criminal enterprises that included an aborted contract killing, insurance and credit card fraud, gambling, and drug sales.

* * *

One night in October 1990, Gia called John Jr. from Florida.

"I don't feel good," she said.

"I gotta call you back," he told her. He couldn't talk because he was getting high.

The next thing he knew, Metro-Dade detectives found Gia faceup on the floor of a $59-a-night room in a motel in North Miami, dead from a drug overdose. There were scratches on her body and wet towels in the room, signs of a bad cocaine high. She was twenty-seven years old and two months pregnant.

Prison authorities allowed Sonny to attend Gia's wake, but he had to remain handcuffed, despite the family's entreaties. When he walked into the funeral home, Gia's boyfriend ran up to Sonny, threw himself at his feet, and pleaded for mercy. He had been trying to get Gia off drugs, he insisted.

The day of Gia's funeral, John was nowhere to be found. Tina called Pearson, who went looking for him. He found John curled up under a desk at the Queens Theatre, smoking crack.

"C'mon," he told him. "You gotta go to your sister's funeral. What's wrong with you?"

Pearson got him showered and dressed and took him to the house, so he could go to the wake.

Michael never showed up.

Back on the streets, John Jr. knew something didn't feel right. He felt sick, and it wasn't normal dope-sickness. He took a tiny sip of beer and threw up blood. He had a 104-degee fever. Usually, he could just push through things like that, but this was different. He called his mother from a pay phone.

In the past, when he called her for money, she would act tough. This time, however, she heard something in his voice.

"I'll pay for a cab if you come home," she told him.

When he got home, Tina took one look at him and drove him to the hospital. He was too weak to protest.

At the hospital, he collapsed. He dreamed of being in water, really cool water, and slept for more than a day. When he woke

up, a woman was standing by his bed. They had put him on suicide watch. It didn't make sense to him. John had never even con-
templated suicide. If he killed himself, he couldn't get his next
hit—and he lived for getting that next hit.

A doctor came in and told him he had severe pneumonia and
had tested positive for HIV, the human immunodeficiency virus
that leads to AIDS.

In 1990, HIV was seen as tantamount to a death sentence; family and friends were nervous about being around him, for fear of
contagion. When he returned home, Tina tried to pretend everything was normal. "He don't have HIV," she insisted.

John knew otherwise.

CHAPTER 20

Colombos Go to War

"If they made up their mind to kill you,
they'll kill you."

FOR A WHILE, JOHN JR. managed to get sober enough to open a pizzeria with his brother-in-law and once again be his father's trusted messenger. One day in late 1990, Vinny Aloi, the son of Sebastiano "Buster" Aloi, the man who sponsored Sonny for induction into the Mafia decades ago, called him into a club in Brooklyn to ask him about Sonny's businesses.

"Well, what do you want to know?" John replied.

Aloi wanted to know where all the cash pickups were made and when.

John knew this wasn't good. They were moving in on Sonny's businesses. He went to Petersburg, the federal prison in Hopewell, Virginia, to talk to his father.

Sonny listened and said, "Give him the list."

Sonny's directive wasn't a capitulation; it was strategic. He knew his men wouldn't go along with giving up their operations, because they'd never be able to make as much money with anyone else. But he also had to do what he could to keep John and Michael alive. Michael's betrayal had badly hurt Sonny's reputation and put his entire family in jeopardy.

John gave Aloi a partial list. Almost immediately, Vinny Aloi's guys started showing up at the Westbury Music Fair, a popular concert venue run by a man close to Sonny. Then, when John went to pick up his weekly $1,500 from a printer, another one of

Sonny's businesses, he was told that another money collector, "Big Lou," had already been there.

"Whaddya mean, Big Lou was here?" John said.

Told it was okay, John said nothing more. He knew well enough to keep his mouth shut. Then Benedetto "Benny" Aloi, Vinny's brother and also in the Colombo family, called him down to his club to talk. "Forget about anything your dad has," he told him. "We'll take care of all of that."

John reeled inwardly. He had never, ever heard anyone challenge his father like that. Aside from Carmine "the Snake" Persico, who was in prison, he knew of no one more powerful or more respected in the family. Something bad was brewing.

He returned to Petersburg and told his father, "Dad, nobody is saying nothing, but there's problems out there that are obvious. Sometimes you've gotta pick a side."

John's words surprised Sonny, but even with his favorite child, he played it close. "Son, you're right. Sometimes you gotta pick a side," he replied, not picking a side.

To John, who had grown up learning to understand the coded language of the street, it was obvious. Tensions were festering between Carmine "the Snake" Persico and his acting boss, Victor "Little Vic" Orena, who was tiring of Persico's micromanaging from prison. Sonny was seen as loyal to Persico. If the Orena faction—and Benny and Vinny Aloi were Orena loyalists—could take something away from Sonny, they'd draw more recruits to their side. Sonny and the Snake would be seen as losing their strength.

John tried to steer clear of the Orena acolytes and stay neutral. He had always liked Junior, as he referred to Persico. As a child, he had loved going over to the Persico household for dinner because Persico and his wife asked their children how they were doing and seemed to actually like them. There were no angry outbursts or criticism, at least not in front of company. Although he knew his parents loved him and showered him with material things, he never felt that they cared about how he felt. He took note of the way the Perscios acted because they were not civilians, who didn't know any better. They were like them, special and wise in the ways of the street.

Despite his efforts to stay away, one day he was called down to a club in Brooklyn to meet with Benny. John went back to Petersburg to confer with his father.

"Dad, why are they calling me down there?" he asked.

Sonny was somber, and his response did nothing to calm John's apprehensions. "Son, all I can tell you is if they made up their mind to kill you, they'll kill you. If they didn't make their mind up to kill you and you don't go, then they're going to kill you."

As John tried to absorb this, Sonny continued speaking. "Look, I told you, I'm in here. I can't help you. If you go and they haven't made up their mind to kill you, you'll be okay. But if you don't go, then you can rest assured they're going to look to kill you, because if they kill my son, it will look really good for them."

John returned to New York fairly certain he could die very soon. He was determined to get through it without letting his father down.

On the day of the meeting, he waited to be picked up and taken to the club, taking long drags on a cigarette. His pal Schwartzy took him to the club. The place was usually packed with people, but on that day, they were the only two men there. As he waited, John ran through the possibilities in his mind: Maybe they thought he was going to shoot someone, maybe they'd take him somewhere and kill him, maybe there was more "trouble" than he had been aware of. The minutes stretched into more than an hour. The waiting was excruciating. Then Schwartzy made a call, turned to John, and said, "Someone's on his way."

All of a sudden, John's cousin Tutti Franzese burst through the door, screaming at him, "I told you to stay out of the way! I told you don't come back. Don't *ever* come here! What are you doing here?"

John was astonished. It didn't make any sense to him. He stood there, speechless. Tutti kept cursing and screaming. "Don't come here no more! Don't bother with no one no more!"

With that, John left, wondering what the hell happened. Tutti had always been close to both Sonny and John. An imposing six-one and 220 pounds, he was an enforcer for the Colombos. Of all the cousins in the extended Franzese clan, he was the one who had been the most reliable support while Sonny was in prison.

About three hours later, John went to his pizzeria, where he ran into another cousin, Chubby.

"John, what are you doing? Tutti's been waiting for you for three hours at his club," he told him.

John dutifully went to Tutti's club, where Tutti was waiting. "Listen, cousin," Tutti said, "there's nothing I can do to help you. Don't come around. Don't ask for nothin'. Don't bother with anything from your dad."

John understood. Tutti had just saved his life. Tutti had made some kind of deal with Benny Aloi and persuaded him not to kill his uncle's son. Later, when John occasionally saw Tutti, he always had a look that made it clear: "I can't save you again."

At Petersburg, he told his father what happened, and Sonny quietly agreed: "Your cousin probably saved your life."

The Colombo war of the early 1990s was on. Though the killings hadn't started yet, Orena had made his move. He had been running the family for two years while Persico was in prison, and he had, in his view, been doing it well. His loyal aide, lawyer Dennis Pappas, had helped him launder millions, and Orena had kicked up copious amounts of money. But increasingly, he complained that the boss was out of touch. He felt particularly aggrieved that Persico was considering a made-for-TV movie on his life, a move that would only turn up the heat from law enforcement.

Orena dispatched his consigliere, Carmine Sessa, to poll the capos on whether they would support installing him as boss. If he won support from the majority of them, it would clear a path for him. Sessa, however, loyal to Persico, warned him of the coup attempt. And capos complained that Orena was cutting them off from their most lucrative rackets. Orena had misread his audience: He wasn't as popular as he thought he was.

The Snake was enraged. He had only made Orena acting boss so that he could keep the seat warm until his son Alphonse "Little Allie Boy" Persico got out of prison and could take over. This was intolerable. From prison, he issued the order: Take Orena out.

On the evening of June 20, 1991, four men waited in a parked car outside Orena's Cedarhurst home. When Orena drove up to his house, he spotted them, immediately made a U-turn, and sped away, very much alive.

After that, the killings started. Bodies were dropping in Brooklyn and on Long Island. In November, gunmen chased down Colombo soldier Gioachino "Jack" Leale in the lobby of the Plainview Plaza Hotel, a quintessential suburban hotel just off the Long Island Expressway. Guests dove for cover as the assailants chased him into the parking lot and shot him seven times in the head and back. In December, a mobster was shot while hanging a Christmas wreath on his front door in Brooklyn. And in March, Michael Imbergamo, who happened to be in the wrong place at the wrong time, was gunned down as he sat in a car with Orena loyalist John Minerva in front of the Broadway Café in North Massapequa.

The murders shook the community. At Imbergamo's funeral, the priest told mourners: "The violence, the blood, the shock, the evil, the horror, the ugliness, the cruelty that is sometimes part of life came to the surface in front of the Broadway Café . . . We can't escape it. We can't wash it away."

The hit squads and drive-by shootings didn't stop. One hit team even ambushed Scarpa, a Persico ally, spraying his car with bullets while he was driving with his family; he and his family, however, escaped unharmed.

Scarpa was helping Persico direct his troops, and yet was still serving as an FBI informant. He fed the FBI information about

Orena, conveniently omitting his own role in killing at least three Orena soldiers.

Law enforcement, alarmed at the carnage, stepped up the pressure, filing indictments against eighty Colombo soldiers or associates.

Surrender was not an option for Sonny or Persico. While in Petersburg, according to the FBI, he approved hits against three men who had been in Michael's crew: Frank "Frankie Body Shop" Cestaro, Louis "Louie" Fenza, and Frank "G" Castagnaro. They had switched sides, and were marked for death.

Castagnaro shrugged it off when he heard about the threat. He later joked with Sonny about it and they laughed.

After two years of bloodshed, in which at least a dozen people were killed and a dozen more became government witnesses, the war effectively ended in December 1992, when Orena was convicted of nine counts of murder and racketeering in connection with murdering one Colombo member and conspiring to kill those in the faction against him. He got three life sentences, plus eighty-five years.

There was no official truce, however, and there were still eleven guys out on the Orena side. It didn't look good to the other families for there still to be a split within the Colombos. Something had to be done.

Joe Colombo Jr. talked to them and came back with a message for John to take to his father: The only person they would negotiate with was Sonny.

At Petersburg, Sonny and Mush Russo discussed it. Sonny came up with an offer to persuade them to come back in, and he dispatched John to a Colombo family wedding in Upstate New York to deliver it.

His message: Sonny guarantees, with Russo's blessing, that the two capos could stay capos and their soldiers could remain with them.

It was a good offer. If the men were put with other capos,

they'd be terrified that they would be killed, one by one. Every-body knew the Snake's reputation and his zeal for murder, and they didn't trust him. On the other hand, they did trust Sonny. They all came in.

For John Jr., who had spent the last six years of his life drug-ging on the street, his role as the messenger in such important ne-gotiations felt amazing. He had gone from wrapping garbage bags around his feet to keep them warm in the winter to suddenly being in the mix of critical business. He felt like Sonny Fran-zese's son again. It seemed as though he might still have a shot at becoming a goodfella.

When the eleven came back into the fold, any vestige of power Orena had left disappeared. Orena wound up at Petersburg, with Sonny and Russo. Sonny, who was always so self-disciplined and controlled, couldn't stand the insult of having to be around the man who had tried to have his son killed. It was too much. One day, he got near Orena and picked up a shank; Russo, who had stayed close, stepped in and stopped him.

At home in Roslyn, Tina was having trouble managing. She worked at Escada, earning a six-figure income, but couldn't, or wouldn't, pay the bills. Normally, she could get away with drop-ping Sonny's name and that would be enough. But by December 1992, even the Franzese name wasn't enough. Mired in debt, she filed for bankruptcy. She never told her family.

She was sure Michael had money, but he didn't give it to her. Besides, he was back in jail after violating his parole in Los An-geles for committing bank fraud. He was sentenced to four years in prison for bouncing checks, falsifying bank loan applications, and failing to pay his rent.

Sonny, after nearly eight long years in prison, got out on parole in April 1994. He came home to discover that even though their house had long been paid off, Tina had remortgaged it and piled up debt. He complained to his mistress, Gina:

"Every time I come out, I'm in debt, half a million bucks. So I gotta do stuff to pay my friends."

He screamed at Tina to stop spending money, but she screamed right back at him: "You *owe* me this money!"

By now, their arguments were openly public. Tina harangued Sonny when his friends were over, and the spectacle embarrassed them. Sonny would try to placate her, tell her anything to quiet her, but she knew he was lying. She'd yell at him, "I know who you are!"

Sonny never beat her, because he didn't believe in beating women, but she liked to threaten him with knives. At Thanksgiving, with all her family gathered around, she pulled out a knife and held it to his face. Everyone tensed, except Sonny. He didn't back up. He just smiled and laughed at her. She put the knife down, and everyone went on as if nothing had happened.

While emotions seemed to be constantly erupting at home, Sonny did his best to calm tensions on the street. The Orena-Persico war was over, but both sides were wary. Often John would drive his father to late-night meetings with people like Thomas "Tommy Shots" Gioeli, where Sonny focused on bringing the family together. If Sonny called the meeting, the old Orena loyalists would come, knowing they could trust his guarantee that they wouldn't get killed. The logistics of such meetings were tricky, as he was still on parole, but in Sonny's mind, they were important. He always stressed that there was strength in unity, not division. They could not afford to look weak.

He was needed on the street now more than ever.

Then in July 1995, Sonny heard some disturbing news: An associate, Fiore "Philly" Caruso, who was his nephew Jerry's partner in the printing business, and who had often been there when Sonny had called from prison, was arrested on serious drug and conspiracy charges. Caruso had been targeted by a joint investigation of the Nassau County district attorney's office and the Drug Enforcement Administration. Authorities seized three kilograms of cocaine, twenty-five pounds of marijuana, and $20,000 cash from his Kings Park home.

The joint aspect of the investigation was what was so disturbing. That meant there had been wiretaps for months and possibly an informant. Sonny was always careful, never leaving a message if someone didn't answer the phone. But he had no idea what other people were saying, and he knew people always used his name. If authorities could tie a high-level organized-crime guy like Sonny to a drug ring, it would be a big coup, and he knew it.

John's friend Dan Pearson knew Caruso well. They had met through John and had become good friends, but Pearson didn't know about his drug dealing. When Caruso's wife, Cheryl, called to tell him about the arrest, he was flabbergasted.

Then he got a call from Sonny, who didn't waste any time with small talk. "Hey, what's going on with Philly?" he asked.

"I don't know," Pearson replied.

"Whaddya mean, you don't know?" Sonny pressed. "You guys are tight as peas in a pod. What do you know about this?"

"Sonny, I don't know anything," Pearson insisted.

Sonny shifted gears abruptly. "I want you to come to the house," he said.

Pearson was a regular at Sonny's home. Tina, who could be harsh with her children and their friends, always treated Pearson warmly, because she knew he looked out for John. He was often there with John, and when they had special guests, like the night they hosted a party with Kool & the Gang. Even though he was usually the only Black person at the house, he always felt accepted there.

But something felt off. There was something in Sonny's tone. It was different. Over the years, Pearson had learned to trust his instincts. He made up an excuse.

"Sonny, I'm in the middle of something right now that I gotta take care of. Can I come later?" he asked.

Sonny didn't say anything. They ended the call.

Pearson wasn't sure what to make of the conversation until he got a call a little later from a friend, Anthony. "Danny," he said, "you got a problem."

"I got a problem with who?" Pearson asked.

"I just talked to the old man. He thinks you're involved with Philly in something. He told me to get you to come to the house. I'm telling you, don't go. I'm risking my life telling you. He thinks you know something. If you go, you ain't gonna walk out."

Pearson got off the phone and tried to absorb it. His relationship with Sonny was valuable, because it opened doors that wouldn't have otherwise opened for a Black man. But he also understood that these people who were his friends always turned on their friends. If for one minute he forgot the type of people he was dealing with, it could be his last.

He didn't go.

CHAPTER 21

John Takes a Fateful Step

"How could you reward him like that?"

COLOMBO SOLDIER Joseph "Joe Baldy" Pistone, sitting in the basement of the federal courthouse in Uniondale, radiated menace. The FBI agents and prosecutors were tough guys in their own right; Pistone, however, with his bulging biceps, shaved head, and Fu Manchu mustache, looked as if he were about to rip through his handcuffs. They eyed him warily.

This Pistone was not the undercover cop who masqueraded as a street guy named Donnie Brasco. This Joseph Pistone had been fingered for a heinous murder by his brother, Peter.

The victim was Louis Dorval, whose body was found in a plastic tool chest floating in the Atlantic Ocean, thirty miles off Fire Island, a long barrier beach just south of Long Island. The killers had shot holes in the chest to make it sink, but it didn't. A U.S. Coast Guard ship on routine patrol happened upon the chest bobbing on the water in August 1994. It became known as the "body-in-the-box" case. The gruesome discovery just offshore from Fire Island, a tourist mecca with pristine beaches and expensive vacation homes, tantalized the media.

Dorval, according to the informant, had been a low-level crook who had failed to kick up enough money to the family, specifically to Sonny Franzese. Additionally, Dorval had been indicted on racketeering charges, and his associates worried he would turn. He was found with bullet wounds to the head. Based on what the Pistone brothers told them, prosecutors believed that Sonny had given the orders for two associates, Joe Baldy and Robert Misseri, to take out Dorval.

They didn't have the evidence to charge Sonny, however, and they stepped up their surveillance. By now, Sonny was in his late seventies. Despite Michael's feeble attempt years earlier to ship him off to retirement in Florida, Sonny wasn't slowing down. It was as if he felt he had to make up for all his years away in prison. He was constantly looking for the next score.

The body-in-the-box case eclipsed the Caruso drug case as an immediate problem for Sonny. It was very high-profile, and it involved a murder. Sonny needed to make sure it was contained, but he also had other business to deal with. He attended a meeting of capos at the Majestic Diner in Garden City. It was a big meeting, with high-level guys such as Tommy Shots Gioeli and Ralph "Ralphie" Lombardo. The feds were watching, and they were taking pictures. One agent went into the diner to listen in on the conversation.

By early 1996, federal authorities had compiled enough evidence to bust him. Sonny was sent back to prison on February 8—his third parole violation. In an ironic twist, the body-in-the-box case wouldn't be resolved for another seventeen years, as the government witness who blamed Sonny turned out to be unreliable. He kept changing his story. The man ultimately convicted of killing Dorval was Christian Tarantino, who shot him because he feared Dorval could implicate him in the murder of an armored truck guard, Julius Baumgardt. Pistone pleaded guilty to murdering Dorval with Tarantino, and Misseri pleaded guilty to money laundering as part of a plea bargain.

Interest in Sonny's story remained high, however. *New York Post* columnist Jack Newfield and screenwriter Nicholas Pileggi circulated a movie treatment entitled *One Free Murder* about his life. The title had come from a dinner party at Newfield's that

Tina had attended. As she walked out, she put her arm around Newfield's wife and joked that if he could prove Sonny wasn't guilty of the bank robberies, "You get one free murder."

The movie treatment, and Newfield's promotion of the story in his newspaper column, attracted enough interest to prompt a Hollywood producer to give Tina $50,000. Tina liked the idea of being in the movies, but, as was often the case with Tina, $50,000 wasn't enough. She called the producer and demanded another $50,000, warning him that if he didn't give her the money, she would have to talk to Sonny. Terrified, the producer called Ori Spado, who had established himself in Beverly Hills and billed himself as the mob's fixer there. Spado called Sonny in prison and explained the situation to him.

"She's crazy, but she ain't all wrong," Sonny told Spado. "See if you can get her more money."

He did. Tina got the additional $50,000, but that wasn't enough. She started demanding complete creative control, and she demanded it in phone call after phone call. It was too much for Hollywood, and the movie never got made.

With Sonny in prison, there was little to keep his family on track. John was back on the street, and his HIV diagnosis did nothing to change his old habits. He had little to live for anyway. With his father incarcerated, he wasn't needed to drive him to important meetings anymore, and he focused on the one thing he cared about: getting high. He'd steal, borrow, or beg for money for drugs. Over time, he found that he was particularly good at creating the look he needed for successful panhandling. He was bearded, unwashed, and usually barefoot on the streets in the winter—he always traded the expensive sneakers Tina bought him for a hit—and the bare feet were always sure to elicit sympathy and a few bucks. And another hit.

John did try to sober up, occasionally attending Narcotics Anonymous meetings. At one meeting, he met a woman and they started dating. He often stayed at her place. One day, he was craving a hit. He looked around her place. She had a gun, which he knew he could sell, and there was also her car. He took them and left.

It was a familiar strategy for John: He would steal from the people closest to him, betting that they wouldn't turn him in. This time, he was wrong. His girlfriend called the police.

On April 29, 1996, Nassau County police pulled him over in her car and arrested him. They found the gun under the seat, which immediately marked him as a dangerous criminal. They hit him with a host of charges: criminal possession of a weapon, equipment violation, failure to produce an insurance card, failure to display a license plate, no seat belt, and unauthorized use of a vehicle. His last name probably didn't help, either.

It was his first arrest, and he was rattled. He didn't have the money for an attorney, and neither did Tina. A Legal Aid lawyer initially represented him.

Five months later, John was sentenced to a year in jail after pleading guilty. He had been nervous about going in, but jail for John turned out to be a place to get warm, get his head cleared out, and make some friends. Although his mother always took him in, her rages made jail seem comparatively pleasant.

One day, Dan Pearson, who had been staying away from the Franzese household after his unsettling conversation with Sonny, went to the Nassau County Jail with Philly Caruso's wife, Cheryl, to visit Caruso, who was in jail awaiting his trial on the drug charges. In the waiting room, Pearson saw an inmate bouncing from table to table chatting with people, joking, laughing. It was obviously a violation of the jail rules, but he somehow was getting away with it. The inmate glanced around, saw Pearson, and his face lit up. "Hey, Danny Boy! Over here! Over here!"

It was John. Pearson couldn't believe it. He was both shocked and delighted to see his old friend. John's family had kept his arrest and jail sentence quiet.

By early December 1996, things came to a head for Tina again financially. She wasn't paying the bills, and the debts piled up.

The Franzese name wasn't enough to stave off all her creditors. She filed for bankruptcy a second time. Once more, she didn't tell her family.

When John got out of jail after nearly a year, he celebrated with a three-day crack run. He stole his younger sister Tina's car and sneaked into the Roslyn house, because he knew his mother and sister weren't home. He got to sleep for a couple of hours, when his sister woke him up by screaming at him for stealing her car. Unfazed, he decided to check the voice mail on the family's phone. It was a message from FBI Agent Robert Lewicki.

FBI agents often reach out to potential informants, knowing that they'll usually be rebuffed. But agents figure it's a numbers game, and maybe one time, their number will come up lucky. The family was used to such approaches, and they always ignored them.

This time, John didn't ignore it. He wasn't sure why. Even though he was out of jail, he felt as if he had nothing. He simply didn't care about life or the people in it. He made a life-changing decision: He called Lewicki back.

"John, I think me and you gotta get together and talk," Lewicki said. "I'm in a position to help you, and you're in a position to help us."

They agreed to meet the next day at a park, a ninety-eight-acre wooded preserve in Roslyn, not far from the Franzese family home. John still had his sister's car, and it was littered with crack vials and beer bottles. Worried he might jam himself up on drug charges, he parked a good distance away from the park and walked in to meet Lewicki.

Lewicki had his own worries. He was meeting the son of a Colombo crime family underboss and had no idea what to expect. He went to the park alone, but wearing a wire, with FBI agents sitting in cars parked nearby listening to every word.

John and Lewicki hadn't met before, but they had grown up in neighboring communities on Long Island. Lewicki, with close-cropped hair and a tough-guy voice, was the kind of man John could relate to. As they were feeling each other out, they discovered that they were just a year apart in age and shared an affinity for the New York Jets and attractive women. They even knew some of the same girls from high school. They clicked.

Lewicki told John that a man who had been in prison with Sonny was offering to refinance the family's house on Shrub Hollow Drive. John recognized the man's name because he had been home when he had called the house and spoken to Tina. Lewicki chose his words carefully, but John understood the message he was conveying: The man was claiming that he was being extorted by Sonny to give money to Tina to save the house. John also understood that the man was an FBI informant.

Rocked by this news, John thought, *Holy cow, my mom is going to lose her house. My dad is not going to come home on parole.*

Sonny was just months away from getting released on parole, and John was terrified he was going to blow it. Even worse, his mother could get charged as an accessory to the extortion and wind up in prison herself.

His mind started racing. John had been trading on his family name his entire life. He had no legitimate career, no work history in the civilian world that he could take pride in. His entire life was wrapped up in the fate of his parents. Though his parents' financial problems were not his fault, he felt as if he had destroyed everything. He felt worthless.

They finished up their conversation and agreed to meet again. The next time, John started probing, asking Lewicki if he was telling him that he really wasn't interested in his father. Lewicki responded that he wanted to know about the family and asked if John could tell him about them.

After a pause, John responded, "Well, I could. When my dad gets home, I would know a lot. But I would only know it through my dad."

In John's mind, he could help his family by helping the FBI. His father would get out of prison on parole; and although Sonny and Tina fought constantly when they were together, at least the bills got paid when Sonny was around. They wouldn't lose the house. He knew he could get killed for cooperating, but he figured he was dying anyway because of his HIV. Besides, it couldn't hurt him to have a friend at the FBI.

He pressed Lewicki. "Rob, is there any way we can guarantee that my dad . . . No one will put my dad in jail while I'm working with you? Because the only way I'm of any use to you is if my dad's out. None of these guys will go near me anymore."

There was no way Lewicki could make that guarantee. "Look, we can't make any promises for your dad unless he was cooperating, too," he said.

"Well, you can forget about that," John said. "Because that ain't never going to happen."

Lewicki changed course, telling John that he could see the logic of his argument. "It is very reasonable to understand that unless your dad comes home, there's very little you're going to be able to do for us," he said.

Then he assured him that he would not have to testify. No one would ever know. As a confidential informant, he would stay just that—confidential.

A deal was struck. They didn't talk about money that day, but John would get regular payments, if he stayed sober. The FBI made it clear that he couldn't get high while he was working as a CI. If he did, the deal was off.

John got sober and got to work. Even before his father got home, he began picking up useful information. A member of the Colombo family, Saverio "Sammy" Galasso III, told him that somebody had paid him money to burn down a dog kennel in Old Brookville. John got upset. He understood giving someone a beating, but not hurting innocent animals. "No way, don't you ever burn down no dog kennel," he told him.

With that, he thought Galasso agreed not to do it. A couple of months later, he learned that someone, indeed, had burned down the kennel. A family associate was building homes in the area and felt that the barking dogs brought down home values. John was pretty sure he knew what happened, and he tipped off the FBI. An investigation ensued, and Galasso, Robert Misseri, and Joe Baldy Pistone all were later indicted in the arson. Misseri and Pistone resolved the charge by agreeing to plea bargains, and Galasso ultimately pleaded guilty to arson.

Meanwhile, in prison, Sonny raged over the financial hole Tina had dug for them. The remortgaging plan had fallen apart, and he was determined not to bail her out again. *I don't give a damn,* he wrote Gina from prison. *I'm letting the house go. I'm done.*

In October 1997, Tina lost the house. It was sold in foreclosure for $360,000, but she didn't have to move out immediately.

In February 1998, Sonny got out on parole yet again and moved back in with Tina. Her relationship with Sonny was more volatile than ever. They fought constantly. In all the years Sonny had been away, Tina had become more independent, and more willing to threaten others in her husband's name. Word would get back to him, and he'd erupt.

"You're not me!" Sonny would scream at her.

Tina fought back in every way she could think of. She kept the house cold just to drive him crazy. He'd walk in and say, "Jesus, it's like a freakin' freezer, you can hang meat in this place!"

In the morning, he'd rant to John Jr., "See how cold it is in here? I'm eighty-some-odd-years old, she's going to kill me!"

It wasn't just the temperature. He hated spending money on air-conditioning, and she knew it. Now that he was home and making money again, she spent it. John had managed to stay sober for several months, and Tina decided he should be rewarded for it. She bought him an $82,000 Jaguar.

John, naturally, loved the car and stayed sober, for a while. Then one night, he went to an exclusive Manhattan nightclub called Marylou's with a record producer. Eager to impress him, John started drinking and getting high. A few hours later, he was driving up to Harlem, selling off the Jaguar, piece by piece. The car's wheels alone cost $1,000 apiece. John Jr. sold them for $15 each. He sold off the airbags and the telephone that came with the car. The money he made from selling off the Jaguar parts fueled a days-long binge of coke parties with prostitutes.

Sonny was furious at Tina when he found out. "How could you reward him like that?" he bellowed.

Tina was unfazed. By then, she was established in her own life. She worked for St. John Knits, a high-end fashion line.

Though in his eighties, Sonny spent more and more time out of the house. He'd often meet a friend of his, who happened to be a U.S. marshal. The friend knew he could lose his job just because he was associating with Sonny, but he didn't care. He had too much respect for Sonny, and besides, Sonny never asked him for anything. Much of the time, Sonny talked about how much he wanted to protect John.

The two of them were together constantly. They'd go to movies during the day—Sonny loved comedies—and dinner at night. Sonny still never paid for a meal; either the restaurant would comp him or someone else picked up the tab. The marshal saw it as a sign of respect. It was also good business for the restaurant owner. Sonny would hold court in places like the Russian Tea Room. Often celebrities would see him and come over to pay their respects.

One night, a famous football player came over to greet him. Then he pulled the marshal aside and said, "You know how me and Sonny became good friends?"

The football player went on to explain that years earlier, a gang of bikers were raping a young woman in a bar in Queens. Sonny single-handedly stepped in and stopped it. That young woman was a friend of the football player's. He was forever grateful that Sonny had saved her life.

Another night, a record producer, Frank Sardo Avianca, came over. He had a similar story. As a teenager, he had stolen a car with some friends, only to learn that, very unfortunately, a wiseguy owned it. The man and his associates grabbed Avianca and were beating him in the basement of a social club. Sonny walked in and said, "What are you doing to this kid?"

"He robbed my car, Sonny," the man replied.

"Yeah, well, why are you trying to make him a rat?" Sonny said. Then he turned to Avianca and said, "Kid, go home."

Avianca never forgot it.

Time and time again, people stopped by Sonny's table to chat. And as usual, law enforcement was watching. They took pictures of the many dinners and the people Sonny met.

The marshal lost his job.

CHAPTER 22

No Turning Back

*" 'Cause the same cocksucker that talked to
you'd be the first guy to rat you out."*

SONNY AND JOHN sat down for coffee with a few guys at a
Starbucks in Greenvale, just east of Queens, in November 2000.
They were chatting with Colombo soldier Leonard "Big Lenny"
Dello and the leader of his crew, Sammy Galasso II, who was
there with his son. At the table next to them were a man and a
woman who appeared to be deeply in love.

In fact, they were FBI agents, and they were taking pictures.

Sonny didn't say anything incriminating, but again, he was arrested for associating with known felons. He didn't come home
for three days, and he didn't call home. Tina was in a panic, until
FBI agents showed her the photos. When Sonny finally called,
she confronted him. She couldn't believe that he had been so stupid to do it again and get caught again. She screamed at him on
the phone.

Sonny did what he always did to try to placate her—he lied.

"Those pictures are lies," he said.

In a fury, Tina hung up, shouting, "I gotta live like this my
whole life!"

It was the breaking point. She split with her husband once and
for all.

A rumor spread that John had been the one who had tipped off
authorities about the meeting, but John swore he wasn't the one.
He pointed the finger at the Galassos.

Six months later, Sonny was back in prison. By now, Tina's rages were like manic episodes. Instead of going on cleaning tears through her children's rooms, she went through Sonny's things and threw out a trunk of personal mementos and photos he had saved. It was his life history, and the loss devastated him. Tina was too angry to care.

Living in California with his second family, Michael reached out to John. He invited his brother to stay with him in September 2001. John jumped at the chance. He loved his brother and his family. He understood that he'd have to stay sober around them. He stayed for three weeks, managing to avoid drugs, and then Michael and his family went away on an overnight trip.

The temptation was too great.

Michael, who hated shopping for new clothes, had ten new suits in the back of his car. John took them and sold them. Then he met up with his old friend Ori Spado and binged on cocaine and prostitutes. Later that night, Spado dropped John off at the hospital, where he spent five hours and was released. Dreading an expected confrontation with Michael, who had come home early with his family, John stalled going back to Michael's house, walking all the way. It gave him time to think.

It suddenly hit him: California is not New York. It's warm year-round, with palm trees, inviting beaches, and a funky scene at the Santa Monica Pier. Best of all, California has—of all things—porta-potties. It felt like a revelation. In New York, people would kill for a porta-potty. Los Angeles just seemed so much more hospitable than the tough streets of New York. If you had to live on the street, California was a whole lot better place to be.

He had noticed a 12-step meeting place around the corner from Michael's house. There were no signs announcing what it was, but he recognized the obvious tells: people standing outside smoking cigarettes and drinking coffee. He walked in. It felt right. He was ready to get sober. He knew this was it. For some reason, he was ready this time. He got financial assistance through a government program designed to help people who had worked in the music industry. John had once worked on a production deal with a well-known singer. Although the deal failed, it was enough for him to get the assistance; he moved into a sober home.

Things were falling into place for him. He even got the date of the day he got sober tattooed on his arm: October 9, 2001.

John took the tenets of the 12-step program to heart and tried to make amends. He went to see his father, who was in a low-security federal penitentiary in eastern Michigan, to tell him he was finally sober. Sonny had pressing business of his own on his mind. He had heard that John was a confidential informant. John swore to his father that it wasn't true. "I would never do that, no matter what kind of trouble I had!" he said, crying.

In fact, the FBI had stopped using John because of his drug use, but not before John had given them useful information about a number of Colombo associates.

Whether or not Sonny believed John, he took him back in the fold. He still needed him for messages, especially to Tina, who wasn't speaking to him. He also had business to conduct. He and an associate, Joseph "Joe D" DiGorga, had made a particularly onerous loan arrangement with a man who, unbeknownst to them, became a federal informant.

In 2002, Tina had to move out of the Roslyn house. John Jr. understood that DiGorga had bought it and didn't give his mother any help. Although she had lost the house to a foreclosure sale years earlier, Tina was shocked that she actually had to move out. She moved to West Los Angeles. She shipped three dogs, two cars, and bedrooms of furniture to a house Michael owned. She needed a rental fast. John's girlfriend, Denyce Marcucci, had a friend who found a place for $5,500 a month. Michael agreed to meet them there and give them the money for the rental.

He never showed. All of a sudden, Tina had a violent asthma attack. Denyce panicked. She couldn't leave Tina, who by then was in her late sixties, on the street. Denyce didn't have a lot of money, but she had just sold her house and had money in the bank. Worried for Tina, she went to the bank and withdrew $12,000 for the deposit and first month's rent as a very temporary loan. Tina promised to pay her back.

She never did. Denyce realized later she had been conned.

Denyce and John had met at the sober house she operated in Santa Monica. A beautiful and brittle woman, she was nearing the end of her third marriage and trying to stay sober after years of battling addiction. She noticed John immediately when he walked into the sober house, mainly because he carried with him a gallon bag of medications he was taking for his HIV. They started talking, and she liked his energy. He was so upbeat, so positive, and he had an old-world gallantry that appealed to her. She used to go to Costco to buy food for the house, and none of the men would help her. John did.

They started sneaking out for coffee and talking. He showed her the book *Murder Machine*, which was about the mob. He had read it more than once and stuffed it with articles about his father. He seemed proud of it.

One day, Denyce told her father, who was originally from New York, that she had a new boyfriend. "What's his name?" her father asked.

"John Franzese," she replied.

Her father paused and said, "Sonny's kid?"

Denyce gasped. She couldn't believe it. Neither could her father. "Stay away," he told her.

She didn't. He would leave sweet cards on her windshield as tokens of affection and sweep her up in warm embraces. He completely won her over by the way he treated her young son, Hunter. John was like a man-child, constantly playing with him. Often he'd take Hunter out, saying, "C'mon, Hunter, let's get outta here, just us guys!" Hunter loved the attention.

They moved in together, and a few months later, they broke up. Then in October 2003, John had a heart attack and was hospitalized. She went to see him. He asked her to sneak him a cheeseburger. She didn't, but it was enough to rekindle their relationship.

* * *

By 2004, John rekindled another relationship—his work for the FBI. He had been working on developing a mob-based television show. It was to be centered on his father, but he had met the producer in Alcoholics Anonymous, not through his father. This project was going to be his, and it was the first time in his life he could claim to have done anything on his own. Word got back to New York, and his cousin showed up in Los Angeles, wanting to know how he could shake down the producer. John was furious. As he saw it, guys in New York had no right to a piece of his business.

It pushed him over the edge. He reached out to Lewicki in October 2004.

Lewicki was receptive. "Listen, you know what, these guys, you don't owe them anything," the FBI agent told him. "They've never done anything for you. When you were down and out in the street, did anybody come and help you? Nobody did."

His words struck a chord with John. He thought about it and called him back. He told Lewicki that he wanted to atone for all the bad things he had done in his life, but it was clear there was something else motivating him—payback. He was so angry that hoods from his former life wanted to hurt his friend, a legitimate guy. He and Lewicki talked some more, and John finally closed the deal by saying, "I'm in."

John Jr. was trying to break away from his old life, but he had always lived off his father's name. The only way he could break away was to live off his father's name again. No FBI agent would have been interested in a low-level street hood like John unless he could lead them to someone bigger.

This time, John was going beyond anything he had done before. He agreed to wear a recording device. The position he put himself in could not have been more fraught. Sonny, out on parole again, had returned at the age of eighty-eight to his old business, and John was still his trusted messenger. If John's wire turned up evidence, he would have to testify. Even if he didn't ensnare his father, the cost would be huge. He knew that anyone in that life who vouched for an informant would wind up dead. Not only was he putting his life at risk, he was putting the lives of his father and anyone else who vouched for him in jeopardy.

By Thanksgiving that year, he and Denyce got married on the spur of the moment and lived in a Section 8 apartment John had been able to get because of his HIV status. It was a hard-to-get garden apartment at the end of a residential street. They settled into a comfortable domesticity.

John used to meet a man at their apartment, and John would make Denyce go in the backyard when he pulled up to the house. She didn't think much about it.

Tina left California, having been evicted from her apartment for failing to pay the rent, and moved back to Long Island into a condo in Northport, a waterside community on Long Island. When Sonny got out on parole, she refused to let him come home to her. He moved in with a sister, but started working on Tina, giving her money and expensive gifts.

At the time, Sonny had been elevated to Colombo family underboss. Carmine "the Snake" Persico, who was still in prison, needed someone he could trust. It was the kind of promotion that not only elevated Sonny's stature in the family, it increased his potential earning power exponentially because so many more men would be kicking up to him. It was also the kind of thing that impressed Tina. Sonny left his sister's house and moved in with Tina.

Word of Sonny's new status circulated swiftly among the ranks. In a recorded jailhouse conversation between Bonanno boss Joseph "Big Joey" Massino and acting Bonanno boss Vincent "Vinny Gorgeous" Basciano, they discussed Sonny's promotion. Massino marveled at his age. "He has gotta be eighty-seven! How much more does he got to live?"

Basciano didn't think Sonny's age was a hindrance. "He's in some shape," he said. "He might live to be one hundred."

Sonny, for his part, was cautious. When people came up to congratulate him on being a boss, he'd say, "Ah, nah, I'm no boss. I'm under him. I'm not the boss."

And he warned John to say the same thing, "'Cause the same cocksucker that talked to you'd be the first guy to rat you out."

John decided that he and Denyce should visit his family for Christmas. John wanted his family to meet his wife, but they didn't have the money for airfare. He knew he could count on his father. As cheap as Sonny was, he never denied his children. Sonny paid for the trip, not knowing he was paying for his own son to come and betray him.

When they arrived, Sonny was sweet to Denyce and grandfatherly toward Hunter. But in Tina's eyes, he couldn't do anything right, and she carped at him constantly. Once, Hunter was hungry and the only thing Sonny could find in the kitchen was a hot dog, so he cooked it and cut it up. Hunter, by then, was twelve, and certainly didn't need his food cut up, but he didn't say anything. When Tina saw this, she yelled, "What a fucking idiot!"

Denyce and Tina took an instant dislike to one another. A stupid argument erupted while she and John were watching television, when Little Tina accused her of not taking care of the dog. Denyce suddenly found herself in a physical fight, with big Tina trying to push her over a bannister. John broke it up, yelling, "Mom, stop! You're going to kill her!"

Rattled, he called Michael. Michael wasn't home, so he explained the situation to Cammy, who burst out laughing and asked him to hand the phone to Denyce. "Welcome to the family!" she chortled.

Unbeknownst to them, FBI agents heard many of Tina's outbursts. Sometimes, when Sonny pulled up to the house—with another informant who was secretly wearing a wire—Tina would greet him at the door screaming about money. Sonny would try to gently rebuke her, telling her, "Don't be a son of a gun."

When he'd get back in the car with the informant, he'd apologize, saying, "I just love her."

FBI agents couldn't believe that a man they knew as a cold-blooded killer would allow his wife to humiliate him like that. It was surprising, but also, in its own way, touching. Sonny never would have tolerated abuse like that from anyone else. Tina was his weakness.

John and Denyce returned to California, but John kept making trips back to New York, funded by the FBI. Denyce thought the trips were for his television show.

While in New York, John got wired up. Agents gave him a transmitter the size of a flip phone and told him to put it in his top pocket. He was sure they were trying to get him killed. The transmitter was heavy and so obvious that it might as well have said FBI on it. It felt like a neon sign. When John saw his friends, like any old-school Italian, he'd kiss them hello. There was no way he could put it in his shirt pocket.

"Rob, I'm a little nervous about this thing," he told Lewicki.

Lewicki told him not to worry, that he should wear cargo pants and put it in the pants pocket. John couldn't believe it. With all the years of experience that the FBI had with electronic surveillance, that was the best they could come up with?

But the cargo pants gambit actually worked. John felt a lot more comfortable and got to work. In March 2005, the FBI announced a major mob takedown, resulting in the indictment of thirty-two Gambino family associates for a range of crimes, from extortion to illegal gambling, which brought in $30 million. An undercover FBI agent had infiltrated the crew of Gambino capo Gregory "Greg" DePalma, who used a nursing home—where he visited his son, who was bedridden in a coma—as a cover for top-secret meetings with his associates.

Sonny watched that news apprehensively and discussed it with John and John's cousin, acting Colombo capo Michael Catapano.

Catapano told Sonny about a couple of Bonanno associates he

hadn't seen around lately. He thought they might be on the lam. Sonny agreed and concluded that they were hiding out because "they must have got information" that the feds were about to make a bust.

Sonny had never liked DePalma, which he made clear: "I always felt . . . I always thought Greg DePalma was an undercover rat. I always felt that way. I done time with the guy, everything. The guy was never no good. The guy would . . . The guy was introducing us to rats. There was a kid there . . . I forget his name . . . in Otisville wanted to go at Greg DePalma. Because the guy in the club, the guy he's partners with, was visiting him on more than one occasion and the kid was going bananas. How could you make a rat come and visit you? And you're introducing him to everybody."

Sonny had no idea of the irony of his comments. John was getting it all on tape.

Sonny told them to monitor the situation with the Gambinos.

"It's not a question that we're interfering with their businesses," he said. "It's a question of their business could affect us. Everybody, all five, all five families, could get locked up."

Catapano said he'd be meeting DePalma that night. "Listen closely what he tells you. Listen closely. And repeat every word the way he said it so we can get an idea how he's really thinking," Sonny told him. "'Cause I believe there's something wrong with this guy."

They discussed another problem that day. John was supposed to pick up a payment from a hair salon owner named Carmine, who had welshed on his debt. Sonny had loaned him $25,000 more than four years earlier, and now, with the accumulated vig, his debt was close to $200,000. Another man, Peter, an attorney, was supposed to come up with half the money, but Carmine kept on giving him stories about where the money was.

John complained about how difficult they were to deal with.

"I said, 'Peter, should you do legal work for free?'

"He said, 'No, I would never do that.'

"So I said, 'Who the fuck? What am I, [do I] look like an idiot?'

"Like he says, 'Well, what, are you gonna come after me?'

"I said, 'Listen, motherfucker,' and Carmine jumped in. Right in the street . . . Carmine jumped in and said, 'Don't even go there, don't even go there.'"

Sonny listened and said, "Well, it seems . . . when you tell me a story, you gotta tell me the whole story. I would have grabbed Carmine and told him, 'Look, you motherfucker rat bastard, go out there and get the money and bring it here! Not [twenty-five hundred]. Five thousand.' And if he don't give it to you, leave him on the floor."

John told his father he was sure Carmine had the money, so Sonny came up with a solution. "You know what you wanna do, John?" Sonny said. "You tell Carmine to come and see ya. Tell him to come and see you, not you go and see him."

John agreed.

"And tell Carmine point-blank, 'Go and get the money, you cocksucker. Your . . . your days are over, and you mother, cocksucker, you fucked people enough. Your days are over.'"

Sonny made it clear that he hated deadbeats and rats.

He had no idea his favorite son was both.

CHAPTER 23

The Tapes

"They don't know they don't need us."

COLOMBO ASSOCIATE Joe DiGorga was worried. He heard that two men who operated the Hustler Club, a strip club on West 51st Street in Manhattan, started by pornographer Larry Flynt, had testified before a grand jury.

"I'm in a lotta fuckin' hot water right now," Joe D told John and Sonny.

"Well, did they give you any money, them guys," John said. "Them guys, can they testify they gave you money?"

Yes, they could, DiGorga replied, adding, "I think they're gonna fuckin' indict me."

The Hustler Club, decorated in a garish red-and-purple color scheme the owners deemed classy, billed itself as "upscale." More important to Sonny's crew, the place practically printed money. DiGorga was the advance man in an extortion scheme Sonny had wrested away from the Genovese family after a sit-down.

He liked to follow Sonny's favored method of extortion: Get friendly with the target, explain that someone else might be creating a problem, and then offer to handle it. As he told Sonny: "It's like you used to tell me, you can't go in and bang their brains out."

Sonny replied, "No."

DiGorga continued, "You gotta go in, you gotta—"

Sonny cut in with, "Slow."

DiGorga concluded, "You gotta make yourself . . . be nice and easy. You gotta take it easy."

The important thing was not to make an explicit threat, but to create the appearance of one, which made the scam that much sweeter. Sonny always told John, with a chuckle: "They don't know they don't need us."

If, however, the appropriate tribute wasn't made, they could be more direct. One night, Sonny and Colombo associate Christopher Curanovic went to the Hustler Club and were shocked when they got a bill from the waitress. Furious at the insult, Curanovic grabbed the manager, shouted, "I should choke you to death" and demanded that he apologize. The manager quickly apologized to Sonny, even kissing his hand. The next time they came to the club, they were immediately shown to the best table in the place.

DiGorga worked out his own side deal with the club: Management paid him $2,000 a month as a consultant under a ten-year contract. Then he saw an opportunity to pull more money out: He pushed John Jr. to stick up the manager, who cashed out at the end of the night.

John didn't stick up the manager, because he was picking up all of it on tape for the government. Over the course of eight months, he recorded hundreds of hours of incriminating conversations. He wasn't merely a passive listener. Sometimes he was cagey, pretending to be confused so that the others would clarify what they said. Other times, he asked questions and goaded and guided the people he was recording, most of them either lifelong friends or relatives.

They talked constantly about money. Sometimes they discussed potentially legitimate deals, like a plan with some rappers to sell Gangsta Cigars, with one cigar line signed by Sonny. Mostly, though, they talked about how much money other people had and how they could squeeze it out of them for themselves.

Unlike most street guys, John was a good listener. He didn't have to dominate the conversation. And when it was just the two of them, his father let his guard down. Although John's handler later said the FBI never directed him to target his father, John taped more than one conversation with just him and Sonny. He understood what the FBI wanted, and he was going to get it for them.

One day, John brought up the Hustler Club to his father.

Sonny chided him. "Don't mention the fuckin' name, John."

John, like a petulant child, responded, "Well, I'm trying to figure out."

Sonny continued to scold him: "Learn how to be evasive. Whisper."

John complained that he wasn't happy with the way the guys at the Hustler treated him. "Let me put a girl in there," he told Sonny. "Like that, I'll show you how much money we'll make. Split her fuckin' tips with her. What, are you kidding? I know what to do in there. Talks to me like I don't know what I'm talking about."

Sonny dropped his guard so that he could soothe his son, and for the first time in their conversation, he said something incriminating: "Well, then, just keep doing what you're doing . . . Don't be pushy . . . Talk sensible . . . You're moving a guy without letting him know he's being moved. Then you're all right. That's what I want you to do."

Sonny always tried to protect John. When he wanted muscle, he could easily turn to other men. That was useful when they decided to move in on the Penthouse strip club. Sonny and Curanovic went there one night and again were surprised when they weren't comped. Curanovic dragged the manager to the edge of a flight of stairs in the storage room and threatened to throw him down the steps, unless he could come up with a way to rid them of the bill "before his head hit the ground." Their bill was comped.

During the time John made the tapes, Sonny actively worked the streets, even at the age of eighty-eight. He oversaw a crew engaged in a remarkable range of criminal activity, from illegal gambling to joker poker machines. At the same time that they were extorting the strip clubs, Sonny was trying to move in on the Garden City Hotel, a historic Long Island hotel, and Ciao Baby, a chain of Italian restaurants, as well as other businesses. No target was too small. He even moved in on a pizzeria, Cugini Due, in Albertson.

In 2000, Angelo Giangrande opened the pizzeria with his cousins, Antonio and Angelo Franzella. Their relationship eventually soured, and Giangrande offered to buy them out for $300,000. They had spent more than $525,000 to open the business, creating an inviting décor, with warm colors and soft lighting inside and umbrella-topped tables outside. The Franzellas weren't interested in selling at such a steep discount.

Giangrande had known Sonny for years and liked throwing around his name. Sonny never minded somebody using his name, because it meant that he'd get his cut. Giangrande turned to Sonny's loyal acting capo, Michael Catapano, and paid him $30,000 to persuade his cousins to get out.

Catapano immediately made an impression on them. One day, he recounted the story to John and Frank "Franky Camp" Campione, Sonny's driver.

He bragged that Antonio Franzella "sees the fuckin' Devil when he sees me."

John chimed in, "Yeah, he abused him."

"I had abused him one day in the fuckin' parking lot," Catapano continued.

Antonio countered that his lawyer told him he didn't have to do anything.

"Let me tell you something," Catapano snarled. "That ain't on the fuckin' table no more. We ain't waiting."

He stepped up his campaign when he visited a hair salon and spa in Williston Park owned by Angelo Franzella. As he told John and Campione, he walked into the salon and said, "Ooh, this is a nice place. I like this place."

John laughed appreciatively.

"I said, 'I could do a lotta things over here.' Nobody said a word. Ya know, and then I says, 'Listen, whattaya think? You gonna talk to your brother?'

"'Yeah, yeah, please don't come toward the customers. They get nervous.'"

John laughed again.

"I said, 'What are you talking about?'"

Angelo begged him to leave the customers alone and not come back. His mother was in a chair, getting her hair done. When she saw Catapano walk in, she fainted. For a moment, Catapano felt bad about her, but only for a moment. He focused on the task at hand.

"I won't come back unless you can do what I gotta ask you to do," Catapano told Angelo. "Otherwise, I gotta come back."

John chimed in, still laughing, "You got a lot of friends with long hair."

A return visit turned out to be unnecessary, however. "Once I showed up in there, then they fuckin' signed the papers. It was all over," Catapano said.

The Franzellas sold the pizzeria to Giangrande for his price and got out. Sonny was paid $10,000.

John was so good in his new role that Sonny proposed him once again as a goodfella. It was a major development. Inwardly John didn't see himself as a gangster. The people he was recording weren't his friends anymore. It wasn't his life. He was working for the government. And yet, on another level, he was genuinely pleased and proud to be proposed; it was a special sign of status in his father's world.

To Sonny, it was a way of making sure his family was taken care of after he was gone.

Sonny told Catapano, who was his nephew, "I'm just trying to make things for you and John so you can have a decent living."

As Catapano and John discussed John becoming a goodfella, Catapano talked about who would sponsor him and offered to do it, a significant favor. John told him he didn't mind who did it, but said, "Truthfully, I'm closer to you than I am with anybody."

It was true. They were close, and not just because they were cousins. John was easy to be around. Like his father, he was an expert at reading people. He always calibrated his responses to make sure they felt at ease.

John assured Catapano they'd continue to be close. "We'll be together . . . We're solid, me and you."

That's what Catapano thought, and he took his role of family protector seriously. He watched the activities of other families warily and warned Sonny when something didn't seem right, as with John Gotti Jr. One day, he told Sonny that another goodfella thought Gotti Jr. was "gonna go bad . . . They were watching 'im. They think he's going bad."

This was not news to Sonny. "I told you that how long ago?" he said.

Sonny later authorized a hit on Gotti Jr. for just that reason, saying that he had met with the crew from Howard Beach— Gotti's home turf—and had given his consent.

Catapano worried about felons getting close to Sonny, causing him to violate his parole again. He talked to John about shielding Sonny, and seemed to worry about that far more than John ever did. John actually complained about having to spend so much time around his father.

Sonny had gotten a job to satisfy his probation officer. This time around, he worked—or more accurately, held court—at Polito Bakery, located in New Hyde Park, run by an old friend. It was an authentic Italian bakery, with much of the space devoted to ovens in the back for baking the fresh bread it was known for. The front part of the store was small and spartan, with linoleum floors and a small table and chairs in the corner. That's where Sonny camped out.

If a customer picked out something Sonny deemed unworthy, he'd say, "You don't want that! It ain't fresh!" Then there was the steady stream of visitors who came to see him who, of course, wanted to sample the wares without paying. Polito got so exasperated that he gave John a wad of cash and said, "Get him outta here. Take him out to lunch and don't come back until a half hour before we close."

Sonny was far better at lining up business for John and Catapano, but a dark cloud always hung over him—Michael Franzese's decision to testify and leave the life. It was the deepest
possible humiliation for Sonny, a man who had done a fifty-year
prison stretch because he refused to cooperate, to have a son who
turned. Most men didn't dare bring up the subject—either out of
respect or abject terror—but some loudmouths did, just to make a
point.

One day, while at Marzullo's Bakery, also in New Hyde Park,
Sonny told John and Franky Camp about an argument he had
with Frank "Chickie" Leto. When Sonny was in prison, one of his
soldiers, Louie Fenza, was moved to Leto's crew. Fenza had
some good moneymaking operations, including the extortion of
the Huntington Townhouse, a popular Long Island catering facility. When Sonny got out, he wanted Fenza and his earning power
back with him. Leto would have none of it. He told Sonny:
"Louie's with me."

Sonny recalled the conversation: "We're talking, me and him,
and, 'Yeah, what are you worried about *marrone* Louie Fenza?
Why don't you worry about your son Michael? That he's a rat,
he's a rat, you cocksucker!'

"I went up, I went at him, like a maniac. That other piece of shit
Ralphie Lombardo's holding me, the other, they're holding me,
nobody's holding him. I couldn't—I coulda killed the son of a
bitch. If I was in good health, I woulda slit his fuckin' throat off."

The fight went no further, but the wound was still raw for
Sonny and his entire family. One day, John Capolino, another
cousin, told John Jr. he had gone after another man with a black-
jack because he had accused him of standing with a rat—
Michael.

"I wanted to kill. I told your father, 'I'm gonna kill this rat.'"

The man was a member of the Bonanno crew. Capolino told a
couple of goodfellas, "I wanna fuckin' kill this kid.

"And they're like, 'No, you know, lemme see, let me go to
their people.'

"I said, 'I don't wanna go to their fuckin' people. Let me just fuckin' do it.'

"I should've never went to them in the first place. I shoulda did it on my own."

John listened and agreed. "Yeah, naturally."

Capolino said he regretted backing off, but assured John, "It ain't over. I'm gonna get this motherfucker."

Capolino eventually went after the man with a rifle, but two other guys stepped in and stopped him.

Guys like that drove Capolino crazy, not just because of the rat insult, but because in his view, he never should have been made in the first place. He was appalled at how far the Mafia's standards had fallen and complained about it to John.

"They run a red light, and they give 'em a fuckin' button. It's unbelievable," he moaned.

If making the recordings was a strain on John, he didn't show it. He had spent his entire life around predators; he could handle it. But he needed to make some money. The FBI paid him, but he wasn't living lavishly. He was traveling back and forth between New York and California and gave Denyce $500 a month toward the rent, but he'd wind up asking for it in small "loans" throughout the month. She put the $500 in a sock drawer, because she knew she'd be giving it all back to him anyway.

Since becoming sober, John had become a fitness buff. He worked out daily, sometimes twice a day. Inevitably, he came across guys dealing in steroids, and he saw an opportunity. At least, that's what he told people. It was his cover story from the FBI.

Lewicki and the FBI got a shock when they learned that John had borrowed $10,000 from Catapano, at three points a week, or $300 a week in interest. John told Lewicki he needed the money for personal expenses. He told Catapano he needed it for his steroid business, but they also discussed doing some extortionate loans together. Interestingly, he did not tape the conversation he had with Catapano about the $10,000 loan.

Whether it was for his own steroid business or the loans was unclear, but it didn't make any difference to the FBI. In November 2005, they shut him down. It was expressly against the rules for a confidential witness to engage in illegal activity. Lewicki told John he could continue cooperating, but that he could not proactively reach out to anyone he had previously recorded. He could return phone calls, and he could tape those. The FBI continued paying him, but a significantly reduced amount.

When he returned to California, Denyce and Hunter were thrilled to have him home. John and Denyce didn't socialize with Michael, even though Michael lived only a few miles away. Their real family was the sober community, and they frequently saw friends in coffeehouses and restaurants. Because she still had money left over from the sale of her house, Denyce always paid. She'd slip John $100 under the table so he could be the man. He always kept the change.

Once, he asked her if she'd like to move somewhere else and start a completely new life. She didn't take him seriously. Her life and her family were in California; she couldn't imagine moving. Then one day, John gave her a business card and said, "If anything happens to me, call this person."

"Yeah, okay," she said, not thinking anything more of it. She lost the card.

More and more, though, John went out with his friends. They didn't like her, and she didn't like them.

Then one night, on September 17, 2006, they had a stupid argument over something small. John told her he was going to spend the night at his friend Joel's place. She threw a bag of tennis balls at him in anger. John ignored it and said, "Love you, D, see you in the morning."

He didn't come home the next morning. At first, she didn't think much of it. Then Spado, worried about a marijuana deal he had discussed with John, called her.

"Where's John?" he asked her.

"I don't know, Ori," she replied.

He said nothing more. The next day, Sonny called her, asking frantically, "Where's that son of mine?"

She didn't know, but she was starting to worry. Spado called again.

"The feds picked him up," he told her. "He wore a wire."

Denyce's head spun. She had no idea, and she didn't really believe it. She went to the police station and filed a missing person report. She returned a week later, and they said they had no open case on John Franzese. "The case is closed," a police officer told her.

Acting on Spado's advice, she went to the U.S. Marshals Service. Nothing. Then she went to the Social Security Administration.

"Here's my husband's Social Security number," she said. "I'd like to know whether he's dead or alive."

They told her the Social Security number she had for John was not connected to anyone.

Denyce didn't know where else to turn. She had run through her savings and had no more money to pay her rent. Worse, Hunter was crushed. He asked her, "Mom, do you think I'll ever see John again?" She changed the subject.

John had entered the federal Witness Protection Program, the very program started in 1968, after his father's associates years earlier had savagely beat a Long Island trucking company owner who feared for his life too much to testify against them.

Denyce never saw John again.

CHAPTER 24

A Protégé's Betrayal

"You can't have a body no more . . ."

WORD OF JOHN JR.'S BETRAYAL spread, but Sonny insisted it was a story planted by the government to rattle him and make him look like a rat by proxy. He wasn't entirely wrong. Lewicki and another agent broke the news to Sonny's loyal aide, Frank "Franky Camp" Campione as he was entering a Key Foods grocery store in New Hyde Park in early January 2007.

"Frank, John is with us. Tell the family. He's with the federal government, and he's safe," Lewicki said.

"I will do that," Campione said. "You have my word."

It was partly to ease the family's anxiety, because Lewicki knew that Tina was in a panic. She called him, crying, desperate to know where John was. Lewicki reassured her that John was fine, much to her relief.

But FBI agents also knew that it wouldn't hurt to rattle the old man. Keeping Sonny off balance was far better for them. He'd be more likely to make a mistake.

Outwardly, upon hearing the news, Sonny maintained his usual stoic demeanor. But then he got angry. He worried about how he might look. When he went to his regular appointment with his probation officer and wasn't arrested, it unnerved him. He became convinced that the FBI was leaving him out on the street to make it look as if he had condoned what John did.

He decided to go to the Dix Hills home of a younger man he

had been grooming for induction into the family, Gaetano "Guy" Fatato, to talk to him. When Sonny showed up unannounced, he explained to Guy's wife that he had heard her husband was ill and he wanted to check on him. Guy's wife, aware that Sonny was important in her husband's world, ushered him to the bedroom.

Fatato was groggy, as he was genuinely ill, but he woke up when he saw who was in his bedroom. Sonny wasted no words. He cocked his hand, tucking his thumb into his palm and jutting out his finger as if it were a gun. He told Fatato that he might have to "call" John and asked Fatato if he would help him do it.

Fatato understood exactly what Sonny was telling him: He wanted Fatato to help him kill his son. He said he would.

Sonny and Guy had gotten to know each other at federal prison in Otisville, New York. Fatato had done his time without flipping on anyone. To Sonny, that was a badge of honor. Though not a good-fella, Fatato had been around wiseguys his entire life. He had been a standout football player in high school in New Hyde Park, near Sonny's Roslyn home, but got involved with selling drugs, which was one of the things that landed him in prison. Like Sonny, he was a hustler, always looking for the next opportunity. And like Sonny, he was never wrong. If confronted with facts, he simply lied his way out of it. Guy and Sonny clicked.

After Sonny got out of prison in 2004, he and Fatato reconnected when Sonny stopped by Fatato's nightclub, the Mirage, in Westbury. The Mirage was a huge Egyptian-themed nightclub modeled after the Luxor Hotel and Casino in Las Vegas. It was the kind of splashy place that attracted guys on the make.

Fatato started driving him around. John often drove his father, but it was always Sonny taking him to his meetings. With Fatato, it was the other way around. He would take Sonny to his meetings. That appealed to Sonny. To him, Fatato was a moneymaking machine, which was very good for Sonny.

"I wanna groom you," Sonny told Fatato. "It takes time, and it'll take a little time . . . but I want you to meet everybody."

The two of them became closer. Sonny liked Guy's hustle and

toughness. At six-two and 220 pounds, Fatato cut an imposing figure. Physical violence didn't bother him, and he embraced the life in a way John didn't. Sonny took him under his wing and started schooling him, sharing secrets with him. He liked to hold court and tell old-time mob stories with him—like the way he forged a critical alliance with Carmine Persico after he hid evidence of a murder for him.

More confidences spilled out, like how Sonny was actually there when the commission "signed the death warrant" for Murder Inc. mob boss Albert Anastasia. Then there was the time Al Capone got slashed in the face.

Fatato wasn't particularly interested in mob history, but the mechanics of murder held his attention. He listened when he and Sonny were talking about the case against then-acting Colombo boss Alphonse Persico in the presumed 1999 murder of William "Wild Bill" Cutolo, a Colombo family member who had sided with Orena in the Persico-Orena war. It was Sonny who explained the importance of making sure a body disappeared:

"You can't have a body no more," Sonny counseled him. "It's better to take that half an hour, that hour, to get rid of the body than it is to leave it on the street."

It was clear Sonny knew what he was talking about. He explained that he wore nail polish on his fingertips to avoid leaving fingerprints and he advised Fatato to wear a hairnet to avoid leaving any stray hairs. And he bragged that he had "done a lot of work" for the family in the 1950s and 1960s.

He even boasted that a newspaper once reported the he was responsible for hundreds of murders.

The FBI was listening to all of it. Fatato was wired.

At the time, Fatato had opened another club, the Rare Olive Lounge, a jazz club in Huntington, with dark-stained hardwood floors, velvet-covered bar stools, and free drinks for women. He had even created a user-friendly website loaded with positive reviews to drive traffic to the club. Sonny frequently stopped by and, as was his habit, never paid. Fatato understood the importance of tribute to Sonny. Whenever he showed up, Fatato handed him an envelope of money.

The envelopes came from the FBI. Agents were banking on Sonny's greed blinding him to any warning signals, and they were right.

In 2004, one of those warning signals flared. Colombo associate Christopher Curanovic heard that Fatato had been arrested in Nassau County on another drug charge and was "whisked" out of the jail. Alarmed that he might have become an informant, Curanovic asked Ori Spado to warn Sonny. Spado did, but Sonny didn't believe him.

"No, I know the guy," Sonny said. "I guarantee him."

In fact, Curanovic's instincts had been accurate. Fatato had been caught selling five ounces of methamphetamines to an informant and knew the cops had him cold. He was facing ten more years in prison, the last thing he wanted to do. There was something else gnawing at him.

Louis Dorval, the man whose body was found in a box floating off Fire Island, ten years earlier, had been Fatato's friend. Worse, Fatato knew that he could have been the body in the box.

In the early 1990s, Fatato ran with Dorval and another man, Christian Tarantino. The three of them constituted a crime wave all their own. They sold cocaine, stole bearer bonds, and staged home invasions. In one December 1993 home invasion, they pistol-whipped a woman and forced a man into a shower and used a Taser on his genitals. Their crimes were frenetic, nonstop, and violent.

Dorval and Fatato were close. Dorval confided in Fatato about an armored truck heist that had gone terribly wrong in June 23, 1994. Dorval, Tarantino, and two other men had ambushed the guards of the Mid-Island Check Cashing company as they delivered the weekly payroll to a graphics business in Syosset. They forced both men to lie facedown in front of the store. As they handcuffed one of the guards, Dorval shot the other, Julius Baumgardt, in the back of the head, killing him. The robbers wore masks—one of them a Halloween mask of a pig—and got away with nearly $100,000 in cash.

Shortly after that heist, later on in the summer of 1994, Fatato went to Umberto's Pizzeria, located in New Hyde Park, to discuss a marijuana deal with Dorval and Tarantino. Dorval stepped out to discuss business with another man, leaving Fatato alone at a table with Tarantino. Fatato tried to make conversation:

"I asked Chris what the . . . happened with the armored car," Fatato later testified. "He looked at me with this cold kill stare and said, 'I had nothing to do with it.'"

That stare unnerved Fatato. He never forgot it.

Shortly after that trip to Umberto's, Fatato learned he had been indicted for selling stolen fur coats and cashing $100,000 worth of stolen bearer bonds. (Secret Service agents successfully traced the bearer bonds to him, because he had been eating potato chips while handling them, leaving perfect fingerprint impressions.) He decided to spend the weekend on Fire Island before turning himself in. Dorval called him there and said Tarantino wanted to pick him up in his boat. He declined. Something didn't feel right.

Fatato returned from Fire Island and surrendered to authorities. While in jail, he called his fiancée. She had terrible news: "Louie's dead. They found him in the ocean, in a box."

The case would remain unsolved for years, but Fatato knew.

After turning himself in, he promised to cooperate, but then changed his mind. He wound up serving about three years on the charges. Over the years, he toyed with the idea of cooperating, but could never quite get himself to do it.

However, by his drug arrest in 2004, he made up his mind. He'd do it. FBI agents, in a nod to his high-school football career, gave him the code name "Audible" for the last-minute change to a play that a football quarterback makes.

FBI agents give confidential sources code names for a simple reason—they don't want someone to slip up and mention the person's name. The anonymity of a source is sacrosanct. Audible fit Fatato well. He was a cut above when it came to being crafty and thinking on his feet, and he moved in and out of dicey situations easily.

He got to work.

Guy Fatato wore a wire for two years, beginning in December 2005, making 242 recordings, covering more than one thousand hours of conversations. He was indefatigable. He was able to elicit information from people by asking questions—but not too many, which would be an immediate tip-off.

In the world of wiseguys, asking questions is tricky, not only for the obvious reasons, but because wiseguys are know-it-alls. Asking too many questions can cause someone to lose status. Fatato managed it well, even when the conversations turned grisly.

One night, they were at the Rare Olive, and Sonny amazed his FBI audience listening to the recording with his ability to toggle from the mundane to the murderous in one conversation. He'd flirt with the waitress, suggest the kind of marble Fatato should install at his club, and then casually talk about how to get rid of a body. He'd talk about dismembering a body in a kiddie pool and then using a restaurant oven—he always did love pizza ovens— to dry out the severed parts.

Fatato asked him, "What do you do with the skull?"

Sonny, who by then was getting hard of hearing, said, "Huh?"

"The skull! The skull! What do you do with the skull?" Fatato shouted over the din.

"Huh?" Sonny repeated.

"What about the skull? The head! It won't fit!"

"Oh!" Sonny replied, explaining that you would tap it so it would crack, and then, "You put it in the microwave."

And after it dried out in the microwave, it could be broken up and stuffed down a commercial-grade garbage disposal, he advised.

In fact, Sonny was personally hopeless at operating simple kitchen appliances, like a microwave or garbage disposal, but he certainly knew how to direct others to use them.

*   *   *

One day, Sonny had Fatato drive him to Roma Furniture, Michael Persico's place in Brooklyn. On the way there, Sonny explained his long-standing ties to them. Junior Persico's brother Alphonse "Allie Boy" Persico had been locked up for the murder of long-shoreman Steve Bove in 1951. Sonny learned who the rat was in the case and was prepared to kill him, until then-boss Joseph Profaci called him off. Nonetheless, Sonny got rid of the car used in the murder, evidence that could have meant the death penalty.

"Allie Boy couldn't get the chair, and that's how we became very friendly," Sonny said.

When they arrived, Michael was standoffish. He didn't grant Sonny the kind of respect other street guys did. Sonny was so well-regarded that even Albanian gangsters in New York dropped his name, but not Michael Persico. Sonny whispered to him, "Tell your brother about my son, but don't worry, he can't hurt anybody."

He then told Michael to "tell Pop and Allie" (after the death of his uncle Alphonse "Allie Boy" in 1989, Alphonse "Little Allie Boy," Carmine's son, and Michael's brother, occasionally graduated to the "Allie" moniker without the diminutive) that he had been with them since the beginning and "would never leave until I die. Guys don't understand, where you were born, you stay."

The meeting concluded quickly, and in the car ride home, Sonny explained to Fatato that Michael "was important to the family," even though he wasn't a made man. "He don't have to be a goodfella. He's doing a different kind of work. One day, I'll explain that to you. Sometimes there's even things I can't tell nobody."

Sonny's freewheeling confidences to Fatato were great for agents building a case, but also worrisome. He had, after all, asked their informant for help in killing his own son. The FBI is obligated to warn any target of such a threat. But by May 2007, the problem was solved. Authorities sent Sonny back to prison—this time the federal penitentiary in Elkton, Ohio—on a fifth parole violation for repeatedly consorting with felons. The information had come from John Jr. Sonny was arrested when he showed up for his regular meeting with his probation officer.

Just a few months after Sonny went away again, Fatato heard some startling news. He and some partners ran a gambling club called the Party Palace in Lindenhurst. They kicked up 20 percent of the profits off the top to Sonny and the Colombos, and Sonny had been actively involved in the operations. The startling news was that two idiot robbers held up the place and got away with $40,000.

In September 2007, the club hosted its weekly high-stakes Texas Hold 'Em poker game. Two young guys, Christopher Verderosa and Andrew "A.J." DeMarco, busted out—in other words, were cleaned out—and left to get more money. The only way to get into the club was to be buzzed in. When they got back to the club, they let in two other men—who happened to be armed with shotguns.

The robbers fired a couple of shells into the walls and took almost everybody's wallets. Miraculously, Verderosa and DeMarco managed to keep theirs. They left quickly.

The wallet lapse was an obvious tip-off to Michael Uvino, the Colombo capo who ran the club. He told Verderosa and DeMarco to meet him there, telling them that it was just to get everybody's money back. It was a cunning lie. If they didn't show up for that, they'd look guilty. They had little choice but to show. Fatato went along, too.

Once they were at the club, Uvino sat down with Verderosa in one room and DeMarco in another. Uvino started interrogating Verderosa.

"We wanted to talk to you about what happened last night. How did you get to the club last night?" Uvino asked.

"My mom dropped me off at the CVS across the street," Verderosa replied.

"Is that normal for your mom to drop you off?" Uvino asked.

Verderosa nervously told him it wasn't. Uvino continued his methodical questioning, asking how exactly it was that they let the stickup men into the club. Verdersosa tried to say they had shoved him to the ground, an obvious lie. Then Uvino said, "Lemme see your wallet."

Verderosa handed it to him.

"He didn't take your wallet?" Uvino said. "What are you, lucky or something?"

"I don't know," Verderosa said.

"What did you guys do after you left the club?" Uvino questioned.

"We went home," Verderosa said.

"You didn't go to A.J.'s house?" Uvino asked.

"No," Verderosa lied, increasingly uneasy. Uvino seemed to know where they went.

Brian Dono, Uvino's hulking associate, was sitting nearby and fuming. He couldn't take it any longer. "You called me a bitch!" he yelled, and he jumped up and decked him.

Uvino jumped in, stomping him. Then he grabbed a metal chair and tried to crush Verderosa's throat with it.

"I'll kill your wife! Your kid!" Dono screamed. "Who's the bitch now?"

"Please don't kill me!" Verderosa begged. "I'll do anything you want!"

DeMarco heard his screams and came running in. They started beating him. DeMarco cried and screamed, "Daddy, stop! Daddy, stop! Please, Daddy!"

They pistol-whipped them and stuck the revolvers in their mouths, threatening to pull the triggers if they didn't give up the names of the stickup men.

"Do you want to walk out of here alive, or do you not want to walk out of here alive?" Uvino shouted.

They gave up the names.

It turned out that Verderosa had butt-dialed Uvino at 5 a.m. the day after the robbery. Uvino and Dono heard Verderosa and DeMarco laughing about the robbery and saying that Dono was so scared he had "acted like a bitch."

After the beating, Uvino and the others debated whether to kill their victims. Fatato intervened. DeMarco had texted his girl-friend: If you can't find me, I'm at the club. Any detectives in-vestigating the murders would look at a text like that, and it would point back to them.

That message saved their lives.

And Fatato got it all on tape.

It was absolutely chilling. As U.S. District Court judge Joan Azrack later said of Uvino: "I've never had a situation where there was more clear and convincing evidence that this defendant is a danger to the community . . . I mean that tape says it all."

The FBI had to immediately shut down the operation and get warrants to arrest Uvino and his associates at 6 a.m. the next day. They had less than twelve hours to get Fatato and his family into hiding, but Fatato was busy. For months, he had been refurbish-ing the Rare Olive and planning a grand reopening. The reopen-ing was that very night.

Fatato's FBI handler tried calling him, but he didn't answer. Around 3 a.m., agents went to the club, which was packed with revelers. They managed to get Fatato outside and explained to him that they had to relocate him, his wife, and two small chil-dren. Thinking it was a joke, Fatato was not amused.

"This is not the night to fuck with me," he said.

They assured him they weren't. Within hours, they packed up the family and moved them.

Word of Fatato's cooperation spread fast, and the damage to Sonny's reputation stung. Not only had he trusted his drug addict son John, but he had vouched for Fatato, even after Curanovic had warned him. Friends were told to stay away.

At home, Tina was threatened with eviction because she hadn't paid the rent on her Northport condo. It couldn't have come at a worse time. Her daughter, Little Tina, who had battled health problems all her life, was seriously ill with cancer. Medical bills were piling up.

Then on June 4, 2008, the Eastern District of the U.S. Attorney's office in New York announced a seventeen-count indictment against twelve mobsters. Any press release about mobsters generates news coverage, but the story of a geriatric gangster—Sonny was ninety-one years old—shaking down strip clubs and a pizzeria made it front-page news.

Three days later, Little Tina died of cancer at the age of forty-three.

CHAPTER 25

John Testifies

"It doesn't bother me no more . . ."

THE U.S. MARSHAL SERVICE didn't take any chances when they picked up John for the trial. They zipped him up in a Kevlar-like sack and put him in the back seat of a literally rocket-proof SUV with tinted windows. John sat in total darkness as they drove—and, worse, he couldn't smoke. When he got out, they led him to a little staircase leading to a vault. They opened it and walked through it to a control room. They went through two more doors, each more secure than the last, and finally reached their destination.

It was a small room, not much bigger than a jail cell. The door was sealed. He felt comfortable there, however. It would be John's home as he waited to do the unthinkable—testify against his father. The trial would be the first time he would see his father, or anyone else in his family, since he disappeared into WITSEC, the program that had become an essential crime-fighting tool of the government, the one started because of his own father.

The Witness Protection Program had been John Jr.'s ticket to freedom. When he wore a wire, he wasn't working off criminal charges or facing the prospect of prison. The freedom he was seeking was from his own life. He had grown up always worrying about his father going to jail, and as he got older, he worried about one of them getting killed. Once he started cooperating, he felt more secure with FBI agents than he had with his friends on the street. And he was hoping that maybe once in his life, he could do something on his own. At the age of fifty, he wanted to find out who he was without someone to lean on.

As he waited in the room, he read, wrote in his journal, and spoke daily to a close friend, a nun. By then, he was accustomed to spending a lot of time in silence. It wasn't hard for him at all.

The trial opened in June 2010. Sonny was out of prison on a $1 million bond and living with his daughter Lorraine in Brooklyn. Tina wanted nothing to do with him.

Sonny wasn't well. Ninety-three years old, he had recently suffered a heart attack and stroke and had hearing aids. He came to the courtroom, a sleek modern affair trimmed in teak and marble, in a wheelchair. In contrast to the days when he had high-powered and very expensive attorneys defending him, this time around, he had a court-appointed attorney. He was, in the words of the court, indigent and therefore entitled to a taxpayer-funded defense.

As John took the stand, wearing a green T-shirt and gold cross, there was a frisson of excitement in the air. He clearly was the star of the trial. For the first time in his life, he would be the center of attention, the one everyone looked to, not his father and not his brother.

The prosecutor asked him to identify his father, who was seated at the defense table with his codefendants. Even in court, the street guys paid attention to rank. Sonny, as the highest-ranking Colombo, sat closest to the lawyers. John pointed toward him and said, "He's the guy in the yellow shirt."

John's testimony had begun.

Tina sat in the press row with the reporters. She was worried about her son, still her favorite child. Although she professed not to care about Sonny, she did care about John Jr. Court proceedings are typically staid affairs, but not when Tina Franzese was around. She made a habit of disrupting her husband's many court hearings, and she was no different now. Onlookers were astonished when they heard screaming in the courtroom halls during a break in the proceedings.

Tina saw Sonny and screamed, "How dare you!"

Lorraine, who had accompanied her father to court, shouted back at her, "Leave him alone!"

Tina, seventy-five, but no less fiery than she was when she was younger, hip-checked Lorraine and commandeered Sonny's wheelchair, pushing him into the men's room. Bystanders heard her screaming at him to plead guilty and give John a break. "I never beat you!" she shouted. "Your mother beat you!"

"Son of a bitch!" Sonny shouted at her. "Shut up!"

A juror heard her screaming about Sonny's mistress.

Tina was frightened for her son, but she also hated the family secrets he was spilling on the stand. On his second day of testifying, he admitted he had HIV—something she had denied to friends and family for years. Worse, John knew she thought he'd collapse under the pressure.

"John was six years old when his father went to prison," she told a reporter. "What kind of childhood is that? When Sonny came out, he sent John on errands. He never let him alone.

"I was the best thing that ever happened to him. But I'm done with him. Finished."

Tina was given a ticket for disorderly conduct and banned from the courtroom.

John, despite his mother's fears, was resolute. He was, by turns, touching, down-to-earth, even folksy, on the stand. He parried the defense attorneys' attempts to rattle him with ease and never seemed to get ruffled. It was the performance of a lifetime, and he knew it.

He testified that Sonny was "a great father" who came to his baseball games to cheer him on. He described growing up not wanting for anything material. His father had a Learjet, they took vacations on the Concorde, and friends at school thought he was the "richest kid in the school." As a teenager, he spent $18,000 a month on clothes.

But he conceded that he had been a drug addict and street thug and that he felt "kind of broken" in life. He decided to wear a wire because "this life absorbs you and you only see one way. And when this thing happened to me in California, I realized there was a whole world out there that I missed, with people that work and try to do the right thing and actually followed other beliefs."

He came across as authentic. It couldn't have been worse for the defense attorneys. They went on the attack.

One attorney, clearly hoping to hit a sore spot, pressed him about entering Witness Protection without Denyce. "Did you leave your wife behind?" he asked.

John didn't take the bait. "Let's just say that my wife chose drugs over me," he said.

It was true that Denyce had battled drug addiction, but she had committed to living a sober life when she married John.

The attorney brought up a book John had written with a friend, *The John Franzese Story: Family Crime, Drugs, Redemption.* He asked whether John had been seeking to cash in on his father's name by trying to sell his life story.

John deftly pivoted to a different storyline. He said his co-writer had been a drunk he was helping and added, "That's part of the work that we do when we go and work in the sober living."

He even conceded that he wasn't above trying to make some money, especially given his reduced circumstances since opting out of a life of crime. "That wouldn't have been a bad avenue at that time," he said, sounding perfectly reasonable.

John didn't come across as a thug, but rather as a man who had changed his life. Like his father, John exuded a natural charm, and he had an uncanny ability to turn things around in a way favorable to him. It couldn't have been worse for the defense.

Another defense attorney, desperate to make John look bad, tried a different tack. He tried to turn John's own words against him.

"And for being a great father, you came here to testify against him, correct? That's the price he's paying, yes?" he asked.

"I am not here to testify because he's a great father," John replied coolly.

"You are an apparition? You are not here testifying before him?" the attorney shot back in mock shock.

John stood his ground. "I am here testifying that he is a member of organized crime," he said.

Stung, the defense attorney quickly dropped that line of questioning.

As he plowed through his questions, the attorney tried to rattle John by going through the transcripts of his recordings in excruciating detail. It was tedious, even for the other lawyers and the judge, who asked him to move it along. Sometimes that kind of technical questioning can throw off a witness. Not John. At one point, the attorney asked him to look at a specific passage, and John, the son of a feared gangster, said, "Okeydokey."

He seemed utterly relaxed.

Throughout his questioning, the attorney tried to make it look as if John had entrapped the defendants. John parried deftly. "I just showed up and kind of let them talk."

And so it went. The defense attorneys' shots at him seemed feeble and, at times, silly. When they called him a liar, he agreed that he had been, but then pointed out the obvious: It was all on tape. Every chance he could, John turned his testimony to talking about how he got sober. He even talked about the role that "grace" had played in his recovery. "I guess I was just ready, and at that moment, I just accepted something that happened to me instead of running away from it," he said.

John might be a rat, but he was appealing. It knocked defense attorneys off balance, but the government needed more than that. The whole purpose of having him on the stand was to provide the testimony to convict his father. They pressed their case.

On redirect examination, a prosecutor asked him, "Who gave you advice about loan-sharking?"

"My father," John replied.

"Who gave you advice about shaking people down?" she asked.

"My father," he said.

"Who gave you advice about what to do if someone did not pay what they were supposed to pay?"

"My father."

It was devastating testimony, and the courtroom audience was riveted.

As John looked over at his father, he saw a beaten man. Sonny, the fearsome mob boss who bragged about his body count, looked weak and old. In fact, he was both. He had to be taken to the bathroom with the help of an aide eight times a day. And he couldn't look at John. He looked down.

Although John knew exactly what he was doing to his father, he felt good. He knew he had handled himself well on the stand. He knew that his old friends—many of them seated in three rows behind the defendants—all thought he wouldn't be able to do it. They thought he was still getting high. It made him happy to show them that he was not the same person, even if the cost of that personal vindication was sending his elderly and sick father to the place he knew he hated the most—prison.

John insisted that he was testifying against the life, not his father. However, few people believed that distinction. It was his father, after all, who would pay the price of his testimony. Like some of his friends in recovery, John found comfort in platitudes and he clung to that one stubbornly.

Guy Fatato, the other informant who had taped Sonny, didn't testify. His appearance would lack the drama of a son betraying his father, but there was a bigger problem. His violent criminal history made him an easy target for defense attorneys, and they were itching to destroy him on the stand. But prosecutors, who had suffered through Fatato's disastrous performance when he was cross-examined in the Uvino trial, were ready. They had prepped him for this trial, and planned to use him to introduce Sonny's admissions on tape about murdering people—which would be a deathblow to the defense.

Although Fatato hadn't been able to record Sonny's threat to kill John, because Sonny had literally gotten him out of bed when he made it, he did record Sonny telling him that he would have to be willing to kill somebody at some point. And he got Sonny on tape bragging about all the people he had murdered.

In an effort to keep that out of the case, Sonny's court-appointed attorney, Richard Lind, called those statements the "Cagney-esque" hyperbole of a vulnerable old man. But Judge Brian Cogan didn't buy it, saying he thought Sonny had done "in substantial part that which he says he has done." More important, he said, he could do it again.

"He can always pick up the phone, he can always talk to people; and for somebody who holds his position in organized crime, that can do a lot of damage," he said.

There was no way Lind could insist that Fatato testify because, if he did, he could recount the chilling gesture Sonny made at his bedside. A jury would be highly unlikely to acquit a man willing to kill his own son.

For the prosecution, the end result was ideal: They could use the tapes and not have to deal with Fatato on the stand.

After nearly four weeks of trial, the jury rendered its verdict: guilty.

The *New York Post* couldn't resist the alliterative possibilities: GEEZER GANGSTER GUILTY.

Sonny remained impassive. He slid the belt out of his pants and reached into his pockets, taking out his wallet, coins, and a wad of business cards wrapped up in a rubber band. He handed all of it to his attorney. He knew all too well what to expect.

Though banned from the courtroom, Tina managed to hover around the edges, occasionally offering a quote to a reporter. After the verdict, she was predictably unsympathetic.

"They had all the tapes," she told a reporter. "What were they going to say? That everyone lied?"

It must have felt like a vindication for her. For years, she screamed that Sonny always lied to her, and that Michael and John went along with his lies. They treated her as if she were crazy. There were certainly days when she acted crazy, but now, she could point to the tapes. Sonny, always so careful and cagey, had been convicted by his very own words.

Tina tried to portray herself as someone who had tried to protect her children from their father's life. In reality, though, she had always known who Sonny was. For a time, she reveled in his power and his money. But now, the money was gone and her favorite child would disappear into the Witness Protection Program and out of her life. Michael's cooperation was bad enough; this was far worse. John was facing a street death sentence, and it terrified her.

When asked earlier by a reporter how he felt about the prospect of prison, Sonny had said, "Who cares? I gotta die someplace."

About six months later, the reckoning came. Prosecutors had prepared an extensive sentencing memo, describing Sonny's long and violent criminal history in the Mafia. They cited his dishonorable discharge from the U.S. Army for "homicidal tendencies," his threat to disfigure his first wife Anna's face with a knife, and that he was charged with raping a waitress in a garage in 1947.

Everyone in the courtroom knew that any sentence would very likely condemn him to dying in prison. Judge Cogan asked Sonny if he had anything to say. He started to mutter something about never having been given a fair shake by the government, until his attorney cut him off. "He has nothing to say, Judge."

Prosecutors decided to use all the ammunition they had at their disposal at the hearing. They hadn't been able to introduce Sonny's threat to kill John at the trial, but they could now. Vincent D'Agostino, Fatato's FBI handler, testified to that incident.

D'Agostino recalled Fatato's account of Sonny bursting into his bedroom and telling him that there might come a time when they would need to "call" John, as he formed his hand into the shape of a gun. Fatato, the FBI agent said, "interpreted that to mean that they would call and kill him."

He also said Sonny told Fatato he put the number of people he killed at around sixty.

Lind pointed out that Sonny had never followed up on his threat to kill John.

Then the lawyers debated the so-called "mitigating factors" that judges consider when determining how long a sentence should be.

Lind argued that Sonny was an old man, hobbled by a litany of serious medical conditions—gout, high blood pressure, impaired hearing, blindness in one eye, an attack of deep-vein thrombosis, a pacemaker, spinal stenosis, anemia, and chronic kidney disease.

He characterized Sonny as a gruff man, but also "insecure and vulnerable to people who would prey upon him," like his son. The claims of committing murders and using nail polish to mask his fingerprints were "pathetic boasts." He asked for a sentence of significantly less than three years because Sonny was "not a risk to the public at this point."

How Sonny, who once had been able to quiet a room with just a glance, felt about being described in such a pitiable way by his own lawyer wasn't clear. He said nothing.

Prosecutors pushed back hard.

"He's never known what it means to get up and go to work every day," said prosecutor Cristina Posa." He's essentially lived as a parasite off the hard work of others by shaking them down, not to mention his extensive and violent criminal history . . ."

She added, "He's largely responsible for the glamorization of the Mafia that has gone on in the past century in this country. Your Honor, I would ask the court to remember the saying 'Live by the sword, die by the sword.' He's lived a life devoted to crime. He's rejected his own family in favor of the Colombo family. For him to die now as a criminal in jail is not an inappropriate response to the lifestyle that he's lived."

She asked that Sonny be sentenced to twelve years in prison.

Judge Cogan acknowledged that Sonny's age and medical conditions were mitigating factors, but noted that when sentencing his codefendants, they cited Sonny's influence, saying they looked up to him as a role model. He clearly struggled with how much he should give him behind bars, noting that Sonny would very likely die there.

"I can't apply the factors in any way to get a sentence that he is likely to survive," he said.

Judge Cogan sentenced him to eight years.

Sonny entered prison in 2011.

Six years later, he surprised everyone. He was released on parole in June 2017, at age one hundred, the oldest inmate in the federal prison system.

Not long after his release, he said he had reached a certain peace about his years of imprisonment.

"It doesn't bother me no more, because I've been incarcerated so long. I was a prisoner. I couldn't do what I wanted to do. Now that I've got freedom, I'm tickled pink," he said.

Sonny had beaten them again. He was out.

CHAPTER 26

Regrets and Reconciliation

"Jesus suffered. He didn't squeal on nobody."

TINA HAD NO PLACE TO GO. She had been kicked out of her Northport condo because she didn't pay the rent. Michael wasn't giving her money, and John didn't have any. In prison and disgraced after John's testimony, Sonny had no more earning power. Though in her seventies, she managed to land a job at a high-end health club. Still, even with Social Security, it wasn't enough to carry her. Her credit history—she filed seven bankruptcies in all—made it impossible for her to con her way into another apartment, and Sonny's old friends were either dead or staying away.

Left alone, without the men who mattered most in her life, Tina became unmoored. She took her two dogs and started living out of her car. It was a stunning fall for a woman who wore only designer clothing and had hosted celebrities at her home. She was tough and she was proud, but she finally broke.

Tina called her former daughter-in-law Roberta and said, through sobs, "I'm homeless. I'm in my car with my dogs. Would you mind if I come and live with you?"

Roberta didn't hesitate. "Sure, Mom," she said. "Come on over. I'll meet you at the house."

Roberta had been married to Sonny's oldest son, Carmine, for ten years. Though their marriage ended in divorce, Roberta and Tina remained close. Roberta loved the way Tina had embraced her, including her in the big Italian Sunday dinners she hosted and family vacations in Montauk in a house that was rented, but Tina always claimed to own. When Roberta was a new mother and panicked over her babies teething or crying, she'd call Tina, who always calmed her down. She felt accepted in a way she had never felt before. Roberta had been adopted as a child and always felt she didn't quite fit in. With Tina and the Franzese family, she did.

Tina moved into Roberta's home in Selden. Before long, she moved in her own furniture, which she had kept in storage, and transformed the look and feel of the place. Roberta's home, a bit worn around the edges as she juggled work and family, suddenly looked like a bed and breakfast. Roberta didn't mind. In fact, she loved it. Tina promised to pay the utilities and did, for a while. Then she used Roberta's name to run up other bills, and things got tense. Tina filed for bankruptcy again—her final one—without telling anyone.

And then Tina became ill. A lifelong smoker, she had quit cold turkey when a doctor told her Sonny would outlive her. "To hell with that," she snapped, and she never smoked another cigarette. But the damage was done, and she was diagnosed with emphysema, chronic obstructive pulmonary disease (COPD), and breast cancer.

She and Michael were estranged. She was sure he had squirreled away millions from the gas tax scam, and it infuriated her that he didn't support her. Though she told friends that she couldn't stand him, her friends knew that she kept track of every appearance he made in his new career as an evangelical preacher, a mob guy saved by God.

Tina was sneaking calls to John, who was living in Indiana under the name "Mat Pazzarelli." It drew them closer. After years of group recovery meetings, John learned to listen to his mother without judging her or pushing back. He began to understand why she had been so angry for all those years. She had expected to be Sonny's partner in marriage, and she was anything but. Lies were the real currency of the Franzese home, and the lying drove her crazy.

As she got sicker, the calls stopped and John knew no way of contacting her. One day, she snapped at Roberta, something she hadn't done before. Later that day, Roberta realized Tina was having a stroke. Tina went to the hospital and then into hospice for her final days. Most of the family made it clear that they wanted nothing to do with her. One member of Michael's crew, Frank Castagnaro, visited her and was shocked to see how emaciated and beaten she looked from her illness. She was embarrassed to be seen like that, no longer beautiful. He left and implored Michael and others to go see her. They didn't.

Roberta begged Tina's family for help, but to no avail. One nephew and a longtime girlfriend visited, but no one else responded to her desperate pleas. Sonny called her from prison to exhort her to do more for Tina. "I'm doing everything I can, Dad," Roberta responded.

Tina died on April 8, 2012, at the age of seventy-seven. Michael made the funeral arrangements. He buried his mother, a woman known for her beauty and love of high fashion, in a hospital gown.

Sonny was in prison at the time. He described learning of her death through a dream he had. He dreamed he was on "an aeroplane" and saw a lot of faces in a cemetery. "I'm thinking, 'Hmm, they look familiar to me. Sure look at that . . . come here . . .'"

When he landed, "They tell me, 'We got some bad news to tell you, Sonny.'

"I said, 'What's that?'

"'Tina died.'"

The news hit Sonny hard. To be sure, they had been estranged, but he had been confident that when he got out of prison—and he was determined to get out—she'd be there.

"You know, it hurt," he said years later from his Queens nursing home. "But she's dead now. What can I do? Can't do nuthin' about it. But she was a fighter. If she was out, I'd never be here. If she didn't die, I'd never be here."

He hated living out his final days in a nursing home. "Well, you know what my tough break was, the mistake I made, is that I never hold on to a woman. Because if I hold on to a woman, I coulda lived with her. I coulda lived with her."

For all their marital battles, Tina always fought for him—and he knew it. "That's why I was hurtin' when she died. That's what I was mad about. When I needed her, she died."

Sonny got out of prison on parole in June 2017. He was 100 years old, the oldest inmate in the federal prison system. He never thought Tina would die before he did.

"Sorry she ever died, but I never figured she'd die. I figured the Devil didn't want her, and God didn't want her," he said, laughing.

"God bless her, wherever she is. May the good Lord have mercy on her, she went through hell. Gotta give her credit. She waited a lot of years for me, and to die like that, you know?"

John, stashed away in WITSEC, didn't attend her funeral. He had been closer to her than any other child in the family, and he couldn't go. He took solace in the fact that they had repaired their relationship near the end of her life. Still, he missed his family.

In hiding under his new identity, he had a regular routine. Every morning, he would send good thoughts to Michael, Carmine, Maryann, Lorraine, Gia, and Little Tina. Then he'd write what he was grateful for—his apartment, food, air-conditioning. He'd read, often spiritual writings, and he'd text affirmations to his friends. He liked sharing bits of wisdom he came across. He started writing in a journal every day. This onetime drug addict and street thug found comfort in writing down his feelings.

He went to church. Raised Catholic, he understood the teachings, but never really thought much about them. His parents made sure their children went through the Catholic rituals of baptism and confirmation, but little else. Sonny always made the sign of the cross when he passed a Catholic church, but that seemed more like a superstition than an act of devotion. To John, making the effort to go to church regularly just seemed like a good thing.

But for all the peacefulness of his new life, John was keenly aware that someone might find him and kill him. He knew what he was like when he was younger, especially with other guys, when they were itching to prove their bona fides. They'd think nothing of jumping a guy and beating him to a pulp if they thought he was a rat. Some nights, he'd barely sleep, jumping at any unusual noise. Mostly, he tried to push the fear aside. Then he decided he'd be better off if he just accepted it.

If ever someone came to kill me, one of the things I hope to happen is me telling him I forgive him, he wrote in December 2012. *Of course, though I would hope it would never happen, though.*

John wrote to his father, but never got an answer. Tina told John that Sonny had read the letters, but wouldn't answer.

John still had HIV, of course, but kept it mostly under control to barely detectable levels with a raft of medications and his strict routine. He didn't think about it much.

However, Sonny did.

In prison, Sonny read everything he could about HIV and AIDS.

"I know he was sick, I know he was sick," Sonny said. "I didn't know what the hell he had . . . And I studied everything up on AIDS because I wanted to see if I could figure where the hell it come from. He don't got AIDS no more."

He couldn't explain John's HIV or, worse, his decision to testify against his own father.

"Can't answer that. I don't know what happened to him. Maybe all the drugs he took. Screwed his mind up. Maybe the medicine he took brought something out of him that we never knew existed. I can't answer that.

"Listen, it broke my heart. He would be the last guy I thought would do that. But he did it."

Sonny didn't buy John's explanation that he really wasn't testifying against him, but against other people and the life of the Mafia.

"Yeah, but he mentioned my name. Why mention my name if you're going to turn on other people? Not that I wanted him to turn on other people. But if that was your thought, in the back of your mind, then what are you talking about me for?"

When Sonny got out of prison the last time in 2017, John reached his own turning point. He had been diagnosed with throat dysplasia, a possible precursor to cancer, and worried he might die without ever talking to his family members again. Then the story of his father being released from prison circulated on the Internet, and someone posted online John's new identity and where he lived. The U.S. Marshal Service called him and told him he had to leave immediately.

He had done that in the past, but at this point, he finally felt settled. He had friends. He felt useful in the sober community. He didn't want to leave. Plus, as long as he was in WITSEC, he couldn't do anything like sell the story of his life.

He signed out of the program.

With the help of a friend, John sneaked back into New York to visit his father. Traveling from the airport to the nursing home was tense. He knew enough to avoid parking ramps because they're an easy place to get killed. But once he got into the nursing home, he relaxed. He walked in and saw his father sitting in a wheelchair. Sonny didn't notice him, and John, no longer lifting weights, was far thinner and older-looking than the last time they saw each other.

"Do you know who this is?" he asked his father.

"It's coming to me, it's coming to me," Sonny hedged.

"Dad, it's John."

"John!" Sonny yelled, stretching his arms out wide. "What are you doing here? You've gotta be careful. They're going to look to kill you!

"Your name? What about your name? Did you sign in?"

John lied. "Dad, Dad, hold on, Dad. I didn't use my name."

Sonny relaxed. They spoke for a few minutes about how John looked, and then Sonny asked his son gently why he testified against him. "That wasn't nice," he said, as if admonishing a small child.

John was nonplussed. No one else had ever asked him why.

"Was it the money? Did they give you half a million dollars?" Sonny asked.

"No, Dad," John said quietly.

"I didn't think so. Was it your mother? Did she convince you to do that?" he pressed.

"No, Dad, it wasn't Mom," John said.

"Was it Rob Lewicki?" Sonny asked.

"Dad, Rob was there. But he wasn't the one who got me to do it. I was testifying against the life, not you. I never meant to hurt you," John said.

That seemed to be enough for Sonny. "Well, you're my son, and I love you," he said. "But you've always been crazy."

Then he looked around furtively, worried that someone he knew might be coming to visit him and see him talking to a rat. "You'd better go," he said, hustling him out.

For John, those few minutes together and the conversation were the reassurances he needed. He never believed that his father was serious about his threat to kill him. Michael believed that Sonny was capable of having him killed; John, always the princeling, was sure in his heart that Sonny wouldn't have hurt him, that he was only posturing. Sonny always told John that, as loyal as he was to the life, his family would not be like other families. Joe Colombo's son knew his father was going to get shot the day he did, and he did nothing to stop it. That was not Sonny's way.

"I'm not going to let anyone hurt my son," he told one friend.

His family was always his weakness. His fervent desire to set up his son in the life, to make sure he was secure, was what had made it so easy for John to betray him.

* * *

John, Michael, and Tina were so mindful of the pain they felt when Sonny went away to prison: The loss of their family's rock was almost unbearable. But they never talked about the pain he felt at not being able to protect them. Watching his family spin out of control while he was behind bars was agonizing to Sonny.

"It gave me a lot of heartaches, not to me, like watching my children, like my son, John," he said.

"I remember, when I come out, when I beat the murder—no, I got out on bail—and I come out, and I come to the house, there's a bunch of people there. And John is in the other room, and they go to John, 'John, your father's home, your father's home.'

"And he says, 'I don't believe it, my father ain't home.'

"So I went in the room, and I say, 'John, what'sa matter?'

"And he comes and he runs in my arms and he's starting, his chest is heaving in and out, like that, and I said, 'John, what'sa matter?'"

He could do little but hold his sobbing seven-year-old son.

"The next morning, I take him to breakfast. I say, 'John, you had me scared, what'sa matter?'"

John hesitated. He didn't want to tell his father.

"I said, 'John, I'm your father, you can tell me.' I says, 'What the hell happened?'

"He said, 'Well, when I was in school, they used to tell me you were a murderer, that you were going to get the electric chair.'

"I said, 'Who told you that?'

"'The kids in the school, the teacher.'

"I said, 'Jeez, that's real terrible.'"

To so many, to his own family, Sonny was larger than life; yet, he couldn't protect his favorite child from taunts in school.

"So a lot of heartaches," he said. "You know, it was a shame. They suffered more than me."

He never told his family about the pain he felt.

* * *

To the end, he believed the government persecuted him. "I had everything. They made me lose everything. For no reason, no reason whatsoever," he said.

"Listen, I'll be honest with you, if I don't get pinched, if I don't get locked up, I don't know how much money I'd be worth. You know? This country destroyed me. I don't know how much money I'd have coming in. You know? It's a shame what they done to me, but listen, that's what they wanted, and they got it," he said.

He could have followed the path of other mob bosses who rolled on their contemporaries, but he never did. "I can't be beaten for no reason. I can't do it. Jesus suffered. He never screwed nobody. Look at what Jesus went through. I'll never forget that man. I says prayers every night," he said.

It's clear that in his later years, Sonny was thinking about an afterlife.

"One day, I was talking to a guy, I said, 'I'll meet Mishler when I die. I'll meet him in Hell.'

"So the guy said, 'Sonny, you're not going to Hell.'

"May God strike me dead if I'm lying to you. He says, 'Sonny, you're not going to Hell.'

"I says, 'What are you talking about?'

"'You're not going to Hell.'

"'What makes you say that?'

"'Sonny, maybe you don't realize it, but the good you've done for people. Why would God take you and make you go to Hell? You helped a lot of people, Sonny.'

"I just kept quiet and walked away. I never knew that much about me—all the help I've done people, and people noticed it. Because everything I've done, nobody helped me. Nobody helped me."

Sonny was unabashed about the life he chose. Unlike Frank Costello, Sonny never craved respectability in the civilian world. He knew who and what he was. When contemporaries like Carmine Persico were confronted with news photographers trying to snap their photos, they crouched and hid their faces. Not Sonny. He never hid his face.

Despite his determined adherence to the code of his chosen life, Sonny didn't want his grandchildren going into it. "There's no more money in crime. If people don't understand, they're crazy. They better go to school. School is the only place. School is stronger than anything," he said.

Sonny came close to dying twice in prison—he said it was from sitting too much—and he couldn't believe he lived as long as he had. "Ain't that something?"

He credited his religious faith. "Jesus is almighty," he said. "Got to give that man a lot of credit. Kept me alive. Because I prayed to Him every night. Every minute I prayed to Him. I was always religious. All the time. I respected my faith."

To Sonny, living so long, outlasting his enemies, was winning.

"Everybody looks up to me. Listen, I'm just a little man, that's all. I ain't lookin' for no glory. I ain't lookin' for no credit. I did what I need."

People constantly stopped him and told him he was a legend.

"I mean everybody, I meet people.

"'You, Sonny. Yeah. Oh, you're the legend.'

"'What legend?' I said. 'I don't know what the hell you're talking about. Legend.'

"I said, 'I thought a legend had to do something great.'

"He said, 'You did a hell of a great thing. You showed the world that there's still guys who will take all the punishment in the world and still stand up.'

"I said, 'I did that?'

"He says, 'Yeah.'

"'You say it, I'll listen to you.'"

As he looked back on his experiences, he chuckled and said, "I've had a helluva experience in life.

"It'd make a helluva story in a book or something."

Sonny's funeral was held Feb. 28, 2020, at Our Lady of Mount Carmel Church in Williamsburg, Brooklyn.

The monsignor presiding over the funeral recalled that when he first met Sonny, he told him, "You know, I've been away at college. Anything you need, call me."

The monsignor paused a beat before adding, "Lo and behold, he went away to school again!"

The mourners laughed appreciatively. Unlike the garish mob funerals of other mob bosses who predeceased him, it was a quieter affair attended by family members and close friends. Two grandchildren eulogized him as a doting grandfather who urged them to pursue their education. For the music, there was a gospel choir—an homage to Sonny's backing of so many Black performers—singing "Amazing Grace." His coffin was draped with an American flag.

Michael and John did not attend.

BIBLIOGRAPHY AND SOURCE NOTES

Aronson, Harvey, *The Killing of Joey Gallo*, New York: G.P. Putnam's & Sons, 1973.

Baggelaar, Kristin, *The Copacabana*, Mount Pleasant, SC: Arcadia Publishing, 2006.

Bonavolonta, Jules, and Brian Duffy, *The Good Guys: How We Turned the FBI 'Round—and Finally Broke the Mob*, New York: Simon & Schuster, 1996.

Capeci, Jerry, *Jerry Capeci's Gang Land: Fifteen Years of Covering the Mafia*, New York: Alpha Books, 2003.

Capeci, Jerry, and Gene Mustain, *Murder Machine: A True Story of Murder, Madness, and the Mafia*, New York: Penguin, 1993.

Carlin, Richard, *Godfather of the Music Business: Morris Levy*, Jackson, MS: University Press of Mississippi, 2016.

Carlo, Philip, *Gaspipe: Confessions of a Mafia Boss*, New York: Harper, 2009.

Dannen, Fredric, *Hit Men: Power Brokers and Fast Money Inside the Record Business*, New York: Vintage Books, 1990.

Darin, Dodd, and Maxine Paetro, *Dream Lovers: The Magnificent Shattered Lives of Bobby Darin and Sandra Dee*, New York: Warner Books, 1994.

DeStefano, Anthony M., *Top Hoodlum: Frank Costello, Prime Minister of the Mafia*, New York: Citadel Press Books, 2018.

DeVecchio, Lin, and Charles Brandt, *We're Going to Win This Thing*, New York: Berkley Books, 2011.

Dwyer, Johnny, *The Districts: Stories of American Justice from the Federal Courts*, New York: Alfred A. Knopf, 2019.

Earley, Pete, and Gerald Shur, *WITSEC: Inside the Federal Witness Protection Program*, New York: Bantam Books, 2002.

Franzese, Michael, and Dary Matera, *Quitting the Mob*, New York: HarperCollins, 1992.

Hearings before the Permanent Subcommittee on Investigations of the Committee on Governmental Affairs, U.S. Senate, One Hundredth Congress, April 11,15, 21, 29, 1988.

Kaplan, James, *Frank: The Voice*, New York: Doubleday, 2010.

Hodas, Romola, and Elizabeth Ridley, *The Princess of 42nd Street*, Riverdale, Bronx, NY: Riverdale Avenue Books, 2018.

Hortis, C. Alexander, *The Mob and the City: The Hidden History of How the Mafia Captured New York*, New York: Prometheus Books, 2014.

James, Tommy, and Martin Fitzpatrick, *Me, the Mob, and the Music*, New York: Scribner, 2010.

Keeler, Robert F., *Newsday: A Candid History of the Respectable Tabloid*, New York: Arbor House, 1990.

Kessner, Thomas, *Fiorello H. LaGuardia and the Making of Modern New York*, New York: McGraw-Hill Publishing, 1989.

Lance, Peter, *Deal with the Devil: The FBI's Secret Thirty-Year Relationship with a Mafia Killer*, New York: William Morrow, 2008.

Lansky, Sandra, and William Stadiem, *Daughter of the King*, New York: Weinstein Books, 2014.

Maas, Peter, *The Valachi Papers*, New York: G.P. Putnam's Sons, 1968.

Mills, James, *The Prosecutor*, New York: Farrar Straus & Giroux, 1968.

Napoli, Tony, and Charles Messina, *My Father, My Don*, Silver Spring, MD: Beckham Publications, 2008.

O'Brien, Joseph F. and Andris Kurins, *Boss of Bosses: The Fall of the Godfather—The FBI and Paul Castellano*, New York: Simon & Schuster, 1991.

Polisi, Sal, and Steve Dougherty, *The Sinatra Club: My Life Inside the New York Mafia*, New York: Pocket Books, 2012.

Puzo, Mario, *The Godfather Papers and Other Confessions*, New York: G.P. Putnam's Sons, 1972.

Raab, Selwyn, *Five Families*, New York: Thomas Dunne Books, 2005, 2016.

Reavill, Gil, *Mafia Summit*, New York: Dunne/St. Martin's, 2013.

Reppetto, Thomas, *American Mafia: A History of Its Rise to Power*, New York: Henry Holt & Co., 2004.

Reynolds Jr., Robert Grey, *The Mafia Slaying of Bank Teller/Go-Go Dancer Irene Brandt*, Self-published ebook, 2019.

Robinson, Paul H., and Sarah M. Robinson, *Crimes that Changed Our World*, New York: Rowman & Littlefield, 2018.

Server, Lee, *Ava Gardner: "Love Is Nothing,"* New York: St. Martin's Press, 2006.

Short, Martin, *The Rise of the Mafia: The Definitive Story of Organized Crime*, London: John Blake Publishing, 2009.

Spado, Ori, and Dennis N. Griffin, *The Accidental Gangster: From Insurance Salesman to Mob Boss of Hollywood*, Denver, CO: Wild Blue Press, 2019.

Turkus, Burton B., and Sid Feder, *Murder Inc.*, New York: Da Capo Press, 1951.

U.S. Treasury Department Bureau of Narcotics, *Mafia: The Government's Secret File on Organized Crime*, New York: HarperCollins, 2007.

Volkman, Ernest, *Gangbusters*, London, England: Faber & Faber, 1998.

Source Notes by Chapter

1: The House on Shrub Hollow Road. 1966 court transcript; FBI agent testimony, 1970; interviews with Sonny, Michael and John Franzese, Vincent D'Agostino, Dan Pearson, Lind DeVecchio, Sal Polisi, Gerald Shur, Vincent Desiderio; *New York Times*, 1967; Gaetano Fatato recording; *Newsday*, 1965, 1960; FBI memos, 1962–63; FBI activity logs.

2: Making His Bones. FBI file, NY-9-0294; interviews with Sonny and Michael Franzese, Angie and John Crispo, Stan Paul Prahalis, Maurice Pierre, Selwyn Raab, Vincent D'Agostino, Gene Kelly, Ori Spado, Ronald Goldstock; *New York Times*, 2020; Bureau of Narcotics; Nassau County police; NY birth records; marriage license; 2011 presentencing memo.

3: Down to Business. Interviews with Roberta, John and Michael Franzese, Frank Castagnaro, Bruce Mouw, sprinkler installer, landscaper, Joe Ligouri, David Shapiro; *Newsday*, 1963–65; FBI memos, activity logs; U.S. Senate testimony, 1988; *New York Post*, 1962–64; Daily News, 1962–63.

4: Dazzling Nights. Interviews with Sonny, Michael and John Franzese, Joey Silvestri, Chip Proser, Gianni Russo, Artie Ripp, Tony Napoli, Sy Presten, Frankie Blue Eyes; *New York Times*, 1973, 1992; *Tampa Times*, 1961; *Billboard*, 1965.

5: Cops Turn Up the Heat. Interviews with Sonny Franzese, Carmine Burzamato, Diane DeRose Gilbert, Michael Nardone, Ori Spado, Robert Greene Jr., Theresa Matthews, Elaine Goldman, Joyce Spivack, Mitch Lambert; *Newsday*, 1963–65; *Daily News*, 1963; unpublished Bob Greene interview; depositions of Carmine Burzamato, Salvatore La Russa; *NBC Evening News*, 1970; FBI Airtel, 1964; *New York Times*, 1964; Gregory Scarpa FBI file; SIC report, 1965.

6: The Hawk Surfaces. Interviews with Sonny Franzese, Ann Zaher, Stephen Rupolo; *Daily News*, 1964; NYPD aided and accident card; *New York Times*, 1946, 1967; Daily News, 1964; *New York Post*, 1964; *Life* magazine, 1968; Sing Sing Prison file; Eleanor Cordero affidavit, 1974; *Newsday*, 1966, 1974; Bethel Police log, 1964; FBI John Cordero file.

7: Sonny Makes Music. Interviews with Paul Vance, Sonny, Michael and John Franzese, Artie Ripp, Ron Dante, Tommy James, Tony and Helaina Bruno, Tommy Gallagher; *Newsday*, 1965.

8: Public Enemy Number One. Interviews with Sonny Franzese, Edward McDonald, Lester Ezrati; *Newsday*, 1958, 1966–67; indictment #1206/66; NY District Attorney press release, 1966; arraignment transcript, 1966; court records, 1966.

9: Sonny Goes on Trial. Interviews with Sonny and Michael Franzese,

Gary von Stange, Warren Coldner, Raymond Dearie, Marilyn Berger Hewitt, Robert Hummerstone, Melvyn Roth, Vincent Potere; *Life* magazine, 1968; *New York Times*, 1967, 1993; *Newsday*, 1967; court records, 1966–67; FBI case notes; *Knickerbocker News*, 1967; *Daily News*, 2017.

10: On Trial for Homicide. Interviews with Serphin Maltese, Sonny Franzese, Kevin and Marian Mosley, Thomas Pattison, Bob Peterson; *Daily News*, 1965–67; *New York Times*, 1967; *Newsday*, 1967; court records 1967; Walter Sher ruling, 1981; *Syracuse Post-Standard*, 1980, 1989; *Life* magazine, 1968.

11: Peep Shows, Porn, and Pop Music. Interviews with Sonny and John Franzese, Romola Hodas, Paul Warburgh Jr., Peter Fabricant, Norby Walters, Angelo Ellerbe; *New York Times*, 1968–75; SIC testimony, 1970; *Daily News*, 1968–72; Nassau County police report, 1963; Hodas court records, 1965; *Newsday*, 1966, 1989; *New York Post*, 1968; Congressional testimony, 1968; *Sports Illustrated*, 1987; *Franzese v. USA*, 1968; FBI memo, 1968.

12: A Home Invasion. Interviews with Lester Ezrati, Milton Ezrati, Sonny, Michael and John Franzese, Gerard Fee, *Newsday*, 1969; Nassau court records; Franzese court records; Gregory Scarpa FBI file; *New York Times*, 1970.

13: Sonny Goes Away. Interviews with Sonny, Michael, John and Roberta Franzese, Kenneth LaMaster, Frank Castagnaro, Tony Napoli, Michael Gillen, Cordero cousin; *Olean Times Herald*, 1971; FBI file on Tuttti Franzese; Newsday, 1970–71; *New York Times*, 1971; FBI arrest warrant, 1971; FBI 302s, 1971, 1975; Nassau police report.

14: Family Fights to Survive Without Sonny. Interviews with Sonny, Michael, John and Roberta Franzese, Bill Ferrante, Ori Spado, Neil Jon Firetog, Kenneth LaMaster, Sydell Topol, Frankie Blue Eyes; *Daily News*, 1973; Tina Franzese letters; *Newsday*, 1973–76; FBI 302s; Eleanor Cordero affidavit; unpublished Manny Topol interview; *New York Times*, 1974; *Vanity Fair*, 1991.

15: Business Behind Bars. Interviews with Sonny, Michael and Roberta Franzese, Chris Mattiace, Dan Pearson, Frank Castagnaro, Theresa LaManna Basilone, Gina Lynch, Thomas Pattison; Tina Franzese affidavit; court records, 1975–76; Sonny Franzese letters; Tina Franzese tax returns; FBI 302s, 1975–76; *Newsday*, 1976; Tina Franzese letter.

16: Easy Betrayals. Interviews with Sonny, Michael and John Franzese, Thomas Pattison, Chris Mattiace, Gina Lynch; Bill Ferrante, Cheryl Zaher DePasquale, Frank Morro; *Newsday*, 1976–78; Sonny Franzese letters; unpublished Manny Topol interview; Lawrence Iorrizzo deposition; FBI teletype 1981; *State of Florida v. Michael Franzese*, 1986.

17: Michael Flying High. Interviews with Michael and Roberta Franzese, Dan Pearson, Robert Creighton, Ori Spado, Jack Weishan, Chris Mattiace,

Bernie Welch, Jerry Bernstein, Frank Castagnaro; *Life* magazine, 1987; Iorrizzo deposition; Florida court records, 1986; *Newsday*, 1986, 1991; U.S. Prisons Bureau; *Sydney Morning Herald*, 2015.

18: John Steps Up. Interviews with Sonny, Michael, Roberta and John Franzese, Frank Castagnaro, Pete Brodsky, Kenneth Steiger, Jack Weishan, Gina Lynch; *South Florida Sentinel*, 1984; Nassau County police reports, 1985–86; Gregory Scarpa FBI file; *New York Times*, 1985–86; *Newsday*, 1986; U.S. Probation Department report, 1986.

19: Family Spins out of Control. Interviews with Sonny, John, Michael and John and Roberta Franzese, Vinny Oliva, Sharyn Arena, Patrick Cotter, Edward McDonald, Frank Castagnaro, Bruce Maffeo, Ron Parr; *Newsday*, 1987–91; *Vanity Fair*, 2012.

20: Colombos Go to War. Interview with Sonny, John and Roberta Franzese, Frank Castagnaro, Gina Lynch, Dan Pearson, Jack Kennedy, Mickey Sochor; FBI files; *New York Post*, 2012; *Newsday*, 1992–95; *New York Times*, 1992; U.S. Bureau of Prisons.

21: John Takes a Fateful Step. Interviews with Joe Conway, Robert Lewicki, Ori Spado, John Franzese Jr., Gina Lynch, James Miskiewicz, former U.S. marshal; *Newsday*, 2000–01, 2012–13; U.S. Prisons Bureau; police and court records.

22: No Turning Back. Interviews with Gina Lynch, John, Michael, Roberta and Denyce Franzese, Ori Spado, Vincent D'Agostino, Joel Freeman, Michael Campione, Jerry Capeci; tape transcript, 2005; *Daily News*, 2005.

23: The Tapes. Interviews with John and Denyce Franzese, Robert Lewicki, Jerry Capeci, Ori Spado; transcripts of recordings, 2005, 2007; memorandum of law, 2009; Lewicki testimony, 2010.

24: A Protégé's Betrayal. Interviews with Vincent D'Agostino, Robert Lewicki, Roberta and John Franzese, Richard Lind, Sharyn Arena; transcripts of recordings, 2007; *Newsday* 2011–13; *Long Island Press*, 2011; trial records.

25: John Testifies. Interviews with Sonny and John Franzese, Vincent D'Agostino, Gina Lynch, *Village Voice*, 2010; trial transcript, 2010; *Newsday*, 2010–11, *Gangland*, 2011; U.S. Bureau of Prisons; *Daily News*, 2010, court records.

26: Regrets and Reconciliation. Interviews with Sonny, John, Michael and Roberta Franzese, Ori Spado, Sharyn Arena, Frank Castagnaro, Robert Lewicki, Lisa Gilbreath, former U.S. marshal; Equinox pay stubs, bankruptcy records; U.S. Bureau of Prisons; John Franzese journal.